Controversial Issues in Adventure Education

A Critical Examination

Scott D. Wurdinger
Tom G. Potter

KENDALL/HUNT PUBLISHING COMPANY
4050 Westmark Drive   Dubuque, Iowa 52002

Photo Credits

Page 2 by Bill Bitzinger
Page 88 by Bill Bitzinger
Page 138 by Scott Wurdinger
Page 194 by Rich Piippo
Page 210 by Scott Wurdinger
Page 246 by Bill Bitzinger

All contributed articles are reprinted with permission of the respective authors.

Dedication

For
Annette, Lauren and Madeline
and
Teresa, Stephanie and Andrew
In appreciation of our daily adventures and meaningful journeys
shared.

Contents

Foreword ix
Preface xi
Acknowledgements xiii

CHAPTER 1

Should Challenge Course Instructors Be Certified? 1

YES—Jeff Boeke and David Lockett 3
NO—Simon Priest 8

CHAPTER 2

Should There Be Rescue Free Wilderness Areas? 19

YES—Ross Cloutier 21
NO—Julie Gabert 28

CHAPTER 3

Are Floating Fee Scales for Corporate and Educational Groups Ethical? 37

YES—Steve Proudman 39
NO—Jasper S. Hunt 47

CHAPTER 4

Should We Use Urban Settings to Promote Adventure Education? 53

YES—Tom Puk 55
NO—Tom G. Potter and Tonia L. Gray 63

CHAPTER 5

Should Modern Communication Systems (Cellular Telephones) Be Used in the Wilderness? 73

YES—Tod Schimelpfenig 75
NO—T.A. Loeffler 78

CHAPTER 6

Do One Day Adventure Programming Activities, Such as Challenge Courses, Provide Long Lasting Learning?   87

YES—Dan Garvey   89
NO—Tom Puk   97

CHAPTER 7

Should Articles on Special Wilderness Places Be Published?   105

YES—Glen Bishop   107
NO—Christian Bisson   116

CHAPTER 8

Have Adventure Programs Eliminated Too Much Risk?   123

YES—Karl Rohnke   125
NO—Camille J. Bunting   129

CHAPTER 9

The Ultimate Goal of Adventure Education Should Be the Improvement of the Individual, Not the Group Within Which the Individual Resides   137

YES—Deborah Sugerman   139
NO—Dan Garvey   145

CHAPTER 10

Should Processing Techniques, Such as Framing and Debriefing, Be a Mandatory Part of Facilitation?   151

YES—Clifford E. Knapp   153
NO—Mark Havens   159

Chapter 11

Is the Process of Experiential Learning (Outside the Classroom) Practical in Higher Education Settings?   167

YES—Iain Stewart-Patterson   169
YES—Tom Puk   178
NO—Scott Wurdinger   187

Chapter 12

✗ Do Contrived Adventure Experiences, Such as Ropes Courses, Hinder Participants from Developing a Connection to the Natural World?   193

YES—Nicky Duenkel   195
NO—Stephen Streufert   202

Chapter 13

Should Wildlands Be Made Available to More People, as Opposed to More Restrictions and Limitations?   209

YES—Alan Ewert and Erin K. Smith   211
NO—Pam Foti   222

Chapter 14

Is It Possible to Justify a "Value-Laden" Position for Ecologically-Based Adventure Education?   227

YES—Holly Bickerton and Bob Henderson   229
NO—Daniel Vokey   237

Chapter 15

↯ Should Gender-Specific Programs, Such as All Women Courses, Be Offered in Adventure Education?   245

YES—Karla A. Henderson   247
NO—Juli Lynch   254

Foreword

Effective leaders in this field must have the ability to make tough decisions. Lead authors Scott Wurdinger and Tom Potter have done an excellent job identifying critical controversial issues, that when examined, will help individuals determine where they stand when faced with such issues. They have collaborated with experts around the world that present their views in this book, which will stimulate critical thinking skills and foster important decision making abilities.

Many of my climbs around the world and the methods used have created controversy in the climbing world. For instance, my long-time partner Reinhold Messner and I were the first to climb Mount Everest without oxygen. We climbed many other 8000 meter peaks using similar methods that were considered by many in the climbing community to be highly controversial, yet we were determined that we could make these ascents in a safe manner and succeeded.

Just as Reinhold and I put much thought into our climbs, Scott and Tom put much thought into this book. Readers will find a variety of interesting topics and opinions written by experts in this field. Enjoy your discussions on these topics!

Peter Habeler

Preface

Adventure education has its own set of unique questions that help to define what it is and how it differs from other fields of education. Adventure education has grown rapidly over the past several decades, and, with its evolution many critical topics for deliberation have emerged. In order for adventure education to mature, we must continue to question assumptions and face controversy, for healthy discussion inspires re-examination and, hopefully, growth. The time has come to examine critical issues at hand and provide a forum to present them for inquiry. *Controversial Issues in Adventure Education: A Critical Examination* includes 15 chapters arranged in a debate format where one contributing author argues the YES side of a particular question and another argues the NO side. Thirty-two adventure education professionals were asked to take a stance on their particular issue for the purpose of generating discussion on some of the most pressing concerns in this field. The book brings forth some of the most salient issues in the field where a variety of topics such as gender specific programming, challenge course instructor certification, mandatory debriefing, use of modern communications systems in the wilderness, and restrictions on wilderness use are addressed.

The book was written for participants, undergraduate and graduate students and professionals interested in adventure education programs. Educators can use the book to set up debates, which will help students and practitioners develop important critical thinking skills. It can also be used to help individuals identify and clarify arguments, examine why some arguments are stronger than others, examine their own personal values on various issues, and expand their own views by examining both sides of an issue. We also believe it will be particularly relevant to aspiring leaders in the field and those who embrace the concept of multiple perspectives in adventure education. Readers should keep in mind that the opinions presented may not necessarily reflect the personal opinions of the authors, but rather were written with the intention of outlining the arguments to promote critical thinking.

Acknowledgements

Scott and Tom would first like to thank their respective families; Lauren, Madeline, and Annette Wurdinger; Stephanie and Andrew Potter and Teresa Socha, for allowing us to make a three year commitment to this project. Such projects always seem to consume more time than what one first expects. Thank you for your patience and unwavering encouragement. To you we are truly grateful.

We would also like to thank all the contributing authors, for without their commitment the project would not have been possible.

Jasper Hunt provided intellectual nourishment and psychological support for the duration of this project. He is truly an inspiration to many of us in the field of adventure education.

Susan Hastings-Bishop, program coordinator of the Recreation Leadership and Management program at Ferris State University, provided support by allowing the time needed to complete the manuscript.

Dave Winninger, John Duman and Margo Millette deserve a special thank you for their wizardly knowledge of technical computer systems and converting numerous files back and forth. Dave rescued us on a number of occasions by converting stubborn documents into readable formats.

We would also like to thank Cindy Roberts for typing several pieces that we were not able to convert from one computer format to another.

Bill Bitzinger and Rich Piippo took valuable time out of their busy schedules to photograph and develop numerous pictures included in the book.

Lastly, a thank you to our students, whom over the years have taught us much and provided us with a great deal of inspiration.

CHAPTER 1

Should Challenge Course Instructors Be Certified?

YES PERSPECTIVE: Jeff Boeke and David Lockett, M.S.
NO PERSPECTIVE: Simon Priest, Ph.D.

Jeff Boeke has been actively involved in implementing adventure education programs for schools, colleges, corporations, camps, and healthcare facilities for over 20 years. Boeke is the owner and CEO of ABEE, Inc., a full service challenge course company which designs, constructs, and implements challenge course programs. Considered by many to be one of the leading challenge course vendors in the industry, ABEE currently has active programs in 42 states and eight countries worldwide. Jeff has been on the Board of Directors of the Association for Challenge Course Technology (ACCT) since its inception and is Chair of the ACCT Technical Training and Operational Standards Committee, and Co-chair of the ACCT Professional Vendor Review Committee. Jeff is married with three children and currently resides in Oconomowoc, Wisconsin.

David Lockett M.S. is coordinator of physical and experiential education at Stevens Point Area School District. Prior to this appointment he was an instructor for the University of New Hampshire Outdoor Education Program and Head Instructor for the University of New Hampshire Browne Center. David has extensive experience facilitating team building activities with a wide range of populations. He was formerly a U.S. Navy Seal and is well adept at numerous technical hard skills. He is married to Monica and has two sons, Frederick and Daniel.

Dr. Simon Priest is a retired full professor from a university in Canada. He also holds adjunct professorships at several American universities and has been a guest or visiting professor at universities in Australia, Czechia, England, Germany, and New Zealand. He has been actively engaged in training outdoor leaders for the adventure programming field for 20 years now.

Should Challenge Course Instructors Be Certified?

Jeff Boeke and David Lockett, M.S.

It is the position of this article that Challenge Course Instructors should be required to comply with a professional certification process. Whereas various types of certification already exist in most viable professional arenas, the real question is perhaps not "should challenge course instructors be certified?", rather "are challenge course Instructors viable professionals?" For the context of this article, the assumption has been made that challenge course services are in fact, very professional in nature. This is seen through the thousands of individuals, organizations, and institutions that financially support themselves through the daily provision of challenge course services. As with most professional venues however, the quality and safety management of the challenge course experience is driven by the skill and ability of the practitioner leading the activity. The appropriate point of discussion, therefore, should not revolve around whether certification is needed, rather, what should certification consist of.

In defining a method and a purpose supporting certification as it relates to the challenge course field, it is necessary to look at the training practices of other Adventure Education disciplines. The existence of certification within a professional practice brings with it the implication of quality, accountability, and order. Levels of certification and licensure within the recreation and adventure fields vary depending on the nature of the activity. All levels of certification, however, typically endorse appropriate standards of practice through a format that is both discipline and milieu specific. A credible certification process is designed to endorse a specific scope of practice as it pertains to perimeters and privileges. Safety guidelines, ethical perspectives, and an outline for quality management procedures are all addressed in viable certification.

The criteria used to outline reputable certification procedures in most cases are written and sanctioned by a professional standard setting organization. For example, the American Canoe Association (ACA) prescribes a certification process for canoeing instructors. This does not mean that one must be certified to teach canoeing skills, but it is well recognized that an ACA certified canoe instructor has gone through a rigorous evaluative process and has a quality endorsement. Other examples include the following: Certified scuba instructors must hold a valid and current instructors card from one of five certifying agencies (i.e. SSI, NASDS, PADA, NAUI, YMCA) to instruct novices and acquire necessary liability insurance, Emergency Medical Technicians (EMT) are certified by a competent medical authority (i.e. Red Cross, American Heart Association, etc.) and must follow specific protocol without deviation, the American Mountain Guides Alliance (AMGA) certifies mountaineering guides, American Camping Association (ACA) certifies for standards of excellence in camping programs, Hunter Education Certification is required in most states to acquire a hunting license for youth and adults, Water Safety Instruction Certification (WSI) is typically required to be a life guard, and National Ski Instructor Certification is required to be a Ski Patrol. These are just a few examples of recreation and adventure venues that successfully implement reputable certification programs. In reviewing these programs it is important to note the common goals they share. These goals embody a commitment to provide state-of-the-art excellence through a set of procedures that are comprehensive, measurable in content, fairly administered, and modeled in accordance with current national operational standards. The challenge course industry, as well as any discipline, would benefit from embracing this commitment.

In considering the need for technical certification in the challenge course industry or for that matter any recreational activity, a clear definition must be established which addresses the notion of risk in measurable terms. It is not enough for instructors to be able to define the differences between *low risk* and *high risk* as they pertain to potential consequences, they should also be able to identify when *low risk becomes high risk*. Only by this identification can reasonable, educated decisions be made addressing the need for certification.

In examining the need for certification it is necessary to note the relationship between "required expertise" and "level of risk". When considering the many activities commonly associated with the field of Adventure Education, remember that viable certification processes are discipline specific. Although risk is present to some degree in all that we do, some activities are obviously more technically intensive than others are. Therefore the need to certify must be based on 1) the level of technical skills required for safe participation, and 2) the potential consequences of improper execution. In short, the greater the possible risk, the more important it is to have instructor certification.

For example, mild terrain hiking is a relatively low risk involvement that brings with it a different set of possible circumstances than class three white water canoeing. Whereas certification may not be appropriate for hiking, it is a common and wise practice in white water canoeing. The simple reason for this is that navigating a canoe in class three white water is a skill driven sport where the lack of knowledge or competence could result in a fatal consequence. A similar comparison might be the sport of fishing in contrast to challenge course participation. Both activities are challenging outdoor endeavors that require expertise, skill, and knowledge for successful execution. Indeed, the potential for professional opportunity exists for both involvements as well. The typical risk factors associated with the two, however, are very different. Though fishing is not by any means risk free, the need for "fishing certification" has not yet shown itself to be necessary. Challenge course instruction, however, brings with it a high level of risk as defined by the dangerous and potentially fatal consequences that could arise from either misjudgment or incompetence. The very nature of challenge course instruction requires the proficient use of "life lines or belay lines" to prevent the occurrence of a serious fall. Consequently, there is a definite need for challenge course instructor certification as it relates to the level of risk.

Another area that needs to be addressed is interpersonal dynamics or "soft skills" as they relate to challenge course certification. Contrary to technical skills that are procedurally consistent and measurable, soft skills are not so clearly defined. For example, the procedure for attaching a climber to a rope can be addressed in a common language that guarantees identical protocol for each participant. On the other hand, the instructor's interpersonal skills may greatly effect the quality of the participant's challenge course experience. Consequently, it is the responsibility of the certification process to address "soft skills" through an educational format that is based on awareness rather than prescribed protocol. Certification must establish clear guidelines and expectations that instructors have the ability to interact and work with people in a skillful, purposeful, and dignified manner. This process however, is more than the simple recognition of an individual's inherent ability to comfortably interact with people. It also acknowledges that the best any professional can do is work within his/her boundaries and seek professional support when needed. Many challenge course programs cater to a diverse cross section of the population. It is not unusual for a program to provide adventure education services to young children on Monday, adults on Tuesday, individuals with behavioral problems on Wednesday, etc. Certification therefore should require challenge course instructors to work within their professional capacity to provide a level of quality and care equal to the demands and expectations of the group.

Utilizing specialized professional resources is a common practice in most human service work. For example, teachers are licensed to provide specified educational experiences to students, and do not ordinarily work outside their area or level of training. Consequently if a student is tested and found to be Learning Disabled (LD), a referral is made to the special education department. If the special education department finds issues with alcohol or chemical dependency, a referral is made to the appropriate counselor and the list could continue based upon the specific circumstances of the child. Likewise, challenge course certification does not imply that instructors are licensed to work with the special needs of cancer recovery patients, or children with Attention Deficit and Hyperactive Disorder (ADHD), or persons with disabilities, or corporate managers, etc. It does imply however, that challenge course instructors 1) have the technical expertise and interpersonal skills necessary to provide a variety of purposeful challenge course experiences to many different groups of people, and 2) honor and respect the many licensures and accreditations that exist for special population focus.

In practical application, "soft skill" aptitude virtually insures or eliminates professional tenure in human service venues. Individuals are typically not eliminated from becoming challenge course instructors through the certification process itself. Rather, in most instances it evolves through the process of 1) natural selection, and/or 2) professional development. Natural selection simply implies that individuals with good "people skills" tend to do well in "people re-lated" professions. The opposite holds true as well. For example, a short career is most likely inevitable for the certified challenge course instructor or the licensed MD Family Practitioner who cannot get along, or work effectively with people. Certified or not certified, challenge course instructors are governed by the same code of reason as all human service professionals. *Professional development* suggests that regardless of the occupation, ultimately, all viable professionals are part of, and governed by, a larger system. Although these systems are situation-specific, they share commonalties including: 1.) methods for assessment (i.e. evaluations, internships, apprenticeships, etc.), and 2.) a means of controlling the quality and mission of the profession/occupation (i.e. supervision). For example, a certified challenge course instructor who works for a public school system must abide by the policies and procedures of the school district, assuming the guidelines are reasonable, fair in content, and in accordance with challenge course standards. Another example might be a Licensed Psychologist whose practice is ultimately monitored by the school, business, or corporation that employs him or her.

In summary, we believe that challenge course certification is a necessary condition for the evolution and continued professional growth of the field. It is our contention that a reasonable argument cannot be made in opposition to a certification process that is comprehensive, measurable in content, fairly administered, and modeled in accordance with current national standards. We did not outline specifics of the challenge course certification process such as: cost information, time allocations, vendor selection, etc., rather, we argued that challenge course instructors are legitimate professionals who work in a viable occupation, and that certification is required for professional advancement, recognition, and acceptance. In short, the development of challenge course certification demands that appropriate and accountable procedures be defined, not through perspectives of relativity, but through solid criteria that represent the industry its intent, purpose, and plan.

The following question and answer format is presented to assist individuals and programs with basic questions they may currently have regarding training and/or certification.

1. What does certification currently mean?

    Challenge course instructor certification means that an individual has been taught and tested in accordance with documented policies, procedures, and standards endorsed by the individual or company administering the certification. It also implies that a "certification document" or "written endorsement" is provided to persons who successfully complete the course. This certificate verifies that specific information and skills were taught and that competency and understanding was demonstrated. It should be noted that although third party professional certification from a professionally endorsed company is typically the best choice, internal certifications can be designed and administered in an effective manner. Serious questions, however, need to be discussed when doing internal certifications concerning state of the art quality and liability considerations.

2. Who is setting the standards for the industry?

    The standard setting body for challenge course programs is the ACCT (Association of Challenge Course

Technology). ACCT is a national trade association organized for the purpose of setting challenge course industry standards. ACCT originated in 1988 as a group of challenge course providers who came together to informally discuss safe practices in the construction of challenge courses. To date, ACCT has evolved into a highly respected trade association credited with the publication of national industry standards for both *challenge course installation* and *technical operations*. With an active membership of over 1000 practitioners, ACCT provides professional vendor endorsement to both small and large companies, ongoing research and development for materials and construction procedures, and networking and resource opportunities of the highest quality. All minimum technical criteria required for challenge course instructor certification is clearly presented in the ACCT Standards Manual.

3. What are they certifying?

    Challenge course certification provides a) a process by which participants are taught and tested, and b) an endorsement by the certifying agent. The process for certification obviously varies depending on the instructor. The general format, however, should include descriptive interpretations of standards allowing for and encouraging site specific application. Protocol for policies and procedures, practical and written testing, discussion of liability considerations, emergency planning and rescue, equipment care, course management, practical skill testing, etc. should all be covered in the certification process. Endorsement of this process is the verification of successful completion.

4. Who is conducting the certification and what are their qualifications?

    It is strongly recommended that a good amount of time and energy be put into choosing a challenge course certification vendor. Unfortunately there are many individuals in the field who claim unsubstantiated expertise in the challenge course "training" arena. Few, however, provide quality certification training. Be wary of the self-endorsed professional who claims that challenge course trainers should not certify. Certification by a quality professional implies that the training entity is confident in their ability to provide a comprehensive curriculum that is measurable, and in accordance with ACCT Operational Standards.

Should Challenge Course Instructors Be Certified?

Simon Priest, Ph.D.

By NO, I really mean YES, if we are talking about certifying the "hard skills" of challenge course instruction. Otherwise, if the certificate encompasses any other competencies of challenge course instruction (such as "soft skills" or "meta skills"), I emphatically stand opposed to that certification in any form. My opposition is founded upon the following reasons:

1. soft and meta skills are difficult (sometimes impossible) to measure, train or assess;

2. testing quality is often poor and minimal (frequently excludes soft and meta skills);

3. certification has everybody doing things the same way, at the expense of creativity;

4. university programs fill the void better, but are impacted by politics and finances;

5. certification can exclude highly experienced and very capable non-certified people;

6. certification does not protect practitioners from litigation or maintain consumer safety;

7. for these and other reasons, some of the best certification schemes no longer certify;

8. practitioners in the field prefer program accreditation to leader certification; and

9. experts in the field have historically agreed on certifying technicians, not leaders.

However, before we investigate these reasons further, I think some clarification around the use and definition of terms is warranted. We need to know the denotation and connotation of words like outdoor leader, challenge course instructor, certification, skills and competence.

DEFINITIONS

An **outdoor leader** is a person who takes others into natural settings or guides them through adventurous experiences for the purposes of changing the way they feel, think, and/or behave in relationships (with themselves, others and nature). In these roles, the outdoor leader holds a subtle combination of legal and moral responsibility for client learning, group supervision, individual safety, and environmental protection (Priest & Gass, 1997).

The **challenge course instructor** is simply a narrower subset of the outdoor leader, because the former works only with challenge courses and not in other settings such as wilderness for the latter. A challenge course is an artificially constructed series of difficult and/or challenging "elements" strung between trees and/or poles and composed of plastic, metal, wood, wire and rope. A client negotiates high elements with a safety line (belay) and low elements with group support (spotting). Early challenge courses were built from rope and thus called ropes courses.

Certification has been defined by literature in our field as a process that guarantees that minimum standards of competency have been met or exceeded as evaluated by a certifying agency following a period of leadership preparation (Senosk, 1977). According to Ewert (1985), certification is "a means to assure that only qualified people may systematically engage in the formal teaching and/or leading of individuals in the outdoor adventure situation" (p.17).

These two authorities have used a mix of carefully chosen words like "guarantee minimum standards of competency" or "assure...qualified...teaching and leading" in their definitions. From this usage, we can interpret their meaning and reason with little argument: *a certified challenge course instructor is a person who is certain to have passed a test of minimum competence and who is thus qualified to teach or lead clients in various aspects of a challenge course.*

definition [handwritten margin note]

Before we can certify someone to be a qualified challenge course instructor, we must agree upon the skills necessary to in-

struct a challenge course experience. Fortunately, members of our field have done this through research studies on outdoor leadership and challenge course competence. From the generic research on outdoor leadership, conducted in the 1980s, the adventure programming field is clear about the skills areas necessary to be an effective outdoor leader (Priest & Gass, 1997):

Hard Skills	**Meta Skills**
technical skills	problem solving skills
safety skills	decision making skills
environmental skills	experience-based judgement
	flexible leadership style
Soft Skills	communication and ethics
organizational skills	
instructional skills	A **Foundation** of personable traits and professional
facilitation skills	knowledge

In comparison, **hard skills** tend to be solid, tangible, measurable, and easy to train and assess; while **soft skills** tend to be amorphous, intangible, difficult to measure, and tough to train or assess. **Meta skills** are higher order core abilities which serve to integrate the hard and soft skills and bind them together in a workable synergy. Consider the illustration of building a brick wall atop a cement foundation (of past learning and personality held by the leader). Hard and soft skills are bricks in the wall. Meta skills are mortar holding those bricks together, thus strengthening the wall of outdoor leadership (Priest & Gass, 1997).

From specific studies on challenge course competence, conducted in the early 1990s, the field of adventure programming seems to be in reasonable consensus about the competencies needed to be a challenge course instructor (Priest, 1995):

Technical (hard) Skills

belaying and spotting techniques

accessing and egressing the course

tying knots and conducting self-transfers

clipping-in or tying-in to harnesses

dressing clients in correct equipment

using specialized equipment

supervising clients in self-transfer/belay

inspecting trees/poles and hardware/software

encouraging clients to stretch and warm-up

knowing construction standards

selecting activity to suit client needs

delivering activity with correct introduction

sequencing activities in appropriate order

picking appropriate props and equipment

setting up/taking down facility components

performing first aid and CPR

carrying out accident response procedures

rescuing/removing a stuck/injured client

identifying negative weather patterns

noticing and avoiding dangers

communicating with effective commands

curtailing dangerous client behavior

reducing damage to the local surroundings

orienting clients to specific safety issues

establishing safety/risk management

screening legal and medical forms

caring for equipment and facility resources

knowing relevant learning theories

managing and supervising staff

writing policies or plans for staff

diagnosing client needs or goals

designing program content and format

planning logistics (food, transport, etc.)

Facilitation (soft) Skills

Recreational (changing feelings)

instructing clients in technical skills

monitoring client challenge by choice

mediating client infractions of activity "rules"

contracting clients for acceptable behavior

observing group dynamics and performance

identifying critical incidents to talk about

having previously participated in the course

determining client readiness to engage

Educational (changing thinking)

debriefing and alternative reflection methods

funnelling (sequence questions in discussion)

direct frontloading techniques

assisting clients to set SMART goals

encouraging metaphor sharing

Developmental (changing behaviors)

isomorphic framing techniques

enhancing transfer techniques

helping clients commit to change

action planning or pledging SMART goals

following-up to check adherence

Therapeutic (changing mal-behaviors)

indirect frontloading (paradox/double binds)

safeguarding client emotions

making decisions within competence limit

exhibiting professional ethical standards

intervening against dysfunctional actions

Once again, we see the familiar division of hard and soft competencies. The hard ones are needed for the challenge course instructor to be an effective technician. The soft ones are needed for the instructor to be an effective facilitator. In addition, the facilitator list is divided into four categories which indicate the depth of adventure programming conducted by the instructor.

A **recreational** adventure program changes the way people feel through enjoyment, entertainment or teaching technical skills. An **educational** adventure program changes the way people think through generating enrichment, teaching concepts or creating awareness. A **developmental** adventure program changes the way people behave by increasing function and positive actions. A **therapeutic** adventure program changes the way people "mal-behave" by decreasing dysfunction and negative actions (Priest, 1995).

The instructor working in a recreational program needs the technical competencies listed and only those from the first part of the facilitation list. The educational program instructor needs all that (technical list plus recreation part) and the educational part of facilitation. In a developmental program, the instructor needs all the technical and all parts of the facilitation lists, except the therapeutic piece. The adventure therapy challenge course instructor needs everything listed.

Although many of the terms used in these lists may not be familiar to all readers, the two key points here are that the division of hard and soft skills is universal throughout outdoor leadership or adventure programming, and that more complex or sophisticated types of adventure programs demand increasing levels of facilitation competence from instructors.

With a clearer understanding of definitions and competencies, we can now turn our attention to the nine reasons on which my opposition to certification is based. These are presented in the order they were first summarized.

Measurement

Soft and meta skills are difficult (sometimes impossible) to measure, train or assess. Working with people (almost all of the soft skills) and reasoning in challenging situations (most of the meta skills) are highly subjective. The field cannot agree upon what the best practices are in each of these cases. Leaders develop these skills by varied means. Humans exhibit these skills differently under different conditions and circumstances. Experts even disagree on what the terms mean.

As a result of the variability listed above, one cannot validly or reliably determine a leader's judgement or compassion. Simply put we cannot measure these parts of the equation. So we are left with two choices: either leave them out (concentrate on hard skills only) or ignore them (and hope they aren't critical)!

My fear with challenge course instructors is that both scenarios are taking place. As with all early forms of outdoor leadership certification, ignorance was bliss and schemes simply measured the tangibles such as ability to do an activity, do it safely and sometimes do it without damaging the environment. These approaches chose to avoid dealing with teaching, or organizing, or facilitating and would never have ventured onto the higher meta plane of judgement, ethics, communication or leadership styles.

The easy way out for administrators is to control for safety and use this as a way to avoid accidents. Many people believe that this will be enough and are not concerned with the quality of the participant's experience or whether that person was traumatized because of unethical coercion or lack of psychological safety procedures. If we only consider the hard pieces of the puzzle, we will never complete the bigger picture of delivering top quality challenge course experiences.

Testing Quality

While writing this chapter, I had just retired and moved to a new state, where I was forced to get a local driving license: **become certified to operate a motor vehicle.** Certification consisted of completing three portions of the examination: an eye test, a written (computerized) multiple choice test, and a driving test.

The eye test consisted of looking into a monitor and reading one line of finely printed eight letters (visual acuity), naming four colours (color blindness), and describing the location of a dot inside or outside a box (depth perception). The answers I provided (all correct) were gleaned from conducting the test with my glasses on, but were also the same answers I had overheard given by applicants lined up in front of me. I could have easily memorized and regurgitated their responses.

I performed the written test of rules and standards, **without** reading the manual, got 5 wrong out of 25, and still managed to pass this portion of my certificate examination! The questions I got wrong had little to do with driving a car and were about subjects like "deadlines for registering the sale of a motor vehicle" and "what kind of identification was acceptable to apply for a license" (a step I had already completed).

When I reported to the window clerk, she asked me how I found the test. I replied; "A very humbling experience" and "kinda scary thinking there are folks out there like me driving around with 80% of the information!" She added; "You think that's scary? Some people miserably fail the test five times and then fluke a pass by accident on their sixth try!"

The driving test was equally interesting. My examiner had just bought the same new car as I had and we spent most of the test time talking about how well they drove on snowy steep mountain roads and how much better they were than our previous vehicles (both pickup trucks). In the end, I don't recall test driving on any major roads with traffic or accessing and egressing the nearby freeway. I certainly completed all the required maneuvers requested of me, however, I couldn't help but wonder whether I was cut a break, now and then, for having such good taste in automobiles!

When I reflected on this experience, I realized it was just like being certified as a challenge course instructor. The eye exam is an example of applicants sharing answers. The written test is evidence of what the lowest possible minimum standard can achieve and how some skills are tested over others. The drive test illustrates the impact of tester favorability and familiarity and again, how certain skills are favored in testing situations. All are indications of how difficult maintaining test quality can be and how easily one can get certified without being prepared. In short, certification testing quality can be poor and minimal, and can exclude soft and meta skills.

Creativity

In Britain, the first country to attempt certifying its outdoor leaders in the 1960s, rigid standards of performance have evolved so that only a few ways of working in the outdoors are considered acceptable. The result of this has been that British leaders do things predictably and in exactly the same manner. As a result British programs are very safe and when an accident does occur, the government simply legislates the noose tighter to provide fewer options for error.

While this legislation keeps participants safe, it also chokes creativity out of programs. New ways of thinking and doing are prevented along with any possible accidents. Leaders no longer rely on their judgement, they simply follow the rules (for an excellent treatise on the dangers of this, I recommend you read Hunt, 1984). As a result, British programs are very sterile and in many places, programs are still operating the way they did twenty or thirty years ago!

If the profession begins certifying challenge course instructors, then I fear that a single way of doing things will become the norm and the very creativity that gave rise to challenge courses in the first place will be lost as it was lost in Britain (the first challenge courses were designed in Britain in the 1940s, but became a mainstay in America in the 1970s before being widely adopted back to Britain in the 1990s).

Today, challenge course builders around the world, who are just beginning with this type of construction and creating the newest innovations, are leveling criticisms at the American builders for lacking vision and foresight concerning course designs. I fear that these rigorous standards, presently associated with course construction, will also find their way into the instructor camp. I fear that all creativity will be lost in the way we prepare challenge course instructors and the way they do their jobs, if we follow the certification line and adopt creativity choking standards.

University Programs

In America, and now to a greater extent in Australia and New Zealand, university and college degree courses evolved to supply the needs for growing numbers of outdoor leaders. Since students could gather experience over four years of their studies, these courses did a better job of preparing outdoor leaders than any certification scheme could manage in a few days.

So noticeable was this advantage, that the Wilderness Education Association arose to incorporate an outdoor leadership certificate into American universities and colleges. Although this certificate was never widely adopted by more than a handful of institutions, it did make excellent headway in the drive for higher quality leaders. Unfortunately, traditional universities and colleges are conservative and unresponsive bodies that must concern themselves with numbers and the bottom line. As a result, the politics and financial crises of the 1980s tended to close many outdoor leadership courses that were considered to be "on the fringe" of academia. In short, these degrees do provide an excellent entry-level opportunity to aspiring challenge course instructors and outdoor leaders, but the tenuous nature of such courses makes them somewhat limited in their ability to deliver all key pieces of the leadership/instructor puzzle.

Exclusive Club

As a student, I was once denied acceptance to an outdoor leadership graduate degree program in Canada, because I didn't have the necessary certificates to demonstrate my competence. When I offered to demonstrate competence by another means (take a faculty member climbing or paddling) I was told that this was an inconvenient way to do things and that the degree program had chosen to measure applicants by the number of certificates held.

Most certification schemes have started out as voluntary and become mandatory because they represent an existing system that is easy for governments to adopt or support. Certification can become a "closed shop monopoly" where noncertified experts are excluded. I fear that working on a challenge course will go the way of requiring a certificate, like changing a light bulb requires a union card on some shop floors of manufacturing plants! What does this do to qualified people that refuse to become certified or who can't afford the time or money to get a certificate?

Now some potentially certifiable readers of this chapter will like the idea that they would be more employable than their uncertified job competitors. In response to this excitement, I ask that you see the bigger selfless picture. You may get a job, but the whole profession is diminished by closed shop monopolies that prevent marginalized or disadvantaged folks from a fair chance.

Protection

People are under the mistaken belief that certificates protect organizations or individuals from lawsuits and therefore will reduce insurance premiums. Neither is true. Litigation arises because lawyers like to sue first and settle later. The threat of litigation no longer revolves around whether negligence was the case, but whether you have fully excluded claims for negligence in your legal paperwork. As a result, more of us can expect to defend against such claims and whether we

are guilty or completely without blame, we will still need to face the lawsuit.

In a lawsuit, the instructor's actions will be compared to those of a reasonable and prudent person (usually an expert witness) and holding a certificate will do little to help. In fact, being certified could be worse than not, because lawyers could claim that a certified instructor should be more prudent and reasonable than the average person: you should have known better!

Adventure programs may get a reduction on their insurance premiums for employing certified challenge course instructors, but those premiums are set based on actuarial data from the industry and will be adjusted based on safety records not staffing. The only remaining argument is that a certificate helps maintain safety and again this is a fallacy: safety maintains safety not certificates!

Historical Shifts

Although it remains a controversial issue, certification has ceased to be the trend it was in the 1960s and 70s (Priest, 1987). The debate around certification went something like this. Proponents stated that certification protected the consumer and the environment, motivated leaders to higher standards, and provided some support in cases of liability and lowered insurance premiums (we now know otherwise). Opponents argued that certification was costly and time consuming, was usually a test of specific skill proficiency (omitting soft and meta skills), and was unable to evaluate competencies such as sound judgement (Green, 1982; Rollins, 1983; March, 1987).

Hunt (1985) summed up the key issue in the certification conflict as "the attempt to conflate being safe with being certified"

(p. 24). Rogers (1979) added that outdoor leadership is not a case of certification, but is rather an ongoing process of preparation which takes place over a great deal of time and is never fully completed for the leader who aspires to be truly effective.

For these and other reasons, some of the best certification schemes no longer certify leaders. Britain (the originator of outdoor leadership certification) has chosen to "qualify" its leaders with a descriptive assessment of their strengths and weaknesses instead of an absolute measure. Britain has moved toward a competency assessment framework and Australia is looking to follow this alternative. The United States has chosen program accreditation as the current answer to safety.

Program Accreditation

Practitioners in the field prefer program accreditation to leader certification. Program accreditation has been defined as the recognition that a program or institution had met certain predetermined standards of operation (Gass & Williamson, 1995). In the accreditation process, a program is evaluated "as a whole" in terms of meeting specific standards of operation. With program accreditation, leadership (certified or not) is considered as one piece of the overall pie.

Several years ago, Wade (1983) suggested accreditation as a viable alternative to certification, stating that "such a system of peer reviews has been in operation within the Outward Bound schools" (p. 6) in the United States for almost two decades. Gray (1990) proposed a voluntary peer review process on a regional basis for AEE. It was modelled after an Outward Bound safety review process detailed by Wade and Fischesser

(1988). Reduced insurance premiums for accredited programs was cited as one immediate benefit beyond the expected improvements in educational quality, accident safety, environmental impact, and ethical behaviors. In Virginia, Cockrell and Detzel (1985) obtained 70% support for the idea of accrediting outdoor adventure organizations rather than certifying individual leaders.

With this in mind, five students surveyed the organizational membership of the Association for Experiential Education (AEE is the lead governing body for adventure programming in North America). They found that about two thirds of the respondents favored program accreditation over leadership certification (Bassin, Breault, Fleming, Foell, Neufeld & Priest, 1992). Respondents further preferred a voluntary scheme done by external peer review and applied over local regions.

In short, organizational members of AEE felt program "accreditation was the only viable alternative to [leadership] certification because more professional credibility would be gained and less dependence was needed on the unpredictable human part of the equation" (p. 25).

Program accreditation retains the strengths of leadership certification without being bound by some of its weaknesses. Accreditation provides adventure programs with the ability to achieve standards without losing the flexibility to determine how these standards are met. It allows leaders to deviate from those standards when doing so is clearly in the best interest of a participant's safety, growth, or psychological well being. Accreditation takes a systemic view of the process of adventure programming rather than dividing it into individualized categories like leadership alone. In adventures, where uncertainty is prevalent, the leaders' best judgment for safely conducting an activity could differ from the standard. In those particular instances, remember that standards are basic guidelines that must be applied to the spirit of the situation, not the mandated letter of practice under all circumstances (Gass & Williamson, 1995).

So Let's Certify Technicians

As the trend of certification slowly died out in the late 1980s, Priest (1988) wrote that:

> "a compromise on the most ubiquitous issue of outdoor leadership certification seemed to be quite possible. Most proponents were in favor of certifying some skills deemed important to an outdoor leader and so were many opponents. Most opponents disfavored certifying some of the key attributes of an outdoor leader and so did many proponents. Could the two groups have wanted the same end product, but referred to it in different terms?...A solution to this long standing problem seems possible...let the certificate be one of [technical] skills and not one of outdoor leadership" (pp. 42–43).

Since experts in the field have historically agreed on certifying technicians rather than leaders, I think the time may be right for a certificate of challenge course technology, but nothing more!

CONCLUSION

I have stood against certification, in most of its forms, since 1982 when, as safety committee chair for the Federation of Mountain Clubs of BC (Canada), I was asked to consider certifying our outdoor leaders. At that time, I wrote that "a certificate can be a false guarantee of good judgement and safe leadership" (March 1987, p. 501). Since then, my antagonism has grown to include:

1. Certification cannot encompass all aspects of leadership competency (ignores many),
2. Testing quality will always be questionably poor due to unavoidable time constraints,
3. Certification mandates a single way of working and thus, it may destroy creativity,
4. Certification is favored by conservative organizations looking for an easy way out,
5. Government agencies move to require certificates and exclude noncertified experts,
6. Certificates offer no more protection than experience and can bring higher liability,
7. Those who have tried certification and failed have found better alternative methods,
8. Accreditation considers leadership (without certificates) as part of the whole system, and
9. People trying to certify challenge course "instructors" probably mean "technicians!"

So for me, this debate depends upon whether we use the term "instructor" to mean "technician" or "facilitator." If we mean technician, then I think it might be possible to certify challenge course technicians. However, if we mean facilitator, then I have great difficulty with anyone saying this is possible, let alone choosing to find his/her market niche by setting up such a certification scheme.

REFERENCES

Bassin, Z., Breault, M., Fleming, J., Foell, S., Neufeld, J. & Priest, S. (1992). An AEE organizational member preference for leadership certification or program accreditation. *Journal of Experiential Education, 15*(1), 21–26.

Cockrell, D. & Detzel, D. (1985). Effects of outdoor leadership certification on safety, impacts and program. Trends, 22(3), 15–21.

Ewert, A. (1985). Certification: Analysing possibilities. *Camping Magazine, 57*(6), 16–19.

Gass, M. A. & Williamson, J. (1995). Accreditation of adventure programs. *Journal of Health, Physical Education, Recreation and Dance, 66*(1), 22–27.

Gray, D. (1990). A pilot model for a New England peer review program. Unpublished manuscript, Association for Experiential Education.

Green, P. (1982). *The outdoor leadership handbook*. Tacoma, WA: The Emergency Response Institute.

Hunt, J. S. Jr. (1984). The dangers of substituting rules for instructor judgement in adventure programs. *Journal of Experiential Education, 7*(3), 20–21.

Hunt, J. S. Jr. (1985). Certification controversy. *Camping Magazine, 57*(6), 23–24.

March, B. (1987). A reply to Wilkinson's comments. In Meier, J., Morash, T. & Welton G. (Eds.) *High Adventure Outdoor Pursuits* (pp. 498–501), Columbus, OH: Publishing Horizons.

Priest, S. (1987). Outdoor Leadership Certification: always an issue, but no longer a trend. *Bradford Papers Annual, 2*, 37–44.

Priest, S. (1988). Agreement reached on the issue of Outdoor Leadership Certification? *Bradford Papers Annual, 3*, 38–43.

Priest, S. (1995). Challenge course facilitator competence: A consensus. *Journal of Experiential Education, 18*(3), 158–160.

Priest, S. & Gass, M. A. (1997). *Effective Leadership in Adventure Programming*. Champaign, IL: Human Kinetics.

Rogers, R. J. (1979). *Leading to share, sharing to lead*. Sudbury, Ontario: Council of Outdoor Educators of Ontario.

Rollins, R. (1983). Leadership certification revisited. *CAHPER Journal, 50*(1), 8–9.

Senosk, E. M. (1977). *An examination of Outdoor Pursuit Leader Certification and licensing within the United States in 1976*. Unpublished Masters Thesis, University of Oregon.

Wade, I. R. (1983). An alternative to certification programs. Unpublished manuscript, Outward Bound USA.

Wade, I. R. & Fischesser, M. (1988). The Safety Review Manual: A guide to conducting safety reviews for assessing and upgrading safety in outdoor adventure programs. Unpublished manuscript, Outward Bound USA.

CHAPTER 2

Should There Be Rescue Free Wilderness Areas?

YES PERSPECTIVE: Ross Cloutier, B.A., B.P.E., M.B.A.
NO PERSPECTIVE: Julie Gabert, M.A.

Ross Cloutier has been actively involved in the adventure industry as a professional mountain guide since 1974. He has organized expeditions and guided journeys to 25 countries around the world and was the climbing leader for the 1991 Canadian Everest Expedition. He has owned two successful international guiding businesses and was the British Columbia Search and Rescue Coordinator from 1989 to 1992. His academic background includes studies in Recreational Administration (BA) and Outdoor Pursuits (BPE), as well as an MBA in International Business. Ross is currently the Chair of the Adventure Programs Department at the Universtiy College of the Cariboo which offers a two-year Guide Training Diploma and a four-year Bachelor of Tourism Management Degree with an Adventure Management major. The department also administrates the Association of Canadian Mountain Guides Training and Certification program.

Julie Gabert, M.A., has been active in the field of Outdoor Education since 1989. She currently works as an adjunct faculty at Northland College in the Department of Outdoor Education and teaches for the National Outdoor Leadership School at various branches throughout the United States.

Should There Be Rescue Free Wilderness Areas?

Ross Cloutier, B.A., B.P.E., M.B.A.

INTRODUCTION

Rescue free wilderness areas are crucial to the very existence of the concept of adventure. Adventure is a state of mind as well as a state of being and it is imperative for the future of humanity that future generations are able to explore and adventure in the manner in which past generations have had the privilege.

The issue of whether there should be rescue free wilderness areas is wide-ranging. It entails elements which encompass philosophical arguments pertaining to the type of wilderness experience users desire and how we define adventure versus sport. It impacts the type of decisions land use managers are making regarding the provision of search and rescue services, health care cost decision making, the impact of commercially generated technology on the adventure experience and how readily wilderness users receive it, as well as issues that surround intergenerational equity and society's desire to protect the right of future generations of wilderness users to experience adventure.

What is wilderness? Is it an area so wild that it limits those who can enter? Is the wilderness definition relative and elastic depending upon the need for rescue? Within the political boundaries, wilderness status limits mechanical intrusions which are frequently waived to allow rescues. Is this an acceptable ethical violation? Technological development has brought us to controversy but should technology necessarily win?

Recently, costs of rescue are making many agencies re-examine their positions. Elemental questions now include, "Who gets rescued?" "Whoever needs to be.", used to be the answer. With the current climate, however, the who and how, and at what cost and risk, has become a controversial issue. Is rescue really a public obligation provided to all wilderness areas of the world?

Should rescue free wilderness areas be established? Is the true definition of a wilderness area where even mechanical intrusion for the saving of lives is prohibited? Perhaps the answer is to take wilderness on its own terms, which include areas so wild that nobody except the user can solve the unforeseen problem.

RESCUE RESPONSE MODELS

There are a wide variety of rescue response models available to agencies tasked with providing rescues. These models include everything from one end of a continuum, where the expectations are the provision of fully professional emergency medical system (EMS) responders utilizing professional paramedic/rescuers and an immediate response period—to the other end of the continuum, where absolutely no response is provided nor allowed in an area. Most response agencies tasked with providing wilderness search and rescue services choose to emulate some varying point on the continuum between these two. From higher service levels to lower service levels these theoretical points may represent any combination of:

1) A fully professional EMS model with professional search and rescue response

2) A fully professional rescue service with volunteers providing search support

3) Organized volunteer search groups with professional rescuer support

4) No agency rescue with organized volunteer groups providing search and rescue response

5) Organized volunteer groups providing search services with non-organized ad-hoc rescue response

6) Ad-hoc volunteer search and rescue response

7) Rescue-available and rescue-free areas (isolation or land manager imposed)

8) Communication/technology bans to protect the wilderness experience

9) No external search or rescues are carried out

10) No external search or rescues are allowed

Any choice of the level of rescue response (or any combination thereof) that should be provided in an area is a jursidictional decision which is comprised of elements of wilderness experience philosophy, rescue philosophy and economics. A more intrusive response policy that supports high levels of rescue response from organized agencies has both the result of impacting the level of experience that is available to the wilderness user, while at the same time increasing the costs to the agency.

"WHITE WILDERNESS" RESCUE AND DANGER

Rescue response is a philosophical decision as it has direct implications on the experience that is available to the user. Reinhold Messner in his description of his concept of wilderness states, "At the beginning of this century, the big adventure was to fill in the white spots on the map. I would prefer to leave the remaining blank spots on the map. It's not necessary to go to wild places and create maps or write guidebooks" (Soles, 1994, p. 24). In addition to the impacts of the creation of maps and guidebooks on the wilderness experience, I would argue that the provision of extensive search and rescue throughout all wilderness areas of the world has the compounding result of providing an unnecessary and unacceptable intrusion into the "white wilderness." Access to rescue changes the mental attitude towards adventure and is, in many cases, inessential and superfluous.

Discussions around whether or not there should be rescue free wilderness areas will increase as the world's true wilderness areas decrease in size and number. This is because human beings will ultimately realize that there is no end to the potential urbanization of the vast spaces; the ensuing backlash will result in our striving to create true white wilderness areas, ones that do not include artificial elements such as rescue.

In addition to retaining blank spaces on the map that enable true exploration, the wilderness experience is characterized by other factors, not the least of which is an appreciation of the potential harm which may result as a consequence of interacting with an untamed environment. No matter how you attempt to package it, outdoor experience without the risk of harm is sport or guided tourism, not adventure. Risk and danger are inherent in the definition of adventure. Fear, as a result of risk and danger, is also part of the adventure experience. If someone starts a route with the knowledge that there is no outside assistance they are likely to be much more careful and much stronger, both physically and mentally. This level of fear is taken away with the expectation that rescue is imminently available. If this fear is taken away, a false sense of confidence ensues and not only are individuals more prone to incident, but they are not experiencing adventure. Adventure occurs only where there is the risk of death. If death is not possible, the activity is not adventure; it is sport (Soles, 1994). In fact, risk and danger are the raison d'être of the activity (Ewert & Hollenhorst, 1997).

THE NEED FOR RESCUE IS A RELATIVE CONCEPT

When lost or injured in the wilderness, the adventurer obviously feels an increased need for rescue. Prior to the accident there was no need for rescue to exist. Injury changes one's appreciation for rescue. When a life hangs in the balance it is easily worth the $2,000 helicopter ride to safety; so too, is the understanding that when it is not required, rescue is clearly an extraneous need.

The concept of what is an extraneous need in the wilderness is very dependent upon a person's individual beliefs, the culture in which they live, the level of their wilderness knowledge, skills, and abilities, their tolerance for epics and whether or not they even know that a rescue option exists. There are legions of stories passed down in adventure folklore of users either calling in unnecessary rescues or waiving off those which rescuers were attempting. I have personally responded to rescue callouts that have included everything from a request for vehicle gas for someone who designated running out of gas an emergency requiring rescue, to a climber who refused to be rescued even though he had a broken leg. Ultimately, the decision of whether or not a rescue is desirable is highly variable and very relative to the individual. So, whose definition of necessary will we use? I trust not the definition which adheres to the logic of, "for any reason, any where, any time, using any means." This is clearly inappropriate in all wilderness areas.

THE IMPLICATIONS OF HIGH-TECHNOLOGY AND COMMUNICATIONS ON WILDERNESS RESCUE

As a result of the physical isolation of many areas of the world (examples might include the Arctic, the Antarctic, Northern Canada, Tibet, etc.) there have effectively been geographically imposed rescue free wilderness areas. However, recent developments in communication technology have given urgency to the discussion surrounding rescue free wilderness areas and have severe philosophical implications for how we view and are able to experience wilderness. Contemporary rescue teams routinely respond to subjects who can communicate with them by cellular or sattelite telephone. While this has desirable effects on both the efficiency and effectiveness of the response, it also has the potential to significantly change the nature and frequency of callouts unless parameters are placed upon the use of these communication systems.

Another high-technology communications item with the potential to impact the wilderness experience is the personal locator beacon (PLB). Operating along the same technological lines as the more familiar emergency locator transmitters (ELT) used in aircraft and the emergency position indicating radio beacons (EPIRB) used on sea-going vessels, the PLB is manufactured and marketed for the use of land-based wilderness travelers. When activated by a user the transmitted signal is picked up via satellite technology and its position is forwarded to the appropriate search and rescue response agency anywhere in the world. Although the concept is sound and the technology works well; there are serious implications for rescue agencies, some of whom embrace the technology while others eschew it. The fact that a PLB transmits only one type of emergency signal gives no clues to the rescuer regarding urgency, which results in all PLB callouts in a jurisdiction receiving the same level of urgency. PLB technology in many jurisdictions is driven by its manufacturers; not as a result of either user or response agency demand. While manufacturer marketing

may subtly allude to high levels of rescue response when they are activated, the truth is that response agencies will set their own policies regarding the urgency given to PLB callouts. These policies may differ widely from manufacturer desires or user expectations. As an example, British Columbia's written policy is to respond to all PLB callouts as though they were a missing person and not as though the subject required a rescue-level response. Volunteer ground search teams are used as the initial response (Amy, 1994). This is likely to be disappointing to a wilderness user who is expecting a helicopter filled with rescue paramedics to come flying over the hill.

The obvious resulting question is what role in wilderness rescue decision making should the manufacturers of high-technology implements be allowed? They have an obvious bias regarding the level of technology that should be used in wilderness areas and philosophical decision-making regarding response levels should be removed from the realm of their influence. It is a fact that communications technology will advance far beyond what is available today and it is crucial for wilderness users to be the ones determining what technology is permitted in wilderness areas.

Although this paper is not particularily intended to argue for or against the merits of high-technology use in the wilderness, it is relevant to any discussion regarding wilderness rescue to consider that by its very existence in the wilderness, the use of high-technology communication impacts the user's experience level. I have never experienced anything as instrusive and disruptive to an expedition experience as carrying out media interview transmissions back to North America from the North Col of Mount Everest. Having experienced it once, I promised myself that this level of high-technology instrusion would never happen to me again. Sponsors thrive on this, while mountaineers sell their souls because of it.

ECONOMIC REALITIES AND PUBLIC AGENCY RESCUE FUNDING

As much as we would like to think otherwise, rescue philosophy is ultimately dictated by economic realities. A rescue agency may strive to provide a level of service based upon its perceived mandate or corporate philosophy only to find that it is inachievable due to inadequate funding sources. Corporate and professional philosophy just met economic reality, an increasingly common occurence in times when rescuers are striving for ever higher professionalism and increased response capabilities while funding agency budgets are ever shrinking. The net result of this conflict is healthy discussion regarding the level of service that should be provided, what level of technology (i.e., communication and helicopters) should be used, who should pay for rescue and ultimately, should rescue be provided in all wilderness areas.

Economic rationalization is positive when it results in a critical analysis of what, where and how rescue services should be provided. It is not necessarily a truism that the default position of rescue providers should be to continually strive for consistent and continually increasing levels of response throughout all wilderness areas. This is a fiscally irresponsible, inappropriate and unlikely scenario that causes much performance frustration throughout the rescue community. Economic rationalization must occur as part of rescue delivery decision making. To

do otherwise would be unconscionable. It is appropriate as part of this rationalization process to consider providing a scaled level of respone; not all areas require similiar response types or speeds. It is consistent with this line of reasoning that some areas require none at all.

RESCUE RESPONSE ZONING

Search and rescue response agencies normally set goals and expectations to the speed with which responders will access an injured person within their jursidiction. Various models have been formulated by agencies to provide guidelines for their response targets; many of which are accompanied by some sort of zoning system that will provide direction as to what type of response time is acceptable within a specific area. This approach to pre-planning response is based upon the assumption that an agency will not be able to provide the same level of service to all areas within its jurisdiction. This is often due only to the varying lengths of time it would take to access all regions it is responsibile for. A sample of one of these models follows:

1. *Near-urban*: Response targets to near-urban incidents will follow the "golden-hour" rule and access all urban and near-urban areas in under one hour.

2. *Front-country*: Response times to front-country incidents will be within one to two hours.

3. *Mid-country*: Response times to mid-country incidents will be between two to four hours.

4. *Back-country*: Response times to back-country incidents will be between two

to twelve hours (Province of British Columbia, 1996).

It is a logical extension of this type of model that there is a place for a *wilderness area* zone that does not have rescue provided. In effect, when an agency starts to base response on a land-base zoning model there are land areas in the world where there is effectively no useful rescue response. Thus, it is appropriate to call it like it is and state outright that these areas are or should be designated as no-rescue areas.

PRIVATE AND PUBLIC RESCUE RESPONSE

In many ways, the discussion around whether there should be rescue free wilderness areas revolves around whether public agencies should provide rescue services to everyone and in all areas. Is rescue really a public obligation to all people in all wilderness areas of the world? It is not. Governments have no moral obligation to assume the responsibility for adventurer behaviours in what are best described as anarchic, antisocial, personal, recreational, non-contributional activities. Without rationalizing one over the other, these accident causing behaviours may include any combination of lack of planning, poor equipment, lack of skill or knowledge, recklessness, acts of God, and bad luck, among others. The reality is that adventuring is high-risk, fickle, and irresponsible from any societal point of view. That is partly why we do it. Placing responsibility upon society to support such behaviour is Machiavellian and misguided at best.

Should wilderness users be able to effect their own private rescue without relying upon public agencies to carry it out or fi-

nance it? Clearly, in most regions, yes. Should the publicly funded response agencies, for callouts that are deemed "extraneous", be able to provide this service on a cost-recovery basis if requested to do so by the user? Clearly, in most cases, yes. Should private alternatives to public agencies be developed to provide an alternate service if the user demanded it? Clearly, in most cases, yes.

Many of the reasons that public response agencies are moving to consider various forms of revenue-generation, cost-recovery or fee-for-service delivery formats are philosophical in nature and not deficit based. Many agencies feel that it is not responsibe for tax-based funds to pay for all rescues in all areas. This is a clear indication of their position that it is unreasonable to provide rescue to all wilderness areas as funded by the public purse.

Rescue costs are directly or indirectly a part of a region's health care costs. Whether these costs are borne by the state, the user, or insurance, will depend upon the particular public policy of the region. Jurisdictions in Canada, the United States and Europe differ widely on their view of this. So, too, will their views on whether there should be rescue free wilderness areas.

INTERGENERATIONAL EQUITY AND FUTURE WILDERNESS EXPERIENCE

The most important aspects of whether there should be rescue free wilderness areas regard what is fair and equitable to future generations of wilderness users. The way we use our resources and the manner in which they are developed are, in effect, policy decisions about intergenerational distribution and equity. The main beneficiaries of rescue free wilderness areas are the inhabitants of the future, as they will then be able to experience wilderness on the same terms that previous generations have. In social decision making, including whether there should be rescue free areas, there is no excuse for treating generations unequally. Decisions made today directly and profoundly impact the experience levels available to future generations. It is unethical and immoral to develop our wilderness areas today in a manner which precludes our children and their children, from experiencing the same isolation, dangers, fears, planning, and contingency challenges that we have been enabled to grapple with. Wilderness is not wilderness with the elimination of these critical elements of adventure!

Intergenerational equity is an obligation to conduct ourselves so that we leave to the future the option and capacity to be as well off as we are today. Distributional equity is an issue between the present and the future, so wilderness management decision-making today becomes a problem of what impact we are prepared to have on future experience opportunities, what we are prepared to do in order to protect future experience options, and what we are prepared to spend to invest in their protection. Current decision making regarding the evolution of rescue response has a tendency to default toward increased coverage and higher levels of service and do not inherently incorporate any concern about the protection of future wilderness experiences.

The provision of rescue free wilderness areas today can be regarded as an act of investment in the type of wilderness experiences available to future generations. I do not want my son to grow up believing that the only definition of wilderness available to him includes the intrusion of rescue teams flying around the wilderness upon the demand of telephone toting urbanites who expect a rescue service to make up in for the knowledge, skills, and abilities with which they should have been trained.

Should there be rescue free wilderness areas? Yes, there should be.

REFERENCES

Amy, G. (1994). *Personal locator beacon response in British Columbia*. The Provincial Emergency Program.

Ewert, A.W. & Hollenhorst, S.J. (1997). Adventure recreation and its implications for wilderness. *International Journal of Wilderness, 3,*(2).

Province of British Columbia (1996). *Land and inland water search and rescue strategic plan for British Columbia: Towards 2000 and beyond* (pp. 151). Provincial Emergency Program.

Soles, C. (1994). On top of the world with Reinhold Messner. *Rock and Ice, 59* (pp. 24–27).

Should There Be Rescue Free Wilderness Areas?

Julie Gabert, M.A.

It's two in the morning, Chris is lying by the side of a river exhausted, soaked, and nearly beyond shivering. Earlier in the day, while attempting to cross a swollen river, Chris lost his footing and was swept downstream. He slammed into numerous boulders until he was finally pushed out onto a sandy bend. Chris sustained a broken leg and moderate head injuries. His pack is gone. He is alone.

In a few days he will be reported missing, but Chris knows that no one will attempt to rescue him. He realizes this because he chose to travel through a "no-rescue wilderness" area. Chris was aware that the management policies of this area forbid official agencies to attempt any rescue operations. In fact, this is why he chose to travel here. In this predicament, Chris knows that he has little or no chance of coming out of this wilderness area alive.

NO-RESCUE WILDERNESS CONCEPT

The concept of rescue free wilderness areas or "no-rescue" zones was first conceived by McAvoy and Dustin (1981). They proposed "an expansion of outdoor recreation opportunities to include wilderness areas in which users would bear the sole responsibility for their personal welfare. Agencies managing areas designated for full-risk use would be absolved, indeed prohibited, from intervening at anytime on behalf of any recreationist in distress" (McAvoy & Dustin, 1981, p. 150).

McAvoy and Dustin felt that the U.S. National Wilderness Preservation System (NWPS) was incomplete, specifically on the primitive end. They proposed the concept of no-rescue wilderness zones in order to accommodate those individuals who desired the "ultimate" wilderness experience. The quest for freedom, self-reliance, and independence fueled this concept (McAvoy & Dustin, 1981).

The no-rescue zone, according to McAvoy (1990), would be managed like any other wilderness area utilizing a user quota system to protect the resource and the wilderness experience. Its uniqueness, he believes, would be that the managing agency would be responsible for informing users of the risks in the area and the fact that no rescue services would be available. However, I will argue that this concept contradicts one of the basic elements of the U.S. Wilderness Act of 1964 and therefore should not be implemented.

PRIORITY ON LIFE

In 1964, the U.S. Wilderness Act set aside designated areas to be preserved as "wilderness." Section 2 (c) states that:

> "wilderness…is hereby recognized as an area where the earth and its community of life are untrammeled by man, where man himself is a visitor who does not remain…Except as otherwise provided, wilderness areas shall be devoted to the public purposes of recreational, scenic, scientific, educational, conservation, and historical use" (Brame & Henderson, 1992, p. 117).

Section 4 (c) of the U.S. Wilderness Act goes on to mention the prohibited uses of wilderness by stating that:

> "there shall be no…permanent road within any wilderness area designated by this Act EXCEPT as necessary to meet minimum requirements for the administration of the area for the purpose of this Act (including measures required in emergencies involving the health and safety of persons within the area)" (Brame & Henderson, 1992, p.118).

Through Section 4, the Wilderness Act of 1964 clearly establishes a priority on human life. A priority that, according to Colin Campbell, Chief Ranger at Grand Teton National Park, still exists today as a policy within the park services (C. Campbell, personal communication, March 13, 1998).

ACTUAL NEED

The question then becomes, can individuals who desire a sense of freedom, self-reliance, and independence attain this in our current wilderness system? McAvoy (1990) says no. He suggests that one cannot approach the edge of life (by potentially gambling with life or death scenarios) if one knows that it is fenced with a rescue policy.

However, according to John Krambrink, Chief Ranger at Mt. Rainier National Park in Washington, "wilderness" truly does exist today due to hazards such as weather, wildlife, and other environmental conditions. "When you travel off trail in a wilderness area, you should not have an expectation of being rescued. People can still get hurt and even killed in wilderness areas today" (J. Krambrink, personal communication, March 5, 1998).

McAvoy (1990) argues that most wilderness users believe they will be rescued if they are overdue, ill, or injured. U.S. Park and Forest Service personnel would argue otherwise due to the wild nature of many existing wilderness areas. According to Pete Armington (1998), Chief Ranger at Isle Royal National Park, the Park Service may intentionally delay a rescue or utilize a slower, more controlled approach in saving someone in order to protect search and rescue (SAR) personnel. In doing so, an individual is entirely dependent upon his/her own self-reliance unless the SAR reaches them in a timely manner. In extreme weather, this could mean countless hours or even days.

In essence, the more rugged, remote, and/or high an area of travel, combined with hazards such as extreme weather, the closer an individual can potentially come to total self reliance. Many winter ascents, for instance, typically offer a very small margin for rescue. In terms of need, Krambrink feels that the concept of no-rescue wilderness areas has "never caught on in the park services because it is really not needed." (J. Krambrink, personal communication, March 5, 1998).

Krambrink believes that "if you truly need 'wilderness,' you can find it."

PERSONAL CHOICE

It is important to remember that individuals seeking total "independence" are not required to carry a radio or cellular phone, and they are not required to call for help or hike out to a roadhead to get assistance. This is a personal choice. Instead of designating an entire area a no-rescue zone, individuals can simply decide that they are the no-rescue type who will not call for assistance. Furthermore, one can easily travel deep into the wilderness and never inform anyone of his/her whereabouts.

The story of Chris McCandless, which was immortalized in Jon Krakauer's (1996) book *Into the Wild*, is a perfect example of an individual who ultimately spelled out his own fateful destiny by choosing to spend four months living alone in Alaska. Many others have taken similar independent journeys, yet lived to tell about them.

MORAL ISSUES

On another note, no-rescue wilderness zones are simply not practical in our society. Armington believes that the no-rescue concept has never been taken seriously by SAR, the National Park Service (NPS), or State and volunteer rescue agencies mainly because it is "too far out to ever be worthy of serious thought. It is just not realistic" (P. Armington, personal communication, March 6, 1998). This potentially powerful, self-reliant concept cannot be realistically implemented in our society due to factors such as morality, legality, and a modern day humanitarian philosophy.

Even though the U.S. Park and Forest Services are not legally bound to rescue individuals in need, they still regard visitor protection as a necessary public service. It would be a crime to prevent rescuers from responding to a plea for help. Armington believes that in the "real world," this no-rescue concept would fall flat due to the high value that we place upon human life (P. Armington, personal communication, March 6, 1998).

Ethically, it is not fair to place SAR and park personnel into a complex ethical dilemma if they know that someone is out in a nearby no-rescue zone in critical need of assistance. Peterson (1987) believes that the immorality of the basic no-rescue premise would compromise the very meaning of civilization. He believes that we have not only the right, but the duty, to attempt to rescue people. The human condition is rooted in an ethics of mutual assistance. He feels that "when we rescue someone in trouble, we say something about the kind of species we are, and aspire to be...we rescue people because we have to live with ourselves and our collective consciences" (p. 41).

In effect, it is not realistic to believe that SAR and Park personnel could comfortably sit and wait in their offices, going about business as usual, knowing that they have the ability to save someone who is dying in a no-rescue zone. Just because someone, on a quest to be "independent," made a choice to travel into a no-rescue zone when entering the wilderness, doesn't mean, that on the brink of death, he or she still agrees with their previous choice.

INDEPENDENCE VERSUS SURVIVAL

It is obvious that the wilderness that once existed during the early frontier days no longer exists today. And, one could speculate that even the most rugged, self-reliant, and independent early explorers would have graciously accepted assistance instead of facing imminent death. Survival is instinctive in humans; as animals, we have an inner drive to live.

Now, say your friend "Chris" is facing his or her final hours, lying injured in a no-rescue wilderness zone where help is potentially nearby. In those last moments, it is hard to imagine Chris not wanting to live...not wishing that someone would help. "Even in the most desperate of situations, each of us will continue to hope for rescue up to the point of death" (Peterson, 1987, p. 42). Take Rob Hall for example, an experienced mountaineer who knew that the possibility of being rescued near the south summit of Mt. Everest was impossible under the conditions he was facing, yet he continued to ask for help even into his final hours (Krakauer, 1997, p. 234).

Perhaps it is true that many travelers could go into no-rescue zones, have incredible feelings of independence, enjoy themselves immensely, and return home safely to celebrate. Yet, it is difficult to ignore those few who wouldn't make it out. McAvoy (1990) argues that too much emphasis has been placed on what could go wrong in no rescue areas instead of what could go right. Yet, in light of all the potential positives, how can we ignore the reality of those who will never return home to their families. "Self growth is learning from your mistakes...to let someone die because of a bad choice or mistake is not growth." (J. Hughes, SAR, personnel communication, March, 1998).

Where is the honor in dying an independent, self-reliant individual if, in your final hours, someone might have been able to save you, yet you chose ahead of time not to have them intervene. Where does society draw the line on independence vs. suicide? "Are we really expected to believe that society will profit from a policy which reinforces apathy and insensitivity for the many, so a few can say they are more self-reliant?" (Peterson, 1987, p. 42).

FAMILY AND COMMUNITY ISSUES

An additional factor that makes the no-rescue concept particularly controversial, centers around the issue of family, friends, and the general public. According to SAR Pilot Tom Jensen, a no-rescue wilderness area would tend to be unfair to the family of a "victim" who might turn up missing. No matter how the "victim" might feel about entering a no-rescue area, Jensen believes that if that person never returned, the family would feel anguish and need the type of closure that a search and rescue or recovery would provide. Without this closure, it is possible that a no-rescue area could have implications which leave family and friends hurt for a very long time (T. Jensen, personal correspondence, March 5, 1998).

The formation of no-rescue zones would definitely compound the problems of a missing wilderness traveller according to Ron Jablonski, Public Affairs Officer for the Rio Grande National Forest in Colorado. Ultimately, untrained family members or friends of a "self-reliant" individual who never returned home might venture out and try to find and save the missing person. In certain wilderness zones, this could mean attempting a vertical rescue for which the friends or family may be untrained to carry out and might result in disastrous consequences (R. Jablonski, personal correspondence, March 10, 1998). It is, therefore, unrealistic to believe that trained SAR personnel would watch on the sidelines as untrained individuals ventured out to attempt to save friends or family members.

In addition, it is difficult to believe that the media wouldn't catch onto the moral debate of rescue free wilderness areas and severely question its legitimacy after the first person came up missing in a no-rescue wilderness zone. One concerned family member could put an incredible amount of pressure on wilderness managing agencies, including the National Park Service, the Forest Service, the Fish & Wildlife Service, or the Bureau of Land Management (BLM), and in doing so initiate an enormous public outcry.

According to Colin Campbell, Chief Ranger at Grand Teton National Park, "some families already put tremendous pressure on rescue operations" (C. Campbell, personnel correspondence, March 12, 1998). Therefore, if pressure is currently being placed on park services for purposefully delaying a rescue due to unsafe conditions, it is hard to imagine the kind of pressure that could be laid forth if the park service becomes legally bound not to assist a person in a no-rescue wilderness area. "The first few deaths due to a lack of rescue would create such a public cry that the restriction would be lifted. For this reason, the formation of a no-rescue area will never go. If it did, it would not last long" (S. Whitehead, SAR, personal correspondence, February 26, 1998).

Another important element to consider is the management of no-rescue areas where Federal land managing agencies would have to determine what type of individuals will be allowed to enter or not enter these no-rescue zones.

MENTAL HEALTH ISSUES

In the United States, mental health therapists can be held liable if they even THINK their client might have gone to the wilderness to kill himself or herself (one no-rescue scenario). Kay Sinclair, MA, LPC, (personal correspondence, March 3, 1998), says that "as a mental health therapist, I am expected to protect a suicidal client from himself. Anyone who is 'independent' or a 'hermit' would certainly fit the no-rescue scenario, but they would also fit the person who would need a mental health evaluation."

Along those same lines, no-rescue could also translate into no law enforcement for those seeking refuge from legal authorities. "We already have quite a problem with drug growers creating hazards for the SAR community" (T. Jensen, personal correspondence, March 1, 1998). No-rescue wilderness areas would open up new opportunities for drug cartels and escaped convicts to find refuge.

Ultimately, in an attempt to resolve the aforementioned issues, it seems that the government would have to require that all individuals interested in entering a proposed no-rescue wilderness area be evaluated by a mental health therapist, be fingerprinted and file searched, undergo a physical exam, be of legal age, take a proficiency test, and pass a sound judgment evaluation before being allowed in. How can this concept realistically be said to encourage less government control?

If, by chance, a person passes all of these requirements, then what? According to Peterson (1987), it seems unreasonable to suggest a policy which would, in effect, allow healthy people who have a zest for life to suffer and die-perhaps needlessly-merely because they wish to be held accountable for their own judgments.

LEGAL ISSUES

Another argument against no-rescue wilderness zones concerns the many legal complications that would surface. For example, would a signed waiver hold up in court if an individual could have been rescued, but instead died? According to Maio, juries might be quite receptive to an emotional plea from a plaintiff's lawyer bringing suit against the jurisdiction "who let this kind, gentle person suffer such a horrible death" no matter what kind of waiver they signed before going into the no-rescue wilderness zone (J. Maio, SAR, personal correspondence, March 4, 1998). In addition, any agency that doesn't investigate and attempt to locate a subject regardless of mental status, could be held liable for the consequences. There is no doubt that the non-responding SAR agency could be dragged to court for negligence or license revocation.

Jablonski agrees that the liability could be tremendous. "Who's going to incur the wrath of family and media? It will probably be the managing agency" (R. Jablonski, personal correspondence, March 10, 1998). Do we really want to see wilderness managers brought to court and sued for a policy that was disagreeable in the first place? What about the lost hiker who happens to wander unknowingly into a no-rescue zone? To solve this potential dilemma, managing agencies will need to fence in all no-rescue boundaries or be held liable when an innocent person wanders in and gets hurt.

It is important to note that the issues are quite complex even though advocates will argue that there will be no legal battles regarding rescue-free wilderness zones. Anyone has the right to sue. And, in these no-rescue circumstances, it is highly likely that someone will.

IMPLICATIONS FOR ADVENTURE EDUCATION SCHOOLS OR AGENCIES

McAvoy et al. (1985) believe adventure education agencies that sponsor trips to no-rescue areas would not have to fear liability problems if they have qualified staff, adequate supervision, inform participants of risks, and have appropriate group responses to handle emergency situations. I can think of no credible school or agency that would agree with this. It is one thing to put yourself into a no-rescue wilderness area, but how could an institution legally or ethically take students into a no-rescue zone knowing that the students are relying completely on their instructors in a life threatening emergency that potentially requires outside assistance. Where is the personal growth here? Whose self-reliance are we tapping into? How is this student benefiting from the concept of "self-reliance" when they are at the mercy of their instructors?

According to Schimelpfenig (1998, p. 8), "we operate in a climate, in both our industry and society, of growing intolerance to the adverse consequences of risk." It therefore appears very unrealistic to even consider this no-rescue concept an option with educational groups.

When I take a group into a wilderness area, we prepare to be completely self-sufficient even in emergency situations. However, I carry a ground-to-air radio that can be used to signal to an airplane flying overhead in the case of an extreme emergency. Basically, if the technology and the resources are available to potentially save a student's life, I want to have access to it. Purposefully taking students into no-rescue wilderness zones should, therefore, be considered negligent. Even though it may enhance the instructor's experience, students will not benefit from this gamble. It is very likely that after the first injury or death, any school or agency involved would fold under litigation. And, since most outdoor education schools and agencies would not be willing to take such high risks, these no-rescue wilderness zones, which legally are considered to be public land, would suddenly be off limits to many schools and agencies.

THE WILDERNESS EXPERIENCE

The idea that individuals should take responsibility for their actions in the wilderness is a very sound one. However, as Allen (1981) points out, "individuals should take responsibility for their actions in all wilderness areas, not just selected ones. To make such a distinction actually demeans the U.S. National Wilderness Preservation System and the spirit of wilderness" (p. 154). Similarly, Peterson (1987) sees the backcountry challenge not simply to survive a wilderness adventure, but to celebrate and savor it. "Not because it is dangerous, powerful, beautiful and, therefore thrilling, and not because it has the potential to help us cope with life. No, wilderness is valuable because it is wilderness. It is that simple" (Peterson, 1987, p. 42).

The "wilderness experience," therefore, takes into account the idea that wilderness is more than just a physical place. Wilderness undeniably offers something different to every individual. It can be viewed as a state

of mind (Nash, 1988), an experience (McAvoy, 1990), a challenge, or a necessity of the human spirit (Abbey, 1968). According to Allen (1981), risk (as proposed by the no-rescue wilderness concept), "is only one component of this wilderness experience, and for many users it is probably subordinate to solitude, nature appreciation and reflection" (p. 153).

ALTERNATIVE SOLUTIONS

The desire for freedom, self-reliance and independence is an incredibly valid need for some individuals. In this sense, the fuel that burns this no-rescue concept is quite valid. Perhaps some alternate solutions already exist that may help ease McAvoy & Dustin (1981), and any others in their search for complete self-reliance in the wilderness.

According to John Lunn, Manager of Tasmania Emergency Services, "To place yourself in a no-rescue situation is not a geographical decision, it is a psychological decision" (J. Lunn, personal communication, March 3, 1998). It can be done easily enough in most places by simply not telling anyone where you are going. Many search and rescue personnel agree with this somewhat obvious solution. "If you don't want to be found, simply don't tell anyone where you are going or when you might return. A rescue mission would never be initiated if there was no clue of where to look or when to begin looking. The burden of the decision to rescue or not rescue would now rest on the subject" (B. Frost, SAR, personal correspondence, March 3, 1998).

On a similar note, Jablonski feels that if you truly want to be self-reliant, don't even venture into a designated wilderness area. There are plenty of other remote areas of land to travel through where no one will go looking for you (R. Jablonski, personal correspondence, March 10, 1998). There are the oceans, the Pole's, the rainforests, and many countries with extremely remote areas available for traveling independently.

Traveling through remote areas knowing that a rescue is a very distant possibility is one thing, yet intentionally going somewhere where the hope of rescue is legally out of the question, even though very capable SAR personnel may have the power to reach you, is an unhealthy twist on self-reliance. It seems to be an artificial or contrived way of attempting to create a new frontier in our time.

My advice then, is be creative. When I truly want to be alone, independent, and self-reliant, I don't have to look that hard to find a place to go. If I don't want to be rescued, I don't broadcast my whereabouts to anyone, I simply slide gently into the mountains without a word. It's that simple.

REFERENCES

Allen, S. (1981). No-rescue wilderness-a risky proposition. *Journal of Forestry, 79* (3), 153–154.

Abbey, E. (1968). *Desert solitaire: A season in the wilderness*. New York, NY: Ballantine Books.

Brame, S.C. & Henderson, C. (1992). *An introduction to wildland ethics and management*. Lander, WY: National Outdoor Leadership School.

Krakauer, J. (1996). *Into the wild*. New York, NY: Bantam Doubleday Dell Publishing Group.

Krakauer, J. (1997). *Into thin air*. New York, NY: Villard Books.

McAvoy, L.H. (1990). Rescue-free wilderness areas. In J.C. Miles & S. Priest (Eds.), *Adventure Education* (pp. 329–334). State College, PA: Venture.

McAvoy, L.H. & Dustin, D.L. (1981). The right to risk in the wilderness. *Journal of Forestry, 79* (3), 150–152.

McAvoy, L.H. & Dustin, D., Rankin, J., & Frakt, A. (1985). Wilderness and legal liability: Guidelines for resource managers and program leaders. *Journal of Park and Recreation Administration, 3* (1), 41–49.

Nash, R. F. (1988). The United States: Why wilderness. In V. Martin, *For the conservation of earth*. Colorado: Fulcrum Inc.

Peterson, D. (1987). Look ma, no hands: Here's what's wrong with no-rescue wilderness. *Parks and Recreation, 22* (6), 39–43, 54.

Schimelpfenig, T. (1998, February). Turning students loose/student independence: NOLS student supervision practices. *NOLS Newsletter*, 7–11.

CHAPTER 3

Are Floating Fee Scales for Corporate and Educational Groups Ethical?

YES PERSPECTIVE: Steve Proudman, M.S.
NO PERSPECTIVE: Jasper S. Hunt, Ph.D.

Steve Proudman, M.S. Adult and Continuing Education, University of Wisconsin—Madison. He is president of the Proudman Group, Inc., a "virtual" organizational development consulting firm. His expertise is in designing and delivering experience-based learning programs for teams and organizations.

Steve worked for Outward Bound, the largest wilderness-based experiential education program in the world, as a field instructor and administrator for seven years. He created and served as the director of the Chicago Outward Bound Center whose primary mission was to serve inner-city youth with urban based adventure programs.

Steve has been an active member of the International Association for Experiential Education for 15 years serving as a Board Member and Treasurer. He is a member of the National Organizational Development Network, the Chicago OD Network and the International Organizational Development Registry, the International Association of Facilitators, the Association for Quality and Participation and the Shivas Irons Society. His passions include backpacking, skiing, running, travel, golf and adventures with his family.

Jasper S. Hunt is Professor of Experiential Education and Leadership Studies and Director of Adventure Education Programs at Minnesota State University, Mankato, Minnesota.

Are Floating Fee Scales for Corporate and Educational Groups Ethical?

Steve Proudman, M.S.

I first asked myself, is this a question about the free market economy and pricing decisions? Is it about the quality of services being delivered justifying higher fees? Is it about the economic freedoms of different institutions with budgets that may be limited? Is it a question about human behavior, greed in particular? On one level this is a question about money which is a social construct that has different definitions attached to it.

In answering this question I had to reflect on my relationship to money as a means to various ends. I think it is helpful to gain some perspective on the meanings we attach to money before exploring the ethics of this chapter's question. I view money as a form of energy that is exchanged for other forms of energy, as either a product or a service. To preface my chapter, I'll share some thoughts on money from Jacob Needleman's *Money and the Meaning of Life* (1991).

> Money, I'm convinced, is an inspired invention by people who understood the play of forces in human life. There must have come a moment when something was needed that could facilitate people's material life in a expanding society. It must have been created as

a means of recognizing that human beings have property rights, but at the same time that no human being or family is self-sufficient. In others words, money was created—by the keepers of the sacred teaching underlying all human societies—to maintain a relationship between man's [sic] spiritual needs and his material needs. What I'm trying to say is that money is intrinsically a principle of reconciliation, of the harmonization of disparate elements. No wonder that in ancient Greece, Hermes was both the god of commerce and the god of communication between man and immortals, the god of the borders, and the god of exchange.

But where there is relationship, there must be contact between things related. For exchange to take place there must be contact between the elements in the exchange. A principle of reconciliation allows this contact to take place. Money was invented to allow contact and exchange between fundamental aspects of human life, the material, external life and the internal life, in the sense of people's relationship to God within and above (Needleman, 1991).

The question to which this chapter offers an answer could be about the degree of acceptability that exists for charging one group of people more for a service than another. In answering this question, I think it is constructive to play with your beliefs and conditioning around your relationship to money. From conch shell currency to plastic, what does it mean to you? Needleman's college students raise some fascinating questions as they contemplate currency:

- How much of myself will I have to sell for money in order to be able to live more fully later, and can I regain what I've sold?

- There is something very frightening about money. I don't understand it. So, apparently, it is not only a material entity, but is tied to inner psychological forces. What can I do to see clearly what money really means?

- Why do jobs that seem to contribute most to people seem to pay the least? Must one choose between material well-being and service to humanity?

- How can I maintain access to the spiritual in myself while living a life of relative affluence and awful money tensions that leave me feeling at times dead and at times in doleful xile from myself?

- How can we reach our own economic and emotional potential without basing it on the destruction of another's?

- I want to feel I deserve to make money, not feel guilty about earning money. I want to keep a balance between the self-respect that money brings me and the search to know who I really am, my inner self. How can I prevent my sense of self-worth from being so dependent on how much money I make?

- Money seems like objective reality, one that can be reasoned about in the form of numbers. But I become painfully confused when I encounter the emotional component of it that seems to erode away all its apparent objectivity. Is money real—like stones and trees? And if not, why does money seem so real? (Needleman, 1991)

I have taken the position that it is acceptable and ethical for providers of Adventure Education to charge differing fees to corporate and educational groups. This is a simple question of business decision making and market based pricing strategy. There is no ethical dilemma at the surface of this question, but it does reflect the ethics of pricing, the principles of fair distribution, and the quality of the services being sold.

I am a small business owner and have to address the question of pricing in determining the price I think the market will accept in valuing the worth of the services I offer. My argument is constructed around the belief in the virtues of a free-market economy. I echo Nobel laureate Milton Friedman's libertarian economics of free markets that goes back to Jeffersonian principles of limited government and minimal regulatory interference in the market economy as the way to achieve growth.

In my opinion, there is no ethical concern with entering into a business venture to make money. The objective of maximizing returns on the investment of time, money and resources is the driving force in a for-profit capitalist system. Private enterprise is predicated on the use of ingenuity, talent, dreams, vision and capitol to create wealth. Pricing is a facet of an open and fair competitive market economy that drives quality and customer choice.

Money is a tool; a form of energy or information used to create material reality from ideas. The accumulation of money or wealth can be used for a lot of ends. The argument here isn't about what those ends are, it's about fairness and discrimination on a level having to do with an organization's orientation to money. By the reality of their existence, corporations tend to have more money available as this is what they generate in providing goods and services (or they don't exist). Educational institutions seem to be always strapped for money as is reflected in their annual budgeting struggles.

The pricing of experiential services reflects their integrity and the value the market will accept. Providers make conscious decisions as to which markets they choose to compete in. If they are serious about their business, their fees will reflect the quality and level of sophistication of their services and the buyers will determine whether those services hold any value. It is assumed that a provider recognizes that staffing qualifications and skills required to serve the corporate market differ from those necessary to serve the educational market. In the competitive corporate training market, the expectation exists that value and benefits will be derived from the expenditure on a training program. The effectiveness and professionalism of the staff delivering corporate programs is reflected in the time invested to acquire necessary skills and knowledge that directly contribute to delivering programs with value and benefit to the customers. Corporate training dollars are investments with expected returns on human resource and knowledge capital. Corporate systems have higher cost flow requirements than educational systems. There are distinctions that exist within educational programs that also reflect the notion of staff having varying lev-

els of training and knowledge to draw from (e.g. working with students requires different skills than working with teachers or administrators). It is unethical to purport the provision of services a provider is not capable of delivering due to unqualified and inexperienced staff.

Assuming that the quality of the facilitation or consulting staff is consistent with the needs of the client, then the ethics of charging separate prices for services delivered to different clients is irrelevant. A profit based business exists in business to realize a vision. Ben & Jerry's, the Hard Rock Cafe, or the Body Shop may have humanistic values driving their operations, but they all value being profitable ventures. Making money has to be a priority at some level to maintain viability in the market place covering its fixed costs and cash flow demands. How a provider chooses to structure its pricing is a business decision made to position itself in the competitive marketplace. The major concern is, does the provider have the staff with the knowledge to add significant value with corporate groups?

A customer's ability to pay will partially determine which supplier they choose. The supplier-customer relationship is a dance between the quality of service delivered and the agreed upon price charged for that service. Different markets typically have differing price points. The higher pricing in the corporate market should reflect the preparation, skill level of staff, and the time invested in training and education. I would argue that it is ethically questionable to charge a corporate group a much higher fee and then provide a program using staff that have not been trained to work with corporate clientele. There is an issue of not having qualified staff, that is knowledgeable of corporate operations delivering such programs. This is the ethical question tangential to the one Dr. Jasper Hunt and I are addressing. Suppliers can adjust their pricing if they determine it will justify the increase in business in that market segment. To claim that charging different fees for services delivered to corporate or educational markets is unethical is an indication that one may not believe in the efficiency of a free-market economy. The ethics question has to do with the justification of the higher price.

An analogy might help illustrate my point. A Yugo is not a Mercedes, but they are both cars. They will both transport you to where you want to go. The price differential of the two machines reflects the quality of the components, performance, styling, and comfort. A ropes course experience is a ropes course experience. The quality differential is seen in the facilitation that accompanies the experience. Corporate groups expect a program to provide credible facilitators that can help link the experience to their business needs. Educational groups have different needs for that experience. Educational groups (students) are not contributing equally to the market economy. The participants in educational groups are learning to become contributing members of the capitalist society. Their current economic value in present terms is less than that found in corporate groups. This isn't good or bad, it just is what it is.

Price collusion is unethical. This occurs when two or more businesses decide to fix their pricing in the market. This is an unfair market practice which is illegal and controlled through regulation. Differentiated pricing is a smart business practice. There is nothing unethical about testing a market's willingness and ability to purchase a quality service at a set price. A business chooses to whom it will sell its services and products to, that is, in which market it consciously chooses to com-

pete. When selling to corporate and educational markets there are fundamental differences in the institutional expectations for the level of service being rendered and the ability and availability of resources to purchase those services. Sliding scale fees are a way to do business in several market segments. It may be necessary and wise for a business to set pricing this way as a strategy for successfully competing in different markets.

The free market will determine whether the price reflects the real value of the service. Clients will decide if they can or cannot afford the price being charged and will find a vendor who satisfies their expectations of quality and/or financial flexibility. In the health care field in the United States it is generally acceptable for the practice of sliding scale fees to exist to provide service for those people with lower incomes. Adventure education is more of a luxury than a necessity such as health care. Our services can and ought to be priced at the level that a provider decides will be in demand in the market. The pricing ought to be in line with the quality of the service, depending on the expertise of staff. I would argue that there is different level of knowledge needed to effectively work with different market segments. Working in the corporate market requires that there be a general level of competence in the staff's ability to gain credibility, use appropriate language, understand business practices, structure and processes of the clients they are serving. Acquiring this knowledge requires an investment that is built into the pricing structures. It doesn't imply that it is better than the knowledge necessary to work with educational groups. There are different skills sets required to work with either corporate or educational groups. A provider entering the corporate market ought to recognize this distinction and work to develop its staff to increase their level of skill sophistication to effectively work with corporate groups. There is a degree of investment that I would say reflects a different state of professional skill that is important to have present when working with corporate groups.

Generally, pricing in the corporate market is higher because staff compensation is scaled higher than in the education market. This reflects the notion that different skill sets required to facilitate in the corporate market have different costs associated with acquiring them. Acquisition costs and opportunity costs exist in any business environment. It isn't realistic to pretend we can structure the world where everything is done on the cheap. Money isn't anything but what society has identified as the currency that is generally accepted in the exchange of goods and services. Higher prices usually equate to higher value, but not always. Sliding scale fees are nothing more than market based segment pricing for profit potential (Nagle and Holden, 1988).

A sliding scale fee pricing strategy is more closely in harmony with the "difference principle" which is defined as, "a strongly egalitarian conception in the sense that unless there is a distribution that makes both persons better off, (limiting ourselves to the two-person case for simplicity) an equal distribution is to be preferred" (Rawls, 1971). In other words, there should be no differences except those that can be justified on grounds of efficiency. In this ethical argument, it is perfectly acceptable to differentiate price, based on market segment, to offer more equal access to services for organizations with differing capabilities to pay. If providers choose to compete in both the corporate and educational markets they will set their prices accordingly. It is efficient to structure pricing to attract business in differentiated markets.

Let's examine the world of competition for a moment. It is widely acknowledged that there are two types of market structures: perfect competition and imperfect competition (Mansfield, 1987). In a perfectly competitive market, a large number of individual sellers compete among themselves, without collusion, to provide consumers with a product or service. There are no external legal, financial, or cost barriers to enter or exit the market. In perfect competition markets a seller sets the price it will receive for its goods or services on the basis of what the buyers are willing to pay. Imperfect competition occurs when monopolies, oligopolies, and/or monopsonies exist on either the supply or demand side. At present, the adventure education field is a more perfectly competitive market.

What constitutes a fair price in a market? In classical economics, the price a company charges its customers for a product or service is the total cost of investment plus normal profit. Price fairness reflects how a society views the theory of justice. There are two broad kinds of material theories of justice, patterned theories and unpatterned theories (Nozick, 1974). Patterned theories judge the fairness of a distribution procedure based on pattern of benefit in the end-state after the distribution actually takes place. Traditionally, material distributions based on utility, need, merit, and equality fall into this category.

There are two dominant patterned theories: egalitarianism, which espouses an equal distribution of at least some social goods in the end-state; and utilitarianism, which promotes distributions that maximize the public good in the end-state (Beauchamp and Bowie, 1993). Hence, the difference between these "patterned" theories is reflected in the kinds of end-state patterns that are deemed morally preferable. A sliding scale fee seen as unethical is probably being argued from either an egalitarian or utilitarian point of view. It might be argued that the fees ought to be flat for any client system, and not discriminate against professionals nor seek profit from the sector that can afford to pay more.

I argue for my ethical position from a belief in the unpatterned theories of justice, such as defended by libertarianism. Libertarians generally reject the notion that any particular distribution found in the end-state is any more fair than any other distribution (Naverson, 1988). Unpatterned theories, "focus on the fairness of the procedures that produce the end-state. Hence, any end-state that is generated by a fair procedure is deemed just or fair, regardless of how the benefits and burdens are distributed in the end-state" (White and Fraley, 1997). A sliding scale fee structure is a fair procedure for entering into a competitive marketplace. Not everyone will receive the same quality of service and the price ought to reflect this just as it reflects the quality and cost of the people facilitating those services.

An analogy that helps illuminate this distinction can be found in the American health care market. Health care services are not distributed by the market deciding who gets what. The government has decided to stake a role in determining how to regulate the fairness of service access, price and distribution. It is seen as a public safety issue and hence ethically questionable to have free market principles in practice in an industry that has life and death implications attached to the quality and accessibility of service. The entire American health care insurance debate is centered on the notions of patterned and unpatterned theories of distribution. In the case of health care, society collectively accepts the notion that there should be accessible and affordable health care available to all the citizenry. To achieve this utopia, a patterned regulated distribution policy is constructed. Health care and free enterprise are a tough mix, evidenced by the current U.S. debate on restructuring health care markets.

In the field of adventure education, seen more as a luxury than a necessity, the free market principles work well for both the suppliers and the buyers. However, I recognize that there are some inequalities that exist. There are classist issues in our society with regard to patterns of hierarchical compensation which often have education as the low end of professional pay scales. The budgeting for public education is set by those governing and often the allocation of funds is less than desirable. Discretionary funds are always in low supply and the competition for how these funds is spent is high. Educational institutions in the public arena do not typically operate in the same philosophical or ideological light as do for-profit corporations. The stakeholders are different in each institution as is the primary purpose for its existence. Like it or not, it is the way American society has come to be structured. And it doesn't change my premise for viewing floating scale fees as ethical.

Lastly in my argument I will make a point for capturing the greater benefits of having higher fees charged for corporate groups. I once directed a not-for-profit business. I made a conscious decision to charge minimal fees to the youth we served in our programs. Many came from lower income households, and the fact that we charged them at all reflected the theory that people will place value on something they have to pay for. Giving services away for free usually resulted in not having people show up, as they had little value invested. We subsidized this portion of our operation with income derived from conducting programming with corporations. We charged corporate groups a premium price and they were glad to pay, knowing full well that we were a not-for-profit operation with a mission to serve inner city youth. With public and private giving being difficult to generate, we chose to enter the market and provide a service that came with an acceptable price as an answer to our need for income to operate.

In retrospect, we provided services we were capable of delivering, doing the best we could at that time to meet our monthly fiscal needs. Cash flow is the bloodstream of an organization. Cut it off, and you start to feel the stress, and eventually die. What would you have done if you were in my position as the administrator responsible for the health of the operation? Sit down and have an inquiry into the ethics of floating fee scales? If you have any business sense at all, you would have followed your entrepreneurial inklings and would have done what it took, within the limits of the law, to survive and thrive. That's the way I see it in the real world.

I make no apologies for floating fee scales. I applaud their use as long as the quality issue in the competency of the staff is managed effectively. There are many businesses operating ropes courses that entered the corporate market for its lucrative returns. I can see the ethical issues involved in these decisions if the administrators are not investing in the staff or hiring competent and qualified staff to conduct these programs. There is an ethical issue with this practice and I would say it is unethical to conduct business in the corporate arena without addressing the efficacy of the staffing requirements to match the quality of the service with the fee being charged.

While working for Outward Bound in Chicago, I made an independent decision to increase salaries for the professional devel-opment staff (PDP). Traditionally, Outward Bound staff in the 80s were paid $80.00–$100.00/day to facilitate corporate groups. I decided their talents were being undercompensated and raised the pay rate to a minimum of $150.00/day. This bordered on heresy in the eyes of Outward Bound administrators. What I learned was that raising salaries had a positive impact on the self-esteem and perceived worth of the PDP staff. The shift created a higher level of professionalism on the part of the staff and the way it worked with the client. The quality of delivery actually began to increase. As staff members were treated more professionally, the overall quality of delivery increased. Let's face it, our markets are maturing and more and more corporations recognize poor quality of program value. This is typically apparent in the staff function. Organization Development professionals have a high level of training and education. These consultants services command a higher fee. If they are conducting adventure programming as a tool for applying their practice they will charge a fee that reflects their skill level and the value they place on their time, not the type of activity they are using to do their work with their clients. This distinction is important. It speaks to the field as a whole in assessing the ongoing professional development interests of the practitioner base.

In the end the market will decide who continues to thrive and who doesn't, unless we become another industry regulated by outside forces. It is in our best interest to examine our own practices and determine individually how we fit into our roles. If we aspire to professionally mature in the field of adventure education (or whatever you call it), then I would argue for continuing to develop our skill sets to justify the higher fees for working with corporate groups. Most practitioners start off working with educational groups. If we end up working with corporate groups, we tacitly know where we stand on our own level of knowledge relating to how effective we can be with those groups. If we are going to float the fee scale, then we should be developing our skills that ethically justify those higher prices.

REFERENCES

Beauchamp, Tom L., and Norman E. Bowie ed., *"Ethical Theory and Business"* fourth edition, Englewood Cliffs: Prentice Hall, 1993.

Mansfield, Edwin ed., *"Microeconomics: Selected Readings"*, New York: Norton and Company, 1979.

Nagle, Thomas T. and Reed K. Holden; *"The Strategy and Tactics of Pricing: A Guide to Profitable Decision Making"*, Englewood Cliffs: Prentice Hall, 1994.

Narverson, Jan, *"The Libertarian Idea"*, Philadelphia: Temple University Press, 1988.

Needleman, Jacob; *"Money and the Meaning of Life"*, Currency-DoubleDay, New York, NY; 1991.

Nozick, Robert; *"Anarchy, State, and Utopia"* New York: Basic Books, 1974.

Rawls, John; *"A Theory of Justice "*, Cambridge: Harvard University Press, 1971.

White, Ronald F. and Sean Fraley; *"Imperfect Competition, Price-Fairness, And The Pharmaceutical Industry"*, College of Mount St. Joseph: Cincinnati, Ohio, 1997.

Are Floating Fee Scales for Corporate and Educational Groups Ethical?

Jasper S. Hunt, Ph.D.

I can remember attending a meeting about 15 years ago of professionals in the field of adventure-based experiential education. We were sitting around talking about various issues and ideas in the field and one of the group members began talking about how much money his program was making by increasing the charges required for participation in his program when clients were corporations and other business groups. He declared that he increased the fees by 100–200 percent and that the clients were willing to pay that amount. The general consensus was that this was an amazing way to make easy money and that we should consider going that route. I can remember becoming very uneasy about the tenor and direction this conversation was taking. I raised a few timid objections but was unable to convince the group that there might be some ethical problems with this practice. Since then I have seen this practice become widespread, even accepted by large numbers of experiential educators.

What follows will be a presentation of various arguments for and against the use of fee differentials with the common thread being that I am suspicious of this practice on ethical grounds. I have been unable to see the arguments put forth by my interlocutor, thus I will be anticipating arguments that will be presented by the other side and I will be formulating arguments of my own concerning this very troubling trend.

THE ROBIN HOOD ARGUMENT

Probably the most common argument I have heard in support of increasing fees for business and corporate groups is what I have come to call the "Robin Hood" argument. Recall that Robin Hood was the legendary character who "stole from the rich in order to support the poor." Robin Hood is often praised by some for resisting social injustice and oppression by taking money from those who did not deserve it and participating in a kind of distributive justice by giving that money to poor people. The argument that I have heard made by many, many adventure education professionals is that *the fundamental ethical justification for fee differentials is to support poor students or clients with the increased revenues derived from wealthier clients.* I hasten to add here that the phrase "Robin Hood Argument" is problematic because no one in adventure education is stealing from anybody. Fee differentials are not theft; therefore, the Robin Hood analogy could be misleading. I recognize this difference but I will still refer to this line of argument as the Robin Hood argument for rhetorical purposes.

I have several responses to the Robin Hood argument. First, on empirical grounds it falls upon those who use this justification to actually show that the increased revenues go directly towards aiding less fortunate students. I suspect that most of these increased monies actually go into salaries for senior administrators, capital improvements, and other uses. It can be argued that unless each and every penny optimized by the fee differentials goes directly to aid others, then the use of the justification is weak, even disingenuous. There are other problems with this argument which will become evident later on in this paper.

THE UPWARD-DOWNWARD ARGUMENT

Imagine for a moment a situation where a patient consults with a physician and after diagnostic workups is informed that he or she needs an appendectomy. The patient is a wealthy corporate executive. The physician decides that the normal fee of say, $1,000.00 for this procedure will be doubled or tripled for this patient. If a physician in this country were to do such a thing, he or she would be in very serious ethical trouble with the medical profession. The same applies to dentistry, veterinary medicine, and the legal profession. Fees are based upon complex market

forces but are not increased for wealthier clients.

Many professionals have "sliding fee" schedules for clients who are unable to pay the full rate. However, this is a vastly different approach that the Robin Hood argument outlined above. I argue that lowering the fee for poor clients is an entirely different approach to the problem of serving poorer people than the opposite approach of raising fees for wealthy clients. What I have seen in the "real world" of experiential education is not the sliding fee schedule *downward for the poor,* but instead is an inverse fee scale *upward for the wealthy.*

Why should it matter? One could argue that it does not matter whether the scale goes upward or downward, as long as the end result is the same. Good ends are achieved, therefore, the technicalities of the means are not too ethically important. My reply is that it makes all the difference in the world. Here's why. By establishing a reasonable fee for a professional service, one removes the delivery of service from the mere achievement of profit. When one is engaged in a professional practice one does what he or she does for two reasons. One is the intrinsic satisfaction one receives from doing that activity. The other is the financial reward one receives for doing that activity. By putting a top limit on the fee schedule (I charge "X" for this particular service), the professional removes himself or herself from the activity exclusively for the obtainment of a profit. And I think that is a good thing for someone engaging in a professional practice.

I think there is a world of difference between selling widgets in the open market than engaging in a professional practice. One sells widgets for the most money that the market will bear. One does not sell appendectomies simply for what the market will bear. Indeed, our culture does not even permit the selling of widgets for what the market will bear in any and all circumstances. When a hurricane, tornado or other disaster hits, hardware stores and other sellers of essential goods and services are not permitted to "price gouge" customers in dire straits.

Back to the Robin Hood argument for a moment. Adventure programs could set a very high fee for their basic services and then say that they indeed are sliding their scale downward, not upward at all. All I can say in reply is that I have never seen this happen in practice. For example, many adventure programs charge $25.00 per person for a high ropes course. The same programs charge the identical service to corporate groups at a rate of $200.00 for person (I do not exaggerate here). Suppose one of these programs were to say, we are not really charging more for the corporate groups, we have as our base fee $200.00 per person per day on the ropes course. Of course, we will adjust this downward for non profit groups. Imagine a brochure put out by an adventure education program, seeking to serve non profit groups, with an advertised rate of $200.00 per person for the ropes course. I suspect that would be a marketer's worst nightmare!

THE FALSE COMPLEXITY ARGUMENT

A third argument against charging much higher fees for corporate groups is that in my experience successful business people are not stupid or idiotic. It may well be that initially people not familiar with adventure-based experiential education programming, will feel that the programming is so technical and dangerous that only very highly trained people are qualified to teach these techniques. In addition, the uninitiated may be willing to pay exorbitant fees at first. However, it may be "penny wise and pound foolish" for programmers to charge high fees. It could be the case that the business people who bring their employees to such programs will quickly realize that the level of training necessary to deliver effective, safe programs is not as high as it initially appeared. They might wise up and realize that for a rather small initial investment, they could build their own adventure facility and hire someone to deliver these programs for far less than the $200.00 per person per day they had earlier been charged. This is an argument from self interest, which would limit huge fee differentials, not for the sake of virtue, but for the sake of not pricing oneself out of the market.

THE CORRUPTION OF CHARACTER ARGUMENT

A fourth argument against tolerating very large fee differentials is what I will call the "corruption of character" argument. I have been struck by how often I have encountered practitioners almost gloating about the huge amounts of money they are making by offering rather simple activities, coupled with sophisticated debriefing experiences. Human nature is such that certain activities are potentially corrupting of human character. Such traits as lust, greed, avarice, power, sexual gratification , and sloth can undo an otherwise virtuous human being. The lust for wealth has long been recognized by philosophers and theologians as one of the most potentially deadly of the vices. History is full of examples of otherwise virtuous individuals who are corrupted by the lure of power and money. A key fear that I have for the practice of adventure education is that once the motivating power of money becomes overly important, that corruption often inevitably follows.

Corruption of character can infect both individuals and organizations. From an individual perspective this occurs when instructors who started out in the field of experiential education because of commitment to the ideals and intrinsic rewards of the profession become sidetracked by the lust of money to the detriment of their own character. I can remember talking to a pediatrician once who told me that he initially started out the practice seeing about 25 patients per day. Each of these patients and their parents had an unhurried appointment which allowed for necessary conversation and a thorough examination, as required by the presenting ailment. However, this doctor realized that by seeing 65 or 75 patients per day he could double his income! He refused to double his income but his colleagues in private practice went that route, doubled their incomes, and in this doctor's opinion corrupted themselves in the process.

The same logic can be applied to programs. There is a huge debate going on right now within the medical profession about HMOs and other managed care programs whereby the doctors working there are required as a condition of employment to routinely see 75 (or more) patients per day. Take an adventure education program for instance that has as its mission statement to further human growth and development and even help with social justice. However, by pursuing corporate contracts with the concomitant fee increases, this program soon becomes dependent upon these contracts for survival. I have even seen programs recently that actually pay staff members who instruct corporate courses more money than staff who work with juvenile delinquents while <u>doing</u> <u>the identical programming!</u> It is arguable that the instructional skills needed to work effectively with disadvantaged juvenile delinquents are much higher and more sophisticated than the skill level required to work with corporate clients. Indeed, it is not uncommon to see the "best and brightest" staff members assigned to corporate courses, while entry level staff get assigned to the less profitable courses. Such outcomes, I will argue, are corrupting of the character of the organization. Once again, the argument is often made that the moral justification for the fee differential is that the corporate courses wind up supporting the social justice courses. If that is the case, then why are the corporate course instructors paid more money then the juvenile delinquency instructors? The potential for self delusion and self justification here is immense. Such delusion and justification can result in corruption of character that is incalculable to the practice of adventure education.

THE INFORMED CONSENT ARGUMENT

This is an outgrowth of the Robin Hood argument. If adventure education practitioners are sincere about wanting to charge higher fees for corporate courses for charitable purposes, then it is reasonable to ask if these adventure educators are willing to tell their potential corporate clients that they will be charged higher fees in order to subsidize other groups. It might well be the case that some corporate groups will be glad to pay more in order to subsidize other groups. However, they might well want to know which groups they will be subsidizing, or they might want to know for sure that the increased fees will in fact go towards the claimed purposes and not be used for other purposes. I am reminded here of recent disclosures about charitable groups who are very efficient at getting services to clients and those who use their donations for high salaries and overhead expenses. Public outrage has often been generated towards those charities who claim to serve the poor but in fact use donations for purposes other than what donors thought the money was being used for. A useful question might be asked of those adventure education programs who have fee differentials: *Are you willing to tell your corporate groups that they are being charged higher fees for identical programming that is offered for other clients?* An unwillingness to state the differential up front could serve as a warning to practitioners that they are on ethically shaky ground. This would be problematic because this unwillingness could deny the corporate group the opportunity for informed consent.

THE IDEOLOGICAL ARGUMENT

I have been struck over the years by what I consider is a disproportionate number of adventure educators who are committed to a left wing, socialistic (even Marxist) orthodoxy in matters of ideology. The Ideological Argument is that fee differentials are justified because, somehow, corporations owe a debt to society and that adventure education practitioners who can succeed in getting large amounts of money from corporations are engaged in a social agenda that is ideologically grounded and pure. These people are generally supportive of progressive tax rates by government and follow this same ideological line of reasoning when applied to fee schedules. Many adventure educators who advocate fee differentials for corporate

groups see themselves in a kind of social crusade for distributive justice following the Leninist slogan "From each according to his ability, to each according to his need." This credo of Soviet ideology is shared by a large number of adventure educators and serves as a kind of moral background for justifying fee differentials.

I find the ideological argument troubling because of what I think is a simplistic and naive set of assumptions which undergird many of these arguments. The vast majority of corporations in the United States are owned by shareholders of stock. These shareholders are very often small investors, pension holders, and owners of mutual funds and other investment instruments. Although a corporation is a legal entity in and of itself, it represents the interests of those who have invested in that corporation. When one penalizes a corporation, one penalizes those who have invested in the corporation. I find it very misguided that many adventure educators have a dislike of corporate entities and find a kind of moral satisfaction when they can penalize a corporation. Efforts which result in penalizing corporations wind up penalizing share holders.

Frankly I doubt that most adventure educators who practice fee differentials for corporate groups do so for purely ideological reasons. Probably most do it for the increased revenues that can be gotten. However, it may well be the case with some practitioners that an ideological overlay is used to in fact hide a simple desire for more money from these groups.

THE CYNICAL ARGUMENT

I hesitate to even raise this argument for justifying fee differentials but I might as well cover it in order to cast as wide a net as possible. Although I have never actually heard this argument used, it does exist as a potentiality. It can be argued that the practice of adventure education is governed by a kind of social Darwinism which makes it morally permissible to get as much as one can in the financial arena without regard to contravening moral considerations. In other words, it might be argued that each and every practitioner is permitted to "watch out for number one", maximize one's profit potential and the hell with any other considerations. Narrow self interest would reign supreme and that would be the end of the discussion. Note here that there is no pretense at a Robin Hood justification, nor any other justification. I mention this not as a viable option for adventure educators, as I have yet to meet or even hear about anyone who operates like this, but human nature being what it is, it seems legitimate to mention this option.

CONCLUDING REMARKS

I have attempted here to cover some of the ethical territory and to look at various arguments that can be made to justify the use of different fee scales for corporate and other groups. It is my position that the use of fee differentials is problematic at best. I know the general plan of this book is for me to take a strong stand one way or the other on this matter and then argue that point. However, I must be content to point out that it is problematic but not necessarily unethical. Probably the most basic concern I have is rooted in the human capacity for self deception and corruption of character. The lure of large amounts of money is intrinsically dangerous

to human character. Although arguments like the Robin Hood argument seek to justify fee differentials, it is very easy for practitioners to lose sight of the intrinsic rewards of being in the profession and, instead, begin to serve the master of money for its' own sake. Herein lies a serious danger for practitioners.

I also recognize the potential for great good to be gained by programs using large profit margins with corporate groups. Programs with financial security are programs that can be creative and innovative with other client groups. Profitable programs can offer reduced rates to less prosperous clients. But once again I offer the warning about these protestations of beneficence being smoke screens for mere financial gain. At the very least I would urge organizations which are considering differentiated fee schedules to consider *downward*, not *upward* differentials as argued earlier in this chapter. It is the raising of prices simply because certain clients have more resources that troubles me ethically. Lowering prices for those less able to pay seems much less troubling ethically than the opposite.

Therefore, my conclusions are that simply raising fees for the identical programming offered for no other reason than the proposed clients will pay extra, is an unethical practice. However, if the fee differentials are grounded in good faith ethical considerations (like the Robin Hood argument) then it is *potentially* justifiable on ethical grounds but I maintain it is very problematic. At the very least the burden of proof lies with practitioners who raise fees based upon ability to pay. Sliding fees that go downward instead of upward present a less burdensome task for ethical justification.

CHAPTER 4

Should We Use Urban Settings to Promote Adventure Education?

YES PERSPECTIVE: Tom Puk, Ph.D.

NO PERSPECTIVE: Tom G. Potter, Ph.D. and Tonia L. Gray, Ph.D.

Dr. Puk is an Associate Professor in the Faculty of Education, Lakehead University, Thunder Bay, Ontario, Canada. He was one of the original developers of Project D.A.R.E (Development through Adventure, Responsibility, and Education), an outdoor program for delinquents started in 1971. He currently teaches (among other things) Outdoor Experiential Education programs as part of a teacher certification, Bachelor of Education program. He has conducted extensive research on self-directed learning and inquiry and is currently conducting research to link quantum theory with curriculum development and also the role of nurturing in teaching and learning.

Tom G. Potter, Ph.D. teaches outdoor adventure education in the School of Outdoor Recreation, Parks and Tourism at Lakehead University in Thunder Bay, Ontario, Canada. Tom conducts research on personal growth in wilderness, outdoor leisure pursuits and family relationships, protected areas and human dimensions. He serves as a journal reviewer for the *Journal of Experiential Education* and is member of the editorial board for *Pathways: The Ontario Journal of Outdoor Education*.

Tonia L. Gray, Ph.D., is a senior lecturer in Health, Physical and Outdoor Education within the Faculty of Education at the University of Wollongong, Australia. Tonia's research interests include program evaluation, burnout, gender issues and spirituality in outdoor education (rather bizarre combination!). She is the Managing Editor of the *Australian Journal of Outdoor Education* and has more than 15 years experience as a facilitator in outdoor adventure education experiences.

Should We Use Urban Settings to Promote Adventure Education?

Tom Puk, Ph.D.

The question above might appear fairly straightforward. However, hidden within it is the problematic nature of defining what adventure education is. In reading outdoor magazines and journals these days, one might come to the conclusion that adventure only exists in exotic and remote locations, e.g., trekking on a wilderness trail far from home or canoeing/kayaking/rafting down a remote river, again far from home. "Free climbing in Southern France, battles of full privation in the water-deserts in the Atlantic, the Pacific or in the deserts of Africa, search for opals in Australia—each continent serves as a large pool of adventure activities" (Becker, 1996, p.67). This gives the impression that adventure can only be found anywhere other than locally. This phenomenon of looking elsewhere, that is beyond the self, for direction and stimulation, is not unique to our topic. We live in a culture which instills at an early age the idea that other people in other places have **the** answers. I would suggest that this image of adventure has some negative side-effects.

The focus on the exotic and remote is not singular to adventure education. In science,

the exotic often gains the media attention. Sound, thorough, effective research of more basic topics is often treated with less respect in comparison to more exotic and romantic explorations, which I would suggest, often mask poor quality, hidden beneath the veneer of the strange and unusual.

The same impression might be given by some research studies. Hattie, Marsh, Neill and Richards (1997) conducted a meta-analysis of 96 studies of adventure programs occurring over the past quarter century. One of the defining characteristics of these adventure programs they list is that these programs were conducted in wilderness settings. One would get the impression that adventure education must occur in wilderness settings in order to be classified as adventure education. In fact, Hattie et al. went so far as to exclude certain kinds of experiences from their study because they tended to involve "nonchallenging experiences" (p.51). Some of the excluded experiences included "a rural retreat that involved tending the farm, building projects, bush walks, camping, and natural science studies" (p.51). These, it would appear, are not challenging experiences.

It would seem that there may be some confusion that adventure education is synonymous with high risk activities. It would appear that is what Hattie et al. (1997) are saying when they exclude some activities because they are not challenging enough to qualify. Camping, bush walks, building projects, tending a farm, etc., are not challenging, perhaps, because they are perceived as not being high risk, they are not potentially life-threatening activities. [Even this assertion seems some what faulty when one considers the risk of grooming a bull, raising a barn, camping in bear country, etc.].

If it isn't already obvious, I disagree with the above elitist view of adventure education. I am of the belief that adventure is in the mind of the beholder and that we should broaden our understanding of just what adventure involves. "Adventure is not in the guide book and beauty is not on the map. Seek and ye shall find" (Russell & Russell, 1973, p.85). You don't have to risk your life to experience adventure. Adventure education does not have to occur "out there". Adventure is all around us, we just have to be able to see it. Admittedly, it does take a little more creative energy to observe and develop adventurous activities in urban settings. Seek and ye shall find. To experience adventure, "means to discover and push the frontiers of new physical or emotional grounds" (Bisson & Luckner, 1996, p.108), where the individual explores the limits of his or her boundaries, not knowing what the outcome will be (Bisson & Luckner, 1996; Priest, 1990). I have seen adult students begin a commando crawl across a one inch manila rope five feet off the ground with as much trepidation as someone doing the same thing thirty feet off the ground, or of someone shooting rapids. The physical experience (of crossing the rope) is the same—which is why I believe adventure to be in the mind. To someone (especially an adult) who has never experienced crossing a thin, swaying rope, s/he is pushing his/her personal physical and emotional frontiers and it is this personal challenge and inner exploration that makes climbing across ropes close to the ground adventurous. Is there risk involved? Yes, a great deal, but perhaps not the kind that some associate with "physical" risk. For some reason the word risk, as it is often used in describing adventure, is used to signify risk to one's life. Those activities with greater chance of causing physical damage or ending one's life are often referred to as "high" risk. To some, this is almost a badge of honour. (Loynes (1996) has argued that in fact physical risk is often used as a marketing strategy). To others, risking one's life in a premeditated manner might be thought of as irresponsible. However, there are other important manifestations of risk that are associated with adventure, including risk to one's ego, risk of failure, risk of appearing foolish or incompetent to peers. These kinds of "emotional" risks can be as forceful and impressionable to the self as physical risk (Keyes, 1985; Wurdinger, 1997). "Often the most obvious fears of physical safety are easily noticed, but the more subtle and possibly more powerful social/psychological fears (threats to one's ego)...are forgotten" (Cryer, 1996, p.20). Emotional risk applies to low ropes courses and to many other forms of adventure that may not involve a high degree of physical risk. It is interesting to note that the symbols of well-being, such as the life-jacket and the carabineer, are provided as standard equipment. Again, these symbols have to do with the physical. We seldom treat social/psychological symbols of well-being in the same manner. We seldom instruct participants that they should view a hug, a kind word, or a smile as standard equipment for protecting one's emotional well-being. Yet, they are just as important.

The point of defining adventure in these terms is that you don't need a wilderness area to build a low-to-the-ground ropes course and you also don't need trees to tie ropes to in an urban setting if you don't have them. Posts, poles, and metal objects can all be used to secure the ropes. Neither does the ropes course need to be built in a permanent manner. Ropes can be untied, retied and moved from site to site, and in this manner participants can be taught to build and experience their own reality rather than experiencing someone else's view of what they should experience. The commercialisation of adventure has also brought about the commodification of adventure, that it can be packaged into predetermined outcomes (Loynes, 1996). However, adventure is dynamic, not static. Participants need to learn first hand that they can create adventure and not just experience it. This pushes the essence of experiential learning to its natural limits.

The question, "should we use urban settings to promote adventure education?" may give the impression that urban settings only contain pavement and concrete and that there is a black and white difference between wilderness areas and urban areas. However, urban settings are not devoid of trees. Most urban areas have within their boundaries lakes, shorelines, rivers, streams, wetlands, gravel pits, ravines, parks, farms, woodlots, etc. Children have found adventure in these areas of urban life long before they were "educated" to believe that adventure could only be found "way out there" in wilderness areas. Children are the experts in creating adventure wherever they find themselves; it is spontaneous and ephemeral. But we educate them to leave behind these "childish" no-

tions and rather engage the true and "manly" kinds of adventure, such as climbing a mountain or anything done under "extreme" conditions. The problem with this impression is that not everyone can climb a mountain and so those who can't may feel inadequate and intimidated and give up their "childish" notions of adventure. Rather, the message is, they should observe through television the "real" adventurers competing with each other as they ford raging rivers, cross glaciers and/or deserts, jump off 2000 foot cliffs, etcetera! The message is that adventure is spectacular rather than educational, that it is a form of entertainment rather than a medium through which one can grow mentally, emotionally and spiritually.

Getting back to rope courses, buildings can also be used to create quite challenging experiences. Yes, I agree something may be lost by going inside. However, it still doesn't negate adventure. On the other hand, I do not feel that indoor climbing in commercial climbing centres is the same as rock climbing. First of all, there usually aren't any rocks indoors. But more importantly, the physical experience, unlike climbing across ropes, is not the same. You can't feel the wind or rain or sun on your face. However, it is different and it is unique to that setting and to some may be quite adventurous; it's just that it isn't rock climbing. Now rappelling in an urban setting is different again. It can be very adventurous, challenging and risky to rappel off the roof and down the side of a building, or down a tower. The physical experience is quite similar and certainly the experience can be just as mentally challenging as rappelling down a rock face, depending upon the height of the building.

Sometimes the exotic trip is so stimulating and overwhelming that the micro aspects of the experience are lost. An individual can only observe and record a limited amount of stimuli. Sometimes we may lose sight of the fact that the reason we encourage adventure education in wilderness settings is to experience the remoteness, and yet it is really the remoteness of the mind that we seek to reach. It isn't the wilderness we are trying to change, it is ourselves. Cutting away excess stimulation may assist the individual in reaching those remote corners of the mind more easily. It brings the focus of the experience right up to nose level. Crossing a rope is an experience involving the mind and the rope. The rope, unlike a set of rapids, does not move except as a consequence of the actions of the participant. On a rope, it is the participant who is creating his or her experience, changing the tempo, changing the resistance, allowing it to swing uncontrollably, or not.

To return to our discussion of what adventure is, I believe that adventure is what one makes of one's experiences and is dependent upon a number of variables, such as age, previous experience and health. For example, laying out a number of different sites in a city that an elementary age student or someone from a rural community must visit, by planning his or her own routes and then taking the bus to find these sites is quite adventurous. This involves challenge, risk, fun, the unknown and the expansion of one's personal limits. Similarly, dropping a group of adults off to explore a neighbourhood in Newark, New Jersey, might also be adventurous (high risk, the unknown). However, after you have taken the bus or subway a number of times, it may be less adventurous. I would suggest that adventure ceases when one's personal horizon ceases to expand. We should keep in mind that this may also apply in wilderness experiences.

In a program operated in Hamilton, Ontario, students experience urban adventure by exploring the downtown section of the city (Lisson, et al., 1996). At times students are led through the city blindfolded and at other times they have to purchase a meal for under $1.00. During these kinds of urban adventures, students might be dropped off without any maps and then visit community organizations and neighbourhoods with distinctive cultural and ethnic backgrounds; they might talk with strangers and taste unusual foods freshly made; they might explore historical buildings; and, if they are lucky, they might get lost. Getting lost in a city can be very adventurous. You can not know ahead of time what incidents you might experience in a downtown setting. New experiences not even expected might occur. Interacting with the people one meets, the architecture, new cultures and organizations can be very exciting and teach one a great deal about adventure. Even doing something you have done previously in new and creative ways can be adventurous. It is how the mind perceives the event that makes it adventurous; it is not primarily the setting.

What are some of the precautions one has to take in an urban adventure, such as found in the Hamilton program? Some include: not causing problems with the people in the neighbourhood—similar to leaving nature alone; safety—similar to wearing life jackets; and whether the group is capable of the activity, similar to the prior experience and skills required to climb a mountain.

City Bound (Welzenis, 1994) is another example of an urban adventure program. Students are given a map, dropped off in the city and have to make their way to a specific destination without asking people for directions. They might visit a hospital, prison or meet with someone with a different cultural background. The program involves social activities instead of physical activities. Nonetheless, Welzenis states that,

> [t]he big city is psychologically less safe than nature. Water, woods, and mountains do not usually change unexpectedly. The psychological dangers are limited and clear in advance. The city, on the other hand is more unsafe because of unpredictable social behavior (p.17).

In other words, dealing with people in an unfamiliar part of a large city can be quite adventurous. As well, Welzenis claims that the knowledge gained during urban adventure programs "is more immediately useful and more directly transferable to daily life" (p.17).

In the above discussion, we have been examining primarily the types of adventure activities that can be accomplished in an urban setting. Now we should turn our minds toward the question of why? Why should we want to conduct adventure education in the urban setting? One of the primary reasons that comes to mind is ecological preservation. Entering the wilderness has been for some time now and will be more so in the future a privileged experience and in some ways an elitist experience. Unfortunately, it can't be done any other way. The wilderness could not sustain the impact of everyone tramping through it. We have known this for some time but it is rather uncomfortable to talk about because it means we are really talking about wilderness experiences for a few. And that few usually means us. The problem is that the "wilderness" is already cluttered. Garbage has been found in deep ocean trenches. Bottles, cans, plastics and oil washing ashore have for some time been found on remote Pacific islands. Trace chemicals have been found in core ice samples taken from the Antarctic. Mount Everest, at one time considered to be the remotest

spot on the earth, is now a big garbage dump as teams leave behind tents, ropes, carabiners, food, bottles, cans, excrement, etc. In fact, Mount Everest has become such a dehumanized and sterile environment that anything can be left behind. On one of the recent Canadian climbs, a dead body left by a previous expedition was found dangling on a rock face in a tangle of ropes. We must, in fact, create adventure in urban settings because we can not afford, from an ecological point of view, to have the masses invade the wilderness. I find it rather ironic and sad, considering what I might have believed in the 1960s, **that in fact we need to encourage urban adventure in order to save the wilderness.** I don't have to experience Polar Bear Park in Northern Canada in order to appreciate its existence. Knowing that these places still exist in the world is worth enough for me. I would rather think of Mount Everest as unspoiled than to contribute to its disfigurement. That is why, for example, indoor climbing may be ecologically more sound.

Wilderness experiences have also become elitist in that it can be very expensive to do in these areas considering user fees, equipment costs, rentals, travel costs, etc. Adventure should not and need not be expensive. You don't need expensive equipment to find adventure. When I take a group out to a stream or a bush lot or an urban park, or at the back of some storage area where packaging has been discarded, I delight in using what I find around me to spontaneously create an adventurous experience. I take some rope with me, and that used in conjunction with what I find, such as fallen tree-limbs, old rubber tires, blocks of wood, packaging, water, hills, bridges, valleys, ponds, etc., can delight even adults for hours and hours. Most of what is used is left where it was found and the adventure moves on to a new setting. This is the spontaneous and ephemeral nature of child-like adventure. It is difficult to commercialize this kind of adventure and to treat adventure as a commodity because it only exists during the experience. The experience is the only real thing and once the experience is over, there are no structures left behind. Adventure has transformed itself into the creative impulses of the participant who carries this feeling of adventure wherever s/he goes. It is always there, not just to be found in the wilderness on occasion, nor even in the structures visited on occasion. Child-like adventure transcends the physical. Afterwards these adults remark with astonishment and humility, how sad it was that they had missed seeing adventure that was all around them. Seek and ye shall find.

Another important reason we should encourage urban adventure is to involve more people in adventure. Our emphasis should be on the majority not the minority. If we believe that the benefits of adventure education are so important, then we should do everything we can to encourage as many people as possible to involve themselves. You don't do that by defining it in a narrow manner. We run the same risk of creating an "adventure elite" as we have allowed to happen in creating a "technological elite" (Puk, 1996). Elitism has a tendency to discourage participation. It intimidates and suppresses. Adventure education should be inclusionary not exclusionary.

For the final reason and perhaps the most important one, as to why we should encourage urban adventure, we have to return to that body found hanging in ropes on Mount Everest. There is something terribly empty about this cold image. Other than the sadness I feel for the indignity of this former life-form being left behind, alone, isolated (treated cal-

lously by the media as just another nameless dead body), it seems to represent the symbol of the quest, perhaps obsession, to find the ultimate form of extreme adventure at whatever cost. Many would say dying in behalf of this quest is noble and they of course have a right to their perspective. It is not the activity that concerns me, it is the symbolism it represents—death and isolation. It strikes me as odd that some of the adventurous things children do, we call "childish" in a pejorative manner, as in what children do is "immature". What is a mature view of adventure? Challenging the boundaries of our inner existence does not need to lead to death. The symbol of adventure should be vibrant life, should be laughter and fun, should be lifelong. Give me children's adventure any time. And the essence of children's adventure is that with a little imagination, you can create your own wherever you find yourself. Perhaps this childish view of urban adventure can breathe new life into an otherwise spiritually-sterile environment.

CONCLUSIONS

Is there something unique about wilderness settings? A ridiculous question of course. As a rule, the development of the feeling of authenticity and the suspension of time correspond very often with geographical places. Out in nature social conventions are missing to a large extent. A mutual almost mythical relation between emotion and place is established through the atmosphere of wild, sublime and lofty mountains, snow-covered landscapes, elegant parks or the deep blue sea (Becker, 1996, p.68–69).

There are aspects of the wilderness that you can not replicate in the urban setting. That isn't the point. The question is, can we afford to give everyone that experience? And while it is a sad, moral dilemma, it is also disingenuous to perpetuate the myth that everyone can experience the wilderness. I doubt, for example, that wilderness areas in China could survive the onslaught of a billion people. Developing urban adventure is crucial to the survival of wilderness areas.

In 1990s, as jobs have become more technologically based and perhaps less adventurous, we have seen the coming of eco-challenges (it is interesting to note how once beautiful words such as ecology, granola, and yogurt are commercialized and turned on end so that they are no longer recognizable in their original form)—teams of competitors thundering through what were once pristine, isolated environments without, it would appear, the slightest concern for the consequences of their hedonistic, selfish pursuits. They seem to give no passing regard for ecological principles, such as "everything in life being interconnected" and "that for every action there is an equal and opposite reaction." "The landscape and its wildlife is increasingly treated as a resource for exploitation by commercial providers" (Loynes, 1996, p.52). And it isn't just the physical damage perpetrated on fragile environments, the crushing of tiny plants in the mad rush to be first that makes one weep. What is perhaps even more disconcerting is the total lack of respect for wilderness, the lack of spiritual connection, a oneness with nature. Wilderness is simply seen as a gymnasium or football field to be abused and to be thought of as simply another venue for humans to conquer. And conquer we do, oh so very well. Will there be an Amazon forest to conquer in the future?

We must not allow the term adventure to be confined to heedless, elitist desires. We need to resist the attempts made to commercialize and "commodisize" adventure. Adventure is everywhere you want it to be and it belongs to everyone who can see its potential and feel its power. Let us agree that there are different these kinds of adventure and different degrees of intensity of different kinds of adventure. Let's make adventure more commonly available to all through urban adventure opportunities rather than just an occasional experience in the wilderness for a few.

REFERENCES

Becker, P. (1996). In quest of paradise: Comments on the current attraction of excitement and adventure. *The Journal of Adventure Education and Outdoor Leadership, 13* (2), 67–70.

Bisson, C., & Luckner, J. (1996). Fun in learning: The pedagogical role of fun in adventure education. *The Journal of Experiential Education, 19* (2), 107–112.

Cryer, J. (1996). Essential strands of managing fear in adventure-based education. *The Journal of Adventure Education and Outdoor Leadership, 13* (2), 20–21.

Hattie, J., Marsh, H.W., Neill, J.T. & Richards, G.E. (1997). Adventure education and outward bound: Out-of class experiences that make a lasting difference. *Review of Educational Research, 67* (1), 43–87.

Keyes, R. (1985). *Chancing it: Why we take risks.* Boston: Little, Brown and Co.

Lisson, B., Park, M., Chant, C., Guyatt, A., Rapcewicz, M., & Mark, L. (1996). Expeditionary learning: Urban community exploration. *Pathways, 8* (1), 17–21.

Loynes, C. (1996). Adventure in a bun. *The Journal of Adventure Education and Outdoor Leadership, 13* (2), 52–57.

Puk, T.G. (1996). A framework for developing expertise in engaging the technological world. *Journal of the International Technology Education Association, 55* (6), 10–14.

Priest, S. (1990). The semantics of adventure education. In J.C. Miles & S. Priest (Eds.), *Adventure education* (pp. 113–117). State College, PA: Venture Publishing.

Russell, J. & Russell, R. (1973). *On the loose.* New York: Ballantine Books.

Welzenis, (1994). City bound: The big city as learning environment for societal-vulnerable adolescents. *The Journal of Experiential Education, 17* (3), 16–19.

Wurdinger, S.D. (1997). *Philosophical issues in adventure education.* Dubuque, Iowa: Kendall/Hunt.

Should We Use Urban Settings to Promote Adventure Education?

Tom G. Potter, Ph.D. and Tonia L. Gray, Ph.D.

While it is certainly possible to use urban settings to promote adventure education, in this milieu the likelihood of instilling meaningful learning experiences which are indelible and profound remains questionable. The non-urban setting provides a unique opportunity for participants to experience first hand, the powerful people-nature nexus. In direct contrast, the urban milieu offers a watered-down alternative. Since the vast majority of participants of adventure education programmes neither live in, nor frequent wilderness areas, wilderness offers a profound divergence from their everyday life experiences: physically, socially, emotionally, culturally and spiritually. In contrast, urban settings cannot provide the depth of experience which is required to fully activate participants' personal, social, emotional and spiritual growth. This paper will argue that adventure education programmes are, from their roots, inherently tied to wilderness, and that adventure programmes conducted in non-urban settings are the more viable pedagogical option. Moreover, the paper will discuss the following six key issues inherent in adventure education: 1. Adaptive state of learner dissonance; 2. Person-nature interaction; 3. Connectedness; 4. Indelible learning; 5. Spirituality; and 6. The potent nature of a non-urban experience.

ADAPTIVE STATE OF LEARNER DISSONANCE

In one of the most influential models in adventure programming, as cited in Priest and Gass (1997), The Outward Bound Process Model describes adventure education as a process in which the learner is placed into a unique physical and social environment and is provided with a set of problem solving tasks (Walsh and Golins, 1976). This process leads the learner to an adaptive state of dissonance, whereby the learner adapts by mastery, which reorganizes the meaning and direction of the learner's experience.

A critical factor in Walsh and Golins' (1976) definition of adventure education is the concept of unfamiliarity, where the learning environment stands in contrast to the participant's home environment. The dichotomy between these two environments inspires participants to open themselves to absorb and process valuable information that they may overlook in their everyday life environments. Furthermore, a wilderness adventure education experience can foster further processing and deepen understandings. The distinguishing and absolute contrasts (physical, emotional, spiritual and social) between everyday life and wilderness experiences have the unique ability to profoundly touch the senses, the mind, the body and soul, and, consequently, create influential experiences that derive inordinate learning and meaning for participants. Within reason, the more polarized the physical, emotional, spiritual and social contrasts are between everyday life experiences and the adventure experience, the greater the potential for learning/growth to occur. Barron (1997, p.25) illustrates this aspect when she states that:

> As a goal of the [adventure] programme, I looked for ways to culturally disorient the students through situations in which normal (city) social mores and habits were challenged—sleeping outside on bare rock under the stars, swimming naked in the rain, jumping from canoes in the middle of the lake, eating wild plants...waking at 5:30 to watch the dawn and articulating our tangible connections to the wild through first-hand contact with moose prints and bear scat.

The Outward Bound Process Model (Walsh & Golins, 1976) further expounds that adventure education is best accomplished in an environment that is multi-sensory, neutral and straightforward. "Upon entering wilderness, one of the first things almost everyone experiences is an enlivening of the five senses. Suddenly we are bathed in (and sometimes overloaded with) new sounds, awesome sights, interesting textures, different smells and tastes. This awakening of our senses, or perhaps better stated, "coming to our sense", is a subtly powerful and underrated experience" (Harper, 1995, p.189). Furthermore, distanced from human cultural norms and rules, wilderness is neutral; the "rules" of the adventure experience are not imposed. Lastly, elements in wilderness are straightforward and present the opportunity for participants to receive direct, immediate and unbiased meaningful feedback (Priest and Gass, 1997).

PERSON-NATURE INTERACTION

Adventure education in wilderness offers participants rare opportunities to emotionally connect with the natural world. Duenkel (1997, p.51) aptly and vividly expresses her true meaning of wilderness adventure, distant from urban settings, when she states that:

> I have journeyed through steep canyon walls that have humbled me and enabled me to grasp my insignificance in the greater scheme of things. I have paddled on lakes and rivers in the mountains, prairies, on the Canadian Shield, and amongst the desert sands that have all taught me to move in accordance with the flow of life rather than countering our own nature and that of the surrounding world. I have hiked on trails travelled by thousands as well on barrens and streambeds likely untouched by direct human presence, both of which have helped me to dispel the myth of dualism and inspired feelings of being a part of, rather than apart from, the natural world. I recognize and celebrate the fact that my wandering has enabled me to become grounded in a deeply felt and profoundly experienced sense of relationship with the Earth. My wandering reflects a deep sense of devotion to an ongoing journey of discovering self and place.

The depths and richness of meanings constructed in a wilderness setting can nurture an openness to view the world from multiple perspectives, create powerful emotions, foster new understandings and ultimately lead to substantial personal growth. Is this reconstruction, this new awareness of self, others and the natural world in the natural world not a critical component, an inherent quality/foundation, of the intra/interpersonal growth potential of adventure education? We believe that it is.

The intra/interpersonal growth potential of adventure education is most meaningfully developed through the forging of a spiritual relationship to the land (Potter, 1993). Adventure education is not the conquest of nature that is embedded within our cultural domain, but the learning of a frame of reference that is fundamentally with nature. As Henderson (1996, p.140) so phrases, "One does not sing the praises of the awe of nature. Rather, one comes to see and accept one's place in a grand design at the level of the comforted soul. This is indeed the true sense of adventure." According to Henderson, one of the challenges for adventure education instructors is "to develop an ecological relationship to nature concerned with the adventure of the spirit" (p. 142).

CONNECTEDNESS

In order to attain Henderson's (1996) challenge, adventure education must return to its wilderness roots and provide opportunities over and away from the growth of technological barriers. Modern technology not only allows, but overtly encourages people to become "cocooned" from first-hand interpersonal contact and be severed from natural rhythms and cycles (Nettleton, 1994). In ad-

venture education we must challenge ourselves to move away from technology, distance our participants from everyday life artifacts and transfer them to a more simplistic wilderness environment. Stapleton (1990, p.20) concurs with this point when he states that:

> With all this [technology] has come a generation of young people who seem to have lost touch with the systems of nature. Nature is almost old fashioned to them. Technology is the go now, and they are convinced that it will be able to solve all problems. They can tell you every known fact about the space program or digital technology, but ask them how to make jam, or how long it takes to boil an egg, or what is the season for apples?

Our nature-estranged way of life concerns many contemporary educators (for instance Kiewa, 1991 and Nettleton, 1994). Furthermore, some interesting issues are raised by Cooper (1994, p.9) when he maintains that:

> There is a lack of purpose in many people's lives. We have become removed from the rhythms of nature, from the seasons, from the day and night, and from the land and sea, from other life. We surround ourselves with surrogates, second-hand experiences vicarious pleasures. These are poor compensations for feeling part of the planet, for having a spiritual belonging, a kinship with the earth.

Being devoid of human interaction and plagued by vicarious reinforcement and second-hand surrogates are spin-offs associated with technology. The holistic nature of education is questionable under a regime such as this. Denying students multi-sensory and indelible learning experiences sounds a death knell as far as adventure educators are concerned.

Urban settings are inextricably linked to a perpetuation of alienation. We live in concrete high storey buildings, which are air conditioned, artificially lit, and devoid of contact with the seasons and elements. We have chosen to become insulated from the reality of our planet, shielded from the authenticity of life itself. Year after year, generation after generation, Western society has distanced itself more and more from the natural world. For example, in our artificial environment the rhythms of the moon barely penetrate the glow of our urban lights. In fact, in our cities, surrounded by the high tension of powerlines (perhaps a metaphor of urban stress) we seem to have abolished the night.

We have succeeded, albeit temporarily, in isolating our physical and emotional beings from the land and in the process, we stand in grave danger of losing a critical portion of our selves, our clarity of vision. Enveloped by modern-day constructs we tend to lose sight, literally as well as metaphorically, of the rhythms and moral significance of nature. By becoming distanced from everyday life, perhaps for the first time, many participants of non-urban adventure education programmes realise that their lives had been obscured by the mechanical order of our society's artifacts. Wilderness can rekindle the reality of humanity's interconnectedness with the natural world and represents a novel, challenging, and meaningful mode of living (Potter, 1993).

Wilderness presents much more than its physical grandeur and associated challenges to participants of adventure programmes. Once immersed in wilderness, people begin to understand that nature is much more than a recreational area and that wilderness has more to offer them than pretty scenery. They sense the intrinsic value of wilderness; that nature and people mutually define one another and that nature encourages the dialectic between self and other. It is in wilderness

that people begin to feel whole and discover elements of selves they did not previously know. Nature, a celebration of life, demonstrates living with meaning. A spiritual landscape exists within the physical landscape. Like poetry, wilderness is inexplicably coherent; it is transcendent in its meaning, and elevates a consideration of human life (Lopez, 1986).

Wilderness defies accurate evaluation; it retains an identity of its own, much deeper and more intricate than we can ever know. Visitors to wilderness began to understand this; they sense that wilderness must be approached with an open mind and feel its variety of expressions: colour, textures, weather, and life. As Lopez (1986) argued, wilderness' mystery must be accepted as wisdom to be experienced; sensations that are felt when something sacred reveals itself.

INDELIBLE LEARNING

First hand experience combined with thoughtful reflection is meaningful, for the fundamental essence of real growth is fostered through meaningful, hands-on learning experiences. According to Knapp (1992, p.2) outdoor/adventure education is placed in a unique position because students use "more of their senses and their whole bodies as they explore meaningful problems ... to understand better the relationships between the school curriculum and community life." In fact many educators and researchers maintain that the utilization of natural environment as an adjunct to the pedagogical process produces learning that is enriching and indelible (Davies, 1993; Hunt, 1990; Jones, 1989 and Knapp, 1992). Arguably, this is much more difficult to attain in an urban environment.

Students must "experience" the pristine environment first hand in order to understand it and develop a meaningful relationship with it; it is here that indelible learning occurs. This was typified in the following passage in a log book of one of our students:

> In textbooks we can learn about [environmental damages]...but still ignore them. When you are faced with the stark bareness of deforestation, it is not so easy to forget. My first experience with this was just outside Gunnison, Colorado. I was working at a guest ranch tucked away in the mountains whose pervading beauty would force smiles to my lips daily. Here I expected a nirvana or utopia of nature; my shock at the truth still bothers me. Every day I saw large trucks coming down a road leading up to the mountains, laden with stripped trees stacked like tinker-toys. I had read about them but had never seen one. I was curious to see where these logs were coming from. On my next day off I rode my bike up that road to a natural reservoir and the source of all this wood. From a high vantage point I could see beautiful thick forest chequered [sic] by land that looked like it had been poorly shaved, stripped bare, leaving only the stubble of tree bases as proof of their existence. I had seen pictures of this in my 9th Grade environment class but never experienced the emptiness and the pain in the land as I wondered what pencil or porch was so important as this. I now wonder at how advanced we can call ourselves when we are so blind at the same time.

Through adventure education in wilderness settings, participants become more aware of nature's intrinsic value and, many for the first time, begin to question humankind's drive to annihilate wilderness areas in pursuit of progress. We believe that adventure educators must take their participants into the pristine wilderness areas, only then will we, as educators, begin to break the cycle of arrogance perpetuated by humankind. To this end, Mortlock (1987, p.101) maintains that "once one becomes *aware*, it is comparatively easy to have respect".

Exposed to the dichotomy of the two worlds (everyday life and wilderness), most participants in wilderness type adventure education programmes no longer "blindly" accept their societal values and everyday way of life. Wilderness experiences foster broader, deeper, more informed perspectives on life which often lead to questions about one's "taken for granted" life style (Potter, 1993).

These kinds of life changing experiences are infinitely more difficult to attain in urban settings. The transition from a taken for granted everyday life to a wilderness life literally alters the way in which people view the world (Potter, 1993). According to Wurdinger (1994), traditional/conventional classroom approaches may not be as effective because they do not teach the last step—application. Similarly, urban settings provide superficial adventure education experiences which don't resonate participants' cores, and thus, fail to have long term effects. In order for learning to accomplishes this, we must teach to participants' emotions; wilderness programmes achieve this naturally. Moreover, Muir (cited by Mortlock 1987, p.103) explains the critical emotional feeling of interconnectedness non-urban areas can achieve:

> Here is calm so deep, grasses cease waving....Wonderful how completely everything in wild nature fits into us, as if truly part and parent of us. The sun shines not on us, but in us. The rivers flow not past but through us, thrilling, tingling, vibrating every fibre and cell of the substance of our bodies, making them glide and sing. The trees wave and the flowers bloom in our bodies as well as our souls.

SPIRITUALITY

The underlying value of the adventure education experience is attributed, in part, to the fact that it provides an opportunity for participants to become reconnected with their "soul". This "soulful" benefit is synonymous with tapping into their spiritual core, which enables participants to evoke a sense of fulfilment, purpose and direction in their lives (Gibbens, 1991 and Warren, Sakofs and Hunt, 1995). Many practitioners refer to this as a "spiritual" component of outdoor education (for instance, Davies, 1993; Gray, 1995; Henderson, 1996 and Potter, 1993). There appears to be no unequivocal definition of spirituality, yet the term is an integral component of health and well-being (Donatelle and Davis, 1996). Breitenstein and Ewert (1990, p.18) reiterate this problematic aspect when they suggest that "while spiritual health is not as easy to define or observe as other dimensions of health, it is accepted generally as a vital dimension of well-being."

On one hand, spirituality may have religious connotations where participants acknowledge a union or affinity with God whilst in the wilderness. On the other hand, some perceive that spirituality may imply a sense of connectedness and unity with nature. Proponents suggest that people are seeking a spiritual inclusion and self-actualization which is inspired by the pristine and majestical qualities of nature (for instance Cohen, 1997 and Henderson, 1996). In many respects, the spiritual empowerment derived from the wilderness experience is instrumental in the self-actualization process. Whatever the interpretation, Breitenstein and Ewert (1990, p.18) conclude that the "wilderness is a sacred space.…[which] helps young people increase congruence between their beliefs and their behaviour."

Clearly, a wilderness episode can be innately satisfying. Frazier (cited by Nettleton, 1994, p.15) corroborates this aspect when he posits that:

> People say that what we are seeking is a meaning for life. I think that what we're seeking is an experience of being alive, so that our life experience on the purely physical plane will have resonances within our inner most being and reality, so that we actually feel the rapture of being alive.

Along the same train of thought, Davies (1993, p.27) posits that humans are propelled to a higher consciousness as a direct consequence of their time spent in natural areas when he articulates that:

> As we develop a sense of awe and wonder, as we identify that which is marvellous in the world, as we fall in love with our planet, and as we develop a sense of concern for humanity, through the warmth of the relationships that we experience, so we begin to find a sense of meaning for ourselves in the midst of all this.

Admittedly, this emotional depth and level of understanding that many adventure experiences foster is not attainable in all adventure programmes. However, most adventure educators who do strive to move their students to such levels of introspection and awareness, will discover that it is difficult—if not impossible—to attain such within an urban setting. Quite clearly, adventure education experiences which occur in urban settings undervalue the inherent potentials of our discipline.

THE POTENT NATURE OF A NON-URBAN EXPERIENCE

Research into nature's healing powers indicates that it is cathartic, energising, rejuvenating, restorative and calming (Burns, 1998; Greenaway, 1995 and Ulrich, 1984) and we use non-urban settings as an escape from the stressors of our frenetic existence. The wilderness provides a naturally recuperative experience—this is where we flee on vacation; others use musical meditation (sounds of waterfalls, birds, dolphins) as a form of stress relief; and others may choose pictures of majestic mountains, endless beaches or calming sunsets. Quite clearly, nature soothes the psyche, and as Cohen (1997,. p.17) states, "our problems are absent in intact natural areas."

Unashamedly, we retreat to the natural environment to restore our sanity. Many would attest to the fact that first-hand contact with the natural environment is healing and *re"creation"al*. Burns (1999, p. 13) concludes that this in part is attributed to the idea that "stimuli in natural environments are softer, more pleasing and have a better "biological fit" than stimuli in human-made environments".

Mortlock (1987, p.98) ascribes to the theory that the "uncivilized people" who live in harmony with the earth, (such as the Inuit, the Herdsmen, the Aborigines), are the innately happy ones. These cultures share a salient commonality; their lives, their well-being are connected to and dependent on a deeply felt and nurtured interconnectedness to the natural world. One of the profound mysteries of wilderness, one these cultures intuitively comprehend, is its ability to provide an impeccable and indisputable integrity we want for ourselves. Upon entering wilderness and opening oneself to it, we often strike a lasting and reciprocal relationship with nature; we aspire to understand that which other cultures (albeit fewer and fewer) fully connected to the land naturally know. Through the beauty of landscape or its frightening environmental conditions, wilderness affects us. Additionally, it provides us with metaphors and symbols through which we can explore the edges of its mysteries as well as the secrets of our own selves.

If we openly enter the land willing to accept its plethora of intra- and interpersonal experiences we may have with it, many difficult to articulate, we may establish a stronger relationship with nature from which greater self-understanding, self-confidence and interpersonal relationships can emerge. With this bond it becomes possible to transfer these enhanced feelings of self, and dignified relationships with others and nature, back into our everyday life. Each relationship, (with self, other and nature), is formed with the same principle. Through nature we can understand that, "the things in the land fit together perfectly, even though they are always changing" (Lopez, 1986, p.405). Similarly, we may wish to order and arrange our life in the same way as nature's. For if we emulate nature we can balance our selves and our relationships with others more appropriately. Hence, to be open to nature and to try to understand her wisdom and richness can mean the unfolding of our human life. Ultimately, it is the enrichment of the human spirit that draws us to wilderness and helps us to appreciate her inherent value.

Gray (1997, p.7–8) suggests that within the adventure education context, "the wilderness experience, at its very simplest involves stripping people of all surrogates, conveniences and artificiality of life and placing them in the bush where they may appreciate nature, both its beauty and wildness." In the process, participants learn self-reliance by discovering or rediscovering literally, how they and the world work (Davis-Berman, Berman and Capone, 1994 and Hedin and Conrad, 1986). This point is reiterated by Miles (1987, p.36–37) when he states that:

Wilderness places also challenge the whole person and thereby contribute to growth. Conventional schooling emphasizes intellectual growth, half-heartedly addressing physical growth and paying little or no heed to the emotional or spiritual sides of the being...modern life plagues us with doubt, alienation, and nihilism and separates us from the natural community and even from ourselves. In wilderness we have a chance to overcome these problems and get in touch with the self and nature.

Interactions between the wilderness environment and the participant activate internal processes (Potter, 1995 and Young and Crandall, 1984). These processes in turn, are catalysts for personal and social growth. Handley (1993, p.3) corroborates with this notion when he eloquently states that:

> ...the wilderness experience is a journey into the unknown where people meet nature as a stranger in kind but a friend in spirit: an experience of risk, of self reliance, of freedom to both fail and succeed, and an opportunity to see ourselves as ourselves, stripped of 'other world' facades and facing the wilderness within.

As can be seen from the examples given earlier, there is a potent nexus between person-nature interaction. Sadly, this cannot be activated to any great depth, within the confines of an urban setting.

CONCLUSION

Urban settings can be used to promote a mere portion of the benefits and meanings that adventure education in wilderness can achieve. However, it must be recognized that urban adventure programmes will be devoid of many of the profound learning opportunities and subsequent social, spiritual and emotional connections, awarenesses and understandings that are so frequently achieved in adventure programmes nested in natural areas. In wilderness, removed from everyday life distractions and many cultural artifacts, the critical social, emotional and spiritual growth is not only a traditional, but a foundational ingredient of adventure education.

We believe that practitioners should use adventure philosophies and practices in urban environments only when the non-urban alternative is unavailable. More importantly, we draw great caution to the dangers of equating the benefits of urban adventure programmes to those that take place in wilderness. It is crucial that practitioners and administrators of adventure programmes understand the fundamental differences between and limitations of these two types of adventure programmes; to attempt to equate the benefits derived from each would do a great disservice to the community and future of adventure education.

REFERENCES

Barron, J. (1997). Nice work if you can get it. *Pathways: The Ontario Journal of Outdoor Education, 9, (5), 24–27.*

Breitenstein, D. & Ewert, A. (1990). Health benefits of outdoor education: Implications for health education. *Health Education, 21 (10), 16–20.*

Burns, G. W. (1999). Nature guided therapy: A case example Ecopsychology in clinical practice, *Australian Journal of Outdoor Education, 2, 9–14.*

Burns, G.W. (1998). *Nature-guided therapy: Brief integrative strategies for health and well being.* Philadelphia: Brunner/Mazel.

Cohen, M. (1997). *Reconnecting with nature.* Corvallis, Oregon: Ecopress.

Cooper, G. (1994). The role of outdoor education in education for the 21st century. *Journal of Adventure Education and Outdoor Leadership, 11* (2), 9–12.

Davies, G. (1993). On becoming human: An examination of the contributions made by outdoor education. *Journal of Adventure Education and Outdoor Leadership, 9* (4), 22–29.

Davis-Berman, J., Berman, D. & Capone, L. (1994). Therapeutic wilderness programs: A national survey. *The Journal of Experiential Education, 17* (2), 49–53.

Donatelle, R. & Davis, L. (1996). *Access to health.* Boston, USA: Allyn and Bacon.

Duenkel, N. (1997). Personal biography in editorial by Duenkel and Henderson: Educating towards deep ecological sensibilities. *Trumpeter, 14* (2), 50–52.

Gibbens, R. (1991). The bliss of solitude. *The Journal of Adventure Education and Outdoor Leadership, 8* (1), 21–23.

Gray, T. L. (1997). *The Impact of an Extended Stay Outdoor Education Program on Adolescent Participants.* Unpublished doctoral dissertation. University Of Wollongong, NSW, Australia.

Gray, T. L. (1995). *Forging synergistic links between theory and practice.* Keynote Address, Victorian Outdoor Education Association. June.

Greenway, R. (1995). The wilderness effect and Ecopsychology. In T. Roszak, T. Gomes, M.E. & Kanner, A.D. (Eds). *Ecopsychology: Restoring the earth, healing the mind.* San Francisco: Sierra Club Books.

Handley, R. (1993). *Opening the black box: How and why it works.* Conference Proceedings of the 3rd NSW Outdoor Education Conference, 1–14.

Harper, S. (1995). The way of wilderness. In T. Roszak, M.E. Gomes & A.D. Kanner (Eds.), *Ecopsychology: Restoring the earth, healing the mind.* San Francisco: Sierra Club Books, p. 183–200.

Hedin, D. & Conrad, D. (1986). Johnny says he is learning through experience. In R., Kraft & J. Kielsmeier (Eds.), *Experiential education and the schools.* Second Edition, Boulder, Colorado: Association for Experiential Education, 258–262.

Henderson, B. (1996). Thoughts on the idea of adventure. In C. Adams (Ed.), *The soul unearthed: Celebrating wildness and personal renewal through nature.* New York: Putnam's Sons.

Hunt, J. (1990). Philosophy of Adventure. In Miles, J. and Priest, S. (Eds.). *Adventure Education* (p.119–128). State College, PA: Venture Publishing, Inc., USA.

Jones, L. (1989). Outdoor education: Can it help our young people? *Youth Studies, November, 8* (4), 22–26.

Kiewa, J. (1991). Education for growth: Outdoor education. *Australian Council for Health, Physical Education and Recreation. National Journal,* Winter, 7–9.

Knapp, C. (1992). *Lasting lessons: A teachers' guide to reflecting on experience.* Charleston, West Virginia, USA: ERIC Clearinghouse on Rural Education.

Lopez, B. (1986). *Arctic dreams.* New York: Bantam Books.

Miles, J. (1987). Wilderness as a learning place. *Journal of Environmental Education, 18* (2), 33–40.

Miles, J. and Priest, S. (Eds.) (1990). *Adventure Education*. State College, Pennsylvania, USA: Venture Publishing, Inc.

Mortlock, C. (1987). *The adventure alternative*. Cumbria, England: Cicerone Press.

Nettleton, B. (1994). Quality of experience in outdoor education. *Conference Proceedings of the 13th Annual Victorian Outdoor Education Association*, November. 15–21.

Potter, T.G. (1995). *Seeds to trees: Towards an understanding of human growth in wilderness*. Proceedings of the Association for Experiential Education 23rd Annual Conference, Lake Geneva, Wisconsin, 211–212.

Potter, T.G. (1993). *A journey through wilderness weekend experiences*. Unpublished doctoral dissertation. University of Alberta: Edmonton, Alberta.

Priest, S. & Gass, S. (1997). *Effective leadership in adventure programming*. University of New Hampshire, NH: Human Kinetics.

Stapleton, I. (1990). *Secondhand and solid: How we built Wollangarra*. Victoria, Australia: Globe Press Pty. Ltd.

Ulrich, R.S., (1984). View through a window may influence recovery from surgery. *Science, 224*: 420–421.

Walsh, V. & Golins, G. (1976). *The exploration of the Outward Bound process*. Denver, CO: Colorado Outward Bound School.

Warren, K., Sakofs, M. & Hunt, J. (Eds). (1995). The theory of experiential education. Dubuque, Iowa. USA: Kendall Hunt Publishing Co.

Wurdinger, S. (1994). Examining the learning process used in adventure education. *Journal of Adventure Education and Outdoor Leadership, 11* (3), 25–27.

Young, R. & Crandall, R. (1984). Wilderness use and self-actualization. *Journal of Leisure Research, 16* (2), 149–160.

CHAPTER 5

Should Modern Communication Systems (Cellular Telephones) Be Used in the Wilderness?

YES PERSPECTIVE: Tod Schimelpfenig

NO PERSPECTIVE: T.A. Loeffler, Ph.D.

Tod Schimelpfenig is an avid outdoor adventurer and ice hockey player who is currently the Rocky Mountain School Director for the National Outdoor Leadership School. Tod started as an instructor for NOLS 26 years ago, and in addition to being a senior staff field instructor has worked in outfitting, program planning, human resources, and risk management. Tod organized the Wilderness Risk Managers Committee and its first annual conferences focusing on safety and risk in wilderness education. Tod has been a practicing EMT for 25 years, volunteers with search and rescue, has taught and lectured on wilderness medicine in the U.S., Kenya and Australia, is a former board member of the Wilderness Medical Society and the author of NOLS Wilderness First Aid. When he can't skate Tod likes nothing better than traveling in the outdoors.

T. A. Loeffler, Ph.D. is an avid outdoor adventurer and ice hockey player who teaches recreation and outdoor education at Memorial University of Newfoundland. For the past fifteen years, she has worked in many facets of outdoor education including summer camps, ropes courses, wilderness-based therapy programs, Woodswomen, NOLS and higher education. When she's not teaching, writing, or chasing a hockey puck, T.A. likes nothing better than strapping on a backpack and going for a long walk.

Should Modern Communication Systems (Cellular Telephones) Be Used in the Wilderness?

Tod Schimelpfenig

This issue catches the attention and ignites the passion of many wilderness educators. It fuels philosophical, ethical, legal and practical dialogue and argument around many wilderness campfires. I'm not trained as an ethicist and will leave that perspective to others. I'm not an attorney or legal expert, but I do have a few comments on the legal angle and developing industry standards. Most of my comments reflect a pragmatic personal philosophy on modern technology in wilderness education programs.

There are still many wild areas where an individual, and an organized wilderness adventure program, has a choice on venturing into wilderness with or without a radio or cellular telephone. The Wilderness Act (U.S.) does not have language specifically addressing celluar telephones, beepers or radios. It gives individual users broad choices regarding communication technology. However, the opinions of legal experts, as they influence insurance companies, boards of trustees and administrators, pressure programs to utilize communication devices. In a few cases land managers have required communication devices of permitted outfitters. The public,

when it reacts with outrage to death and injury in wilderness, and with its expectation of access to expedient rescue, wants the best of the wilderness experience and the benefits of rescue technology. As well, communication industry advertising creates mis-perceptions about the effectiveness of these devices.

Carrying a radio or cellular telephone is, in my opinion, not an industry standard, although it is becoming more common. Program use of cellular telephones is driving the industry, but the actions of one program, do not dictate another wilderness adventure program's position on this issue. If a program chooses not to carry a modern communication device, or if its reliability is limited for its program area, it needs to clearly articulate to participants the limits of access to rescue or medical support.

Celluar telephones are a lightning rod for discussions on technology in wilderness. However, weather radios and global positioning systems are also utilized by wilderness adventure programs, and in some cases portable cassette players are carried by staff as well as students. The avalanche beacon, essentially a radio system, is accepted without question as a lifesaving tool in avalanche terrain.

Resistance against the use of modern communication systems subsides when the device supports evacuation for legitimate emergencies. In my 25 years of wilderness search and rescue experience I've never once had a patient, or trip leader, request an urgent evacuation be handled without a radio, or refuse a helicopter and demand to be carried from the field.

Recently, I hiked into the Fitzpatrick Wilderness in the Wind River Mountains accompanied by my two teenage sons. We stopped at the boundary sign and talked about legislated wilderness and my thoughts on its value. It would have been an interesting experience, and one I may well try sometime, to carry across that boundary only items made by my hand with natural materials. However, we didn't drop our packs and leave behind products of technology that increase our comfort in the wilderness. I wanted my polyester pile clothing, Dacron filled sleeping bag, my stove, matches, fuel, insect repellent, Powerbars®, the map developed with satellite accuracy, my nylon rope, fiberglass fishing pole, and my prescription sunglasses. I also didn't leave my cellular telephone or epinephrine syringe behind. I carried these in, just in case of a medical emergency.

Most of us routinely use technology, or the products of technology, on our wilderness trips. Using technology isn't the issue. The issue is how communication technology impacts the quality of the wilderness experience. I began living in wilderness before portable music players, modern communication systems or computers were even a dream. This experience, and the values of remoteness and self-reliance, paint the picture of my ideal wilderness trip.

We already utilize technology to make ourselves more comfortable, to manage risk, and as rescue tools in wilderness. I cannot argue for omitting a cellular telephone, radio or beacon, which could access emergency support and may save a life, while I carry technology, such as a stove, polyester clothing and light nylon tents, that all help to increase my comfort. I can understand a program committed to a primitive wilderness experience not utilizing any modern technology. I could not explain to a grieving parent why I chose not to carry a radio, yet I brought along my walkman, or my polyester jacket.

I know that there are downsides to cellular telephones. I fear that a radio or cell phone will become a distraction and interfere with the focus on the wilderness and the group, what pilots call situational awareness, and will contribute to a poor decision. I've carried a radio or cellular telephone for several years now. I've yet to make a distracting call, but I know of others who have had their attention diverted by calling home or work from the middle of the wilderness.

I fear cell phones will substitute for competence and that scenarios such as the tale of two hikers with global positioning devices and cell phones, but no maps or compass, will become common. They knew exactly where they were, but hadn't the faintest idea how to get from point A to point B. Rescuers had to assist them down the mountain. Radios are often incorrectly labeled as safety devices. In reality we most often use the radio as a rescue tool after an accident or illness in the backcountry. Regardless of these fears, I choose to use cellular telephones in wilderness. The challenge is to utilize a cellular telephone prudently, and to not abandon self-reliance and our ability to act decisively and independently.

I had several long wilderness experiences where I cooked only on fires and navigated with hand drawn maps. Things change. Many of my current wilderness companions, students and fellow staff, have a different image of an ideal wilderness experience. They are barraged with gear and gizmos in climbing, paddling and skiing magazines, and in the role models provided by their instructors and guides. It is inevitable that cellular telephones will become commonplace equipment with wilderness users. At some point, popular backpacking magazines will have feature articles discussing which cellular telephone is the lightest and most reliable. Wilderness adventure programs, because they think it's appropriate, or in response to legal pressure, will increasingly use communication devices. Participants, and their parents, will increasingly expect effective emergency communication. Regardless of my personal opinion,

this will happen. As a wilderness educator, my best tool to manage this issue of technology in wilderness is to model and teach wilderness values, to make sure users understand the impact of communication technology on a wilderness experience, and to teach them to use it wisely. We need to foster attitudes and habits in leaders to carry only what they need into the wilderness and to set aside distractions to concentrate on safety and enjoyment of a wild area.

END NOTE:

The official position of NOLS on this topic is stated in *Cell Phones at NOLS* in Wilderness Risk Management: Proceedings of the 1995 Wilderness Risk Managers Conference. National Outdoor Leadership School. Lander, Wyoming. U.S.A.

Should Modern Communication Systems (Cellular Telephones) Be Used in the Wilderness?

T.A. Loeffler, Ph.D.

Many claim that communications technology (cellular phones) will only be used as a tool in the wilderness user's toolbox and that the technology will not change people's expectations and behaviors. Given the way technology is embraced in the current society, it is impossible for such expectations not to change. The use of technology is seductive. One need only look at microwave ovens to see this influence—many people have given up cooking, switching instead to "heat and eat." I have refused to purchase a microwave because I'm not sure I could hold out against the siren's call. I even returned a microwave that I'd been given as a housewarming present because I wanted to retain my emphasis on cooking my food from scratch rather than heating ready-to-eat products; I didn't trust that I wouldn't give into the pull of the microwave.

In a similar way, the facsimile and the internet have changed people's expectations about the availability of information. Where in the past, people would have requested information from an agency by mail, expecting to receive it in two or three weeks, now people expect to receive information almost instantly through fax or the internet. Much of technology reduces the time it takes to accomplish tasks. With technology in place, people's expectations change and the reduced time frame is expected, not appreciated. If cellular telephones are readily carried into the wilderness, a similar shift from appreciation to expectation is predicted. In other words, there would be a change from appreciation of rescue efforts to an expectation of them. And, not only would there be an expectation of rescue, it would be expected rapidly. Glick (1997) identified this trend as the "help-on-demand syndrome" (p. 59) and he predicts that it may be leading to a dangerous mindset where people believe help is only a call away.

Proponents of the use of cellular phones often cite increased safety as a rationale for their use in the wilderness. That is, if an accident were to occur, help could be summoned more quickly utilizing the technology. In some instances, this more rapid response is possible but in many cases, it is not. It is feared, with the expectation of readily available rescue being only a call away, people will venture into situations where they do not have the skills or experience to be and will place themselves and rescuers in great danger. Glick (1997) relays the story of a group of climbers who were caught in a vicious hailstorm high in the Grand Teton mountains.

> Terrified and desperate, they did what any self-respecting backpackers of the 90's do—whip out the cell phone and yelp for help. Rescuers found a group of tenderfoots astonishingly unprepared, clad in shorts and T-shirts, without extra supplies. Ranger Tom Kimborough asked them to explain. "I looked at the big pile of gear and I looked at the phone," a climber said. "And the phone was a helluva lot lighter" (p.59).

Unfortunately, the story above is not unique. Glick (1997, p. 59) states that the "lore of the foolish cell-phone caller is growing among the ranks of search-and-rescue squads." There is the story of the man who called to be rescued in Washington state because he was dehydrated and could not go on. The three rescue teams that responded found that he had not carried adequate water but that he did have a cellular phone, GPS, and laptop computer along (Vines, 1998). Or the many stories of individuals calling 9-1-1 and asking for flashlights or directions or sleeping bags because they went out unprepared (Glick, 1997; Wheatley, 1996). Wheatley (1996, p. 1) reports that "this past summer, a business man called the Forest Service from the crest of the Presidential Range and demanded a helicopter ride out because he was late for a meeting." Finally, Wheatley (1996) sums up the problem of cellular phone use in the wilderness by stating that:

> These intrepid outdoors people apparently feel safer with their expensive electronics. But this is a dangerous illusion. These gadgets don't keep them out of trouble. They just make it possible for them to call for help when they find themselves inconvenienced or in danger, incurring public expense, using up scarce emergency resources, and in some cases jeopardizing the safety of others (p. 1).

There is a common assumption that the use of communications technology in the wilderness has saved lives. This potential is often listed as the major rationale for employing its use. The potential is there, but along with it, can be the dangerous expectation that it will solve all problems.

Current communications are becoming increasingly reliable, but there are many reasons to be skeptical. First, the technology is based on fragile electronics. Wilderness journeys involve rugged travel through varieties of weather. Eventually, even with the greatest care, backpacks are dropped, water gets into dry bags, and unexpected snow soaks through the tarp. Second, if the cellular phone survives the rigors of wilderness travel, it needs power to run. Generally, this power comes from some form of battery. Batteries are known to lose their charge frequently in cold weather and so they must be recharged or spares carried. Recharging involves carrying another device and usually depends on solar power, which is weather dependent. Third, if the unit survives the trip and has adequate power, it may still not be dependable because of coverage zones and shadow areas. Cellular communication technology depends on repeater towers or cells. You cannot use a cellular phone in areas that are far removed from these towers. Also, in valleys or canyons, cellular reception is frequently not possible. Often getting reception depends on climbing to the highest point around and hoping. The Boy Scout Wilderness Emergency Preparedness, Communications and Training Manual (1998) suggests that the way to deal with the above difficulties is through redundancy. The manual suggests that "having multiple spare batteries, more than one phone, and phones with different carrier companies is essential" (p. 1). As highlighted in this manual, the question could evolve from "should I carry a cellular phone into the wilderness?" to "how many phones and batteries do I need to carry to ensure successful communication?"

A recent canoe expedition to Northern Quebec and Labrador retraced the expedition of Mina Hubbard and used satellite communications technology to transmit the details of the adventure out to an expedition web site (Pratt, 1997). The necessary technology weighed one hundred pounds and included a satellite phone, digital camera, two laptop computers, and a solar-charging system. One of the expedition members declared "shoveling our mountains of gear out of the truck at Sept-Iles station, we stuck out like sore thumbs" (Pratt, 1997, p. T10). The expedition's challenges were described in this way:

> ...harsh unforgiving weather, legions of blackflies and mosquitoes, churning kilometres of challenging rapids and the occasional frustrations of hauling temperamental and heavy technology across the waves with them (Pratt, 1997, p. T10).

Related to the third difficulty of using communications technology in the wilderness listed above, the expedition's greatest technological problem was keeping all of the batteries charged. The phone was described as a "power pig" and they found that it was difficult to keep the three solar charging panels (three to five feet long) anchored on the decks of their boats through rapids and frequent portages.

Last year, I returned from taking students on an overnight camping experience. The director of my department asked me if I had taken a cellular phone on the trip. I said "No, I didn't think I needed one." He replied, "What if something happened? You would need to have the phone to summon help quickly." I answered that I had a solid risk management plan and that I could summon help reasonably quickly because we were just an hour away from a phone and that I feared the experience would be changed if I took a cellular phone along."

This year, at his request, I took a cellular phone with me. When I tested the phone, we had no reception at our campsite because we were surrounded by high sea cliffs. I climbed up to several of the high spots around to test where I would need to go to assure adequate reception. It took me three hours to find a spot that would work and that spot ended up being an hour and a half's hike from camp. I could get out to the roadhead in about an hour. In a true emergency, I may have used up valuable time attempting to use the technology rather than using a more effective and less technologically based solution.

There is concern about how using communications technology would effect the experience of being in the wilderness. I frequently use computers in my office work. When the technology works well, it is a beautifully efficient tool. On other occasions, by insisting I use a computer, I have added hours to a task because of software or hardware difficulties. Having communications technology on a wilderness trip, may encourage and/or require people to spend much of their time maintaining, testing, and attempting to get the technology to work, both prior to and during an emergency.

This is especially apparent in wilderness education programs. The use of communications technology is quietly and seductively becoming the standard of care for wilderness programs in the name of safety, risk management, and liability insurance coverage. The danger in this is two-fold. As the use of communication technology becomes standard operating procedure, programs will lose the ability to make that decision based on their program's aims, objectives, goals, and course areas. With the use of communication technology becoming the standard of care, there comes the expectation that the technology will be infallible and that rescue can be accessed quickly. Currently, the technology is fallible and rescue efforts can easily be hampered by weather, terrain, and other factors. There will need to be an increased diligence on the part of wilderness instructors to ensure that the communications technology they are carrying is in working condition. The time involved for this could easily translate to over an hour a day, time that was formally available for instruction or other tasks. Also, with outdoor organizations and consumers accepting and expecting that the use of communications technology is standard, there becomes the expectation that the technology will work, and that there will be great liability if the technology fails to operate.

The use of communications technology in the wilderness could soon be out of the hands of individuals or programs. With pressures from legal experts and insurance carriers, the use of such devices is moving toward being the standard of care. What level of technology will be sufficient? Is a cellular phone enough? Are two cellular phones enough? What about a 20 pound, typewriter-sized satellite phone? What about location transmitters? Currently, if an individual wishes to hike in the backcountry of Gros Morne National Park in Newfoundland, Canada, he/she is required to carry a radio transmitter so that the park service can find them easily if they do not return on schedule (Flanagan, 1996). You cannot convince me

that this invasion of technology into the wilderness does not affect one's experience of it. What does this do to the sense of freedom and self-reliance that traveling through the wilderness brings?

It is often argued that people use many different forms of technology in the wilderness so there should be no problem assimilating another piece of technology into the milieu. The argument is expressed like this: "if you use Goretex clothing or avalanche beacons, how can you be opposed to cellular phones? They are both technology." To me, there is a major difference between technology that is utilized within the wilderness and technology that provides two-way communications in and out of the wilderness. It is this two-way communications ability that makes people question the use of communications technology in the wilderness because it can create a barrier between the user and the wilderness. The ability to communicate with the "outside" world prevents people from being fully present in the wilderness since they can be in contact with friends, call for weather reports, or ask for more rations at a re-supply.

I have frequently observed this barrier when leading trips in the Grand Canyon in Arizona. At the start of every trip, I ask participants to share their goals and expectations for the trip. Many express goals such as seeking solitude, getting away from the pressures of everyday life, get closer to nature, and experiencing the Grand Canyon. I usually lead one of two routes. One route takes the group through Phantom Ranch, a small enclave of civilization at the bottom of the Grand Canyon, and the other route travels west along the Tonto Plateau. Participants are often surprised by what they find at Phantom Ranch: flush toilets, running water, and pay phones. I notice a shift in my participants as we spend time at Phantom Ranch. They become preoccupied with the phone. They frequently plot about how to squeeze in one last phone call before bed and before we hike to our next campsite the next day. They lose connection with the magnificent place they are in and are transported back into their worlds they wanted to leave behind. Instead of exploring Bright Angel Canyon, they stand in line waiting for a chance to use the phone. Glick (1997) reported a similar story in which three brokers were out fishing on the Russian River in Alaska at 3:00 in the morning. Before they had even caught any fish, they used their cellular phones to work the markets in New York and Singapore.

I fear that if I carried a cellular phone in the Grand Canyon, this preoccupation would be present for much of the trip. The presence of the phone would slow or prevent the transition from everyday life to life in the wilderness. Ideally, there would be no transition between these two places, and these two states of being, but I've found for many there is a great difference. It is this difference that impels people into the wilderness. As Thoreau (1992) reflected, "I went into the woods because I wished to live deliberately" (p. 61). I believe the presence of communications technology interferes with the ability to live deliberately, to separate from everyday strains and concerns, and to connect deeply with the land we travel on and the people we travel with.

Don Starkell, veteran of many extraordinary expeditions, echoed this sentiment when he explained why he wasn't taking communications technology on his expedition to the Canadian Arctic.

> Just don't want to carry the weight and the worries of protecting it and depending on it. A radio would make me careless, knowing that I could ask for rescue at any time. It

would give me the security to take more risks, risks that I can't afford to take. Most important, it would not allow me to think and feel like the Inuit and the adventurers of the past (Starkell, 1995, p. 106).

Thinking back to the Grand Canyon, I remember that when I lead groups on the other route which has no access to phones, the topic never comes up. The group moves into the experience with a minimum of distractions.

What is the experience of wilderness? What does it mean to voluntarily choose to be in wilderness? What is lost by taking communications technology into the wilderness? In an attempt to answer this question, I turn to the words of John Muir. This passage, written over 100 years ago, is equally apt today:

> The tendency nowadays to wonder in wildernesses is delightful to see. Thousands of tired, nerve shaken, over-civilized people are beginning to find out that going to the mountains is going home; that wildness is a necessity; and that mountain parks and reservations are useful not only as fountains of timber and irrigating rivers, but as fountains of life. Awakening from the stupefying effects of the vice of over-industry and the deadly apathy of luxury, they are trying the best they can to mix and enrich their own little ongoings with those of Nature, and to get rid of rust and disease (1971, p. 32).

What is lost, then, is access to true wildness. By taking communications technology into wild places, we blur the line between our civilized lives and our wild lives. A line which provides for the separation of simplicity and complexity, quiet and noise, and self-reliance and dependence. Through the loss of this difference, we lose the ability to awaken. Thoreau (1992) suggests that "we need to learn to reawaken and keep ourselves awake, not by mechanical aids but by an infinite expectation of the dawn" (p. 61). Muir (1971, p. 32) agreed, suggesting that "in wildness, is the preservation of the world."

It is often proposed that communications technology will only be used in the wilderness in cases of extreme emergency. Even if this is so, I believe the wilderness experience will be tainted by the presence of communications temptation. I can imagine realizing that my group is going to be two hours late for the pick-up and being tempted to call basecamp. I can imagine it being my partner's birthday and being tempted to call expressing birthday wishes. Even if I do not pick up the phone and dial, my wilderness experience has been impacted by having to think through and make a decision about using the technology. During the time I am thinking and deciding, I am less available to the group I am leading and I am less present in my environment.

It is clear that cellular phones have a huge potential to influence the experience of being in wilderness. It is time to consider, as well, the reciprocal of that question. How is the wilderness influenced by the presence of cellular phones? According to the Appalachian Trail Conference (1998):

> technical innovations, combined with the federal Telecommunications Act of 1996, have led to lots of antennas sprouting up over the countryside, and industry experts anticipate a dramatic surge of new antennas nationwide during the next few years...as companies expand their services beyond metropolitan areas (p. 1).

The Appalachian Trail Conference is concerned about this trend because much of the Appalachian Trail is on high ground that is ideal for telecommunications antennas and they fear that the siting of antennas near the Trail "could have a huge cumulative impact on hikers and on the 'AT Experience'" (1998,

p. 1). Similar concerns were expressed by Senator Patrick Leahy, "I do not want Vermont turned into a giant pincushion with 200-foot towers indiscriminately sprouting on every mountain and in every valley (1997, p.1). As greater cellular coverage is demanded by consumers, the greater the number of cellular antennas that will adorn high places. As wilderness travelers demand the ability to communicate from wild places, so too, will come, the antennas to wild places. As well as being an "environmental eyesore, these transmission towers may pose a great danger to the health and well-being of those who live near them" (Davis, 1996, p.1).

Many people are concerned about the health risks of exposure to radio frequency (RF) and microwave radiation emitted from cellular phones and cellular transmission facilities (Bergman-Venezia, 1996). Hatfield (1995) comments that:

> Forty-five million cell phones are in use today, over one-hundred thousand cell towers loom over our skylines in the US, thousands of additional wireless communications facilities are under construction and concerns of health effects including learning disabilities, cancer, leukemia, DNA damage, blood disorders, brain tumors, electrical sensitivity and other serious adverse health disorders are brushed aside in the name of progress. We are irrevocably altering the electromagnetic signature of the world and we are doing this with no clear understanding of the implications to humans and other species (p. 1).

Davis (1996) suggests that "we don't know the price we will ultimately pay for the convenience of all the new toys we think we need" (p. 1). As a result of such concerns, many communities are mobilizing to fight the siting of cellular transmission facilities in their communities, especially the placement of cellular towers in school yards and playgrounds because some studies have shown that children are especially at risk from RF and microwave radiation (Bergman-Venezia, 1996). In fact, New Zealand recently passed legislation preventing the siting of cellular towers on school property (Bergman-Venezia, 1996).

The cellular phone industry claims that the technology is safe, however, the research on which that claim is based, is not definitive (Goldberg, 1993). It is easy to become enamored with new technology and ignore its possible health and environmental concerns. Realistically, it could be decades before the true effects of cellular communications technology are fully understood (Bergman-Venezia, 1996).

What will be the price we will have paid, in twenty or fifty or one-hundred years, of choosing to embrace communications technology so fully today? What will be the health costs? What will be the environmental costs? What will be the psychological costs? Can you put a price on the loss of wildness? What will be the ultimate price we pay for the ability to communicate from every place on earth? Do we want or need to pay it? These are questions I pose to those who wish to use cellular telephones in the wilderness; please ponder them before you head out to the woods with a cellular phone in your backpack or canoe.

REFERENCES

Appalachian Trail Conference. (1998). *Telecom Towers Issue Page*. (http://members.aol.com/atconf/Towers.html).

Bergman-Venezia, C. (1996). *Cell tower static: Consumers cause interference in the race to a wireless world*. (Available from EMR Alliance. 410 West 53rd Street, Suite 105, New York, NY 10019 USA).

Boy Scout Wilderness Emergency Preparedness, Communications and Training Manual. (1998). (http://www.macscouter.com/Survival/WildPrep.html)

Davis, R. (1996). *Vermont: Mugged and unplugged: The health and policy threat of the wireless revolution*. (http://members.aol.com/Health4VT/index.html).

Flanagan, C. (1996, January 14). Radio tracking beepers bargain and boon for lost hikers. *Evening Telegram*, p. 4.

Glick, D. (1997). Cell phones: A call from the wild. *Newsweek (130)*, 4. p. 59.

Goldberg, R. B. (1993). The cellular phone controversy: Real or contrived? *EMF Health Report (1)* 1.

Hatfield, J. B. (1995). Cellular towers exposure levels and public health. *EMF Health Report (3)* 2.

Leahy, P. (1997). *Vermont: Mugged and unplugged: The health and policy threat of the wireless revolution*. (http://members.aol.com/Health4VT/index.html).

Muir, J. (1971). In wildness is the preservation of the world. In J. Opie (Ed.), *Americans and environment: The controversy over ecology* (pp. 32–40). Lexington, MA: D.C. Heath and Company.

Pratt, L. (1997). Going wireless in whitewater: A team of canoe trippers puts satellite and Web-site technology through the telecommunications torture test. *Financial Post (10)* 37, p. T10.

Starkell, D. (1995). *Paddle to the Arctic*. Toronto: McClelland & Stewart Inc..

Thoreau, H. D. (1992). *Walden and resistence to civil government: Authoritative texts, Journal, reviews, and essays in criticism* (2nd ed.). W. Rossi (Ed.). New York: W.W. Norton & Company.

Vines, T. (1998, March 20). No easy fix for beartooth panic. *The Wall Street Journal*, p. 16.

Wheatley, R. H. (1996). *Cell phones in the wilderness: Try bringing a swiss army knife instead.* (http://www.pookas.com/cols/col.12-13-96A.shtml)

CHAPTER 6

Do One Day Adventure Programming Activities, Such as Challenge Courses, Provide Long Lasting Learning?

YES PERSPECTIVE: Dan Garvey, Ph.D.
NO PERSPECTIVE: Tom Puk, Ph.D.

Dan Garvey is a faculty member in Outdoor Education at the University of New Hampshire. He is the former President and Executive Director of the Association for Experiential Education (AEE). He received his Ph.D. from the University of Colorado and has written and researched extensively in the fields of moral development, international experiential education, and educational reform. Before joining the faculty at UNH he had a twenty year career as an administrator and practitioner, ending as the Director of the Merrowvista Education Center and the Vice President of the American Youth Foundation. He has also served as Executive Director for the University of Pittsburgh, Semester Sea Program.

Dr. Puk is an Associate Professor in the Faculty of Education, Lakehead University, Thunder Bay, Ontario, Canada. He was one of the original developers of Project D.A.R.E (Development through Adventure, Responsibility, and Education), an outdoor program for delinquents started in 1971. He currently teaches (among other things) Outdoor Experiential Education programs as part of a teacher certification, Bachelor of Education program. He has conducted extensive research on self-directed learning and inquiry and is currently conducting research to link quantum theory with curriculum development and also the role of nurturing in teaching and learning.

Do One Day Adventure Programming Activities, Such as Challenge Courses, Provide Long Lasting Learning?

Dan Garvey, Ph.D.

INTRODUCTION

The question before us is whether one-day adventure programs can have long-lasting effects on clients. This is a wonderful question to be addressed in a book focused on controversial issues within the field of outdoor education, because some outdoor educators and clients have raised concerns regarding the possible positive results associated with short-term programs. Our clients often look to us for reassurance that a one-day ropes course activity or series of team building exercises has the potential to benefit the individual and the group. Clients also wonder if the learning resulting from these programs can be long lasting. We may ask ourselves if the work we do is making any difference to our clients in the long run. Given only one day to work with a group, we are often unsure what, if any, learning may have occurred. Even if the client has a self proclaimed intense learning experience, how long is this likely to last? These questions and misgivings reinforce the need for thoughtful reflection regarding the potential potency of one-day programming.

In this article an argument will be made for the positive benefits of one-day programs. The article is organized into six sections and a conclusion.

1. We should expand our thinking regarding the question of one-day programs.

2. The history of outdoor education is based on long-term programs, but the direction of outdoor education field favors shorter programs.

3. There is an increased demand for short one-day programs because these programs work.

4. Learning theories in outdoor education support the effectiveness of one-day programs.

5. The short-term experiences are potentially powerful.

6. Personal experience teaches us that brief experiences can have long-lasting results.

This argument in support of one-day programs does not minimize the effectiveness of longer programs, each program model has its place in the full array of outdoor programming. One-day programs can be highly effective for our clients, however, this does not negate the effectiveness of multi-day programs. The increasing demand by our clients for short, intense experiences leaves little doubt that one-day programs are viewed as being worthwhile.

We Should Expand Our Thinking Regarding the Question of One-Day Programs

To answer the question of the possible effectiveness of one-day programs, we may be inclined to seek objective research. Unfortunately, very little research is available that specifically focuses on the effectiveness of programs based on the time clients spend in a particular activity. We know very little about the minimum or maximum time needed in order for successful learning to occur in an outdoor program.

Three studies, that indirectly relate to the topic of this chapter, support the idea that short-term outdoor activities can have positive results. Priest and Lesperance (1994), and Priest, Kichar, Gibson and Bronson (1992) provide some evidence that the length of program time is less important than the skill of the group facilitator. Wagner and Roland (1992) conducted a study involving more than one hundred and fifty participants working for the U.S. Department of Defense. In this study, participants were pre/post tested following a one-day program. The subject group was also compared to a control group of employees matching the characteristics of the subjects, but not taking part in the program. Those subjects who attended the one-day programs showed significant positive improvement in the areas of: "problem solving, group awareness and group effectiveness" (p.7).

While these studies are informative, they do not directly answer the question of the long-lasting effects of one-day programs. We may learn some important information from the limited research reporting on short-term programs, but research data is an inadequate source to fully understand the impact of one-day programs. To gain a fuller understanding, we need to use both objective facts, when we have them, and logic based upon related theories and our subjective experiences.

A word here about the difference between objective facts and subjective beliefs. An objective fact is one that exists regardless of whether we happen to believe in it. For example, gravity. Gravity exists, not because we believe it exists, but quite independent of our belief. Our belief in gravity is not a necessary condition for its existence. A subjective belief is one that requires our belief for it to be true. For example, honesty. There is no objective form of honesty. Yet, we may believe we can identify honesty when we see it. Many of us seek the certainty of objective facts. We want "hard" answers to questions like: "Do one-day programs have long lasting results?" We desire to live in a world where things can be proven, often by counting.

The problem we encounter immediately is that objective facts do not really exist in the social world. The laws and rules that appear to govern our physical world do not have a corresponding certainty in the social world. To answer the question of the efficacy of one-day outdoor adventure programs, we can't rely entirely on the examination of the "objective facts" that have been assembled on this topic. We must look at this question from several directions and apply our subjective reasoning to see if we can gain a fuller and more accurate understanding of the potential benefits of one-day adventure programs.

The History of Outdoor Education is Based on Long-term Programs, but the Direction of the Outdoor-education Field Favors Shorter Programs

The roots of outdoor adventure education in much of the world are connected to Kurt Hahn's Outward Bound Program. Outward Bound's "standard" course was/is 28 days. Subsequently, the 28 day course became a common time block for a plethora of outdoor programs that were modeled after Outward Bound. One might assume that a preference for relatively long (28 day) courses is grounded in well researched educational theory, unfortunately this may not be the case.

It's interesting to recall how Outward Bound established the 28 day course. The first Outward Bound Course was in 1941, at the Aberdovey Sea School/Outward Bound Centre (Zelinski, 1991, p.7). This course length neatly corresponded to the normal pay period for the British merchant seamen who were often forced, as a condition of their employment, to take part in these courses. Therefore, the 28 day course may have had more to do with the ability of an employer to guarantee participation by an employee, than the pedagogical superiority of this time span. We don't know if Kurt Hahn was in favor of the near month-long courses, but we do know there were strong economic and social control reasons present to make this course length preferable.

Based upon this historical preference for long courses, it might be understandable that some outdoor educators might find one-day programs to be a threat to the roots of outdoor adventure education as created in the Outward Bound Schools.

There is An Increased Demand for Short One-day Programs Because These Programs Work

From this beginning of near month-long courses, we have witnessed a steady reduction in the amount of time some clients are willing to spend participating in adventure activities. In the 1970s and 1980s, during an era when public schools began bringing students on outdoor adventure activities, week-long programs were very popular. This week of adventure activities replaced or supplemented the week of environmental education that was part of the junior high school curriculum in many states. As we progressed from the 1980s, there has been a tendency for school groups to book two and three-day programs at outdoor adventure education centers.

This trend by schools for shortened programs was accelerated in the 1990s due to a reduction in the amount of federal money available to school districts for out-of-class activities. Consequently, the result has been a dramatic increase in the desire by schools to have one-day adventure activities for their students.

Corporate training programs, using outdoor adventure activities, have also had a great impact on the growth of one-day programs. Most corporate clients are seeking the greatest program impact using the least amount of time. If a week long program can be condensed into a weekend retreat, that's preferable. And, if the learning gained in a weekend can be realized in one day, all the better. Corporate training in the United States blossomed in the past decade to an estimated $100 million dollar industry (Thompson, 1991). This large and growing sector of outdoor programming, corporate training, is currently demanding short, one to three day programs for their clients.

Learning Theories in Outdoor Education Support the Effectiveness of One-day Programs

Gass (1985), in his article on the transfer of learning, helped connect the learning theories of Bruner (1960) and Bacon (1983) to the outdoor adventure education field. Gass suggested that there are three overlapping categories of learning activity as one attempts to make sense of new educational experiences. Profound, long-lasting learning can take place on one-day programs because, according to Gass, despite the relatively short time of only a single day, one-day programs meet the essential conditions necessary for *specific*, *non-specific* and *metaphoric* transfer of learning to occur. Each of these terms is described below.

In the specific learning phase, the participant is interested in acquiring new information about tangible concrete skills. For example, if a participant took part in a one-day ropes course activity, it might be reasonable to assume that this participant could leave the program knowing how to protect someone during a fall, since "spotting" techniques are taught in most outdoor programs. If the participant had any use for spotting techniques in other areas of his/her life, one might conclude that the introduction of the skill of spotting during the one-day outdoor adventure experience had the long lasting effect of enabling this participant to, forever more, spot a falling person.

In the second area, non-specific transfer, the participant gains the ability to connect the general principles learned through an outdoor activity to another activity at a different location, at another time. For example, a participant in a one-day course learns that a group of strangers functions better if people spend time getting to know each other before they are asked to perform complex tasks. The participant transfers this new learning to his/her job, resulting in team building activities at their company. This new knowledge, allowing group members to get to know each other before attempting to perform tasks, was a direct result of the one-day program.

The third area of learning is the more abstract, metaphoric transfer. Metaphoric transfer refers to learning that has the potential to transform one's underlying understanding of the world. All learners have deep beliefs about how the world is ordered. These belief systems are often recognizable in the values and definitions we apply to abstract concepts, for example, the concept of honesty. Honesty can not be measured in any quantitative way. But the need for honesty may become apparent as a result of an outdoor adventure activity. A participant may transfer the need for honesty that is necessary between the belayer and the climber on a ropes course, to a broader understanding of the need for honesty as a more generalizable human quality. The climber/belayer relationship serves as a metaphor for the relationships we have with each other in our daily lives, where one person is often dependent on the support and attentiveness of another for safety and success.

It's in this third area, metaphoric transfer, that many of us are most interested in knowing if change is possible. The vast majority of adventure educators are not content to teach skills alone. We are glad participants might have gained the ability to spot another person, but this is not a sufficient outcome for us to work toward as educators. While we are interested in the more non-specific or metaphoric learning associated with outdoor programs, we are often most interested in helping clients identify, and if desired, change their underlying assumptions regarding how a person views the world and his/her place in that world. The one-day program contains great potential for this deeper, more meaningful metaphoric transfer.

Short-term Experiences Are Potentially Powerful

For confirmation of the belief that one-day programs can have profound long-lasting effects, we must venture from the limited field of outdoor education research and theory to the more expansive social-psychological theories. The broader question which might be asked is: Do brief experiences of any sort have the potential to produce long-lasting cognitive change? In this chapter we are concerned with those brief experiences that might take place on a one-day outdoor adventure program. But, can any short-term experience alter our thinking in a long lasting way? Two theories may be useful to support the notion that profound learning and change is possible.

Perhaps the most compelling rationale for the belief that one-day programs can have a lasting effect is found in Abraham Maslow's "Peak Experience Theories" (1943, 1970). Maslow believed "peak experiences" to be states of extreme happiness and rapture where a person becomes lost in the experience. A "peak experience" has the potential to alter a person's preconceived cognitive structure because the intensity and learning in the experience is powerful. Maslow viewed "peak experiences" as an overlapping or fusion between facts and values, and identification of the "intrinsic values of being." A "peak experience" is that state of being when

one is fully connected to the experience. It is a time when one has great insight and understanding about the nature and structure of the world around and his/her place in this world. It's as if the light were suddenly turned on and one is able to view a previously darkened area of misunderstanding, seeing the patterns and qualities of an experience with new vision and clarity.

The other theory that might support the idea of short-term experiences containing the potential for long-lasting change is based on the work of Mihaly and Isabella Selega Csikszentmihaly's "Flow Experiences" (1988). The theory of "flow experience" is based on the notion that individuals are constantly engaged in activity. Some of these activities are directly related to meeting our basic human needs: food, water, safety, etcetera. Other activities we engage in because they are "engrossing, intrinsically rewarding, and outside the parameters of worry and boredom" (Csikszentmihaly & Csikszentmihaly, 1990, p.150) these activities are known as "flow experiences." The Csikszentmihalys make a well-grounded argument that adventure activities help foster the potential for a flow experience. "Adventure activities, having few extrinsic rewards, are a way of challenging oneself to participate in experiences that are removed from everyday opportunities, that may use skills not called for in daily routines, or conversely, as a way of developing skills that one admires and would like to acquire" (Csikszentmihaly and Csikszentmihaly, 1990, p 154).

In both, Maslow's (1943) "peak experiences" and the Csikszentmihalys' (1975) "flow experiences" the duration of the experience is often very short, certainly within the one-day format we are examining. Those professionals who have led one-day outdoor adventure programs often witness and hear participants talk about the new insight they gained following a particularly relevant activity. We might refer to these as the "ah-hah" statements that occurs during a debrief of an experience. The client suddenly understands how his/her behavior is being interpreted by other members of the group.

One-day adventure experiences help create the potential for "peak experiences" because they place the participant in a novel learning environment. The client, unfamiliar with the environment of the outdoor program, is able to view behavior with new clarity. The habitual, patterned problem solving techniques that have helped the individual function in the real world are examined. It is the newness of the activity and the location that contribute to the power of the experience. These novel environments were cited by both Maslow (1943) and the Csikszentmihalys' (1988) as contributing to the possibility for powerful learning. A one-day outdoor adventure program can satisfy the necessary conditions for each of these theories.

Personal Experience Teaches Us That Brief Experiences Can Have Long-lasting Results

In addition to the theories of renowned psychologists such as Abraham Maslow and the Csikszentmihalys', our lives have taught us that brief experiences can have lasting effects. For example, a short conversation such as; "Pat, I really still love you, but I think it would be best if we were just friends", could have a tremendous long-term effect on Pat and how Pat thinks about trust, relationships, and possibly forgiveness. The length of Pat's experience of listening to another person redefine a relationship, may be very brief, but it can produce long-term results. The frequency with which Pat has this same experience

with other people, unfortunately, may have an even greater effect on Pat's understanding. But the initial experience was powerful in its own right.

In a similar fashion, clients arrive at a one-day program fresh from the experience of living their lives in the "real" world. They have patterns of frequent behavior that are often unrecognizable, even to themselves. A one-day program has the potential to help people understand these patterns of behavior in a supportive environment. A one-day outdoor adventure program may alter the person's sense of whom he/she is and how he/she functions, if such an experience occurs at a time when the person is predisposed for change.

For example, people may not realize how important being in control of information might be to them until they are part of a group problem-solving task where they are not able to access the information they think is needed. In real life, individuals might be at the center of the information of their organization, but on an outdoor activity they may not be in control of information. The way in which people handle new roles can be very interesting, and exciting new knowledge may result.

The timing of powerful experiences in a person's life effects the impact on the person. If a participant has a great learning experience on day three of a multi-day program, it may be that this same learning would have surfaced in a one day program because the person, as a thinking organism, was about to gain this new and deeper understanding. The learning experienced by the person may result from the intensity of the particular experience, rather than the accumulated intensity of the multi-day program. If for instance, day three of a multi-day trip is when the group attempts a novel experience, such as rock climbing or navigation by map and compass without the guidance of the instructors, it may be the intensity of this particular experience that helped produce the learning. The participant has experienced a change because the discrete activity occurred on day three, not the length of the program within which this experience was embedded.

CONCLUSION

Short-term experiences can create long-lasting learning in our lives. As has been demonstrated by Wagner and Roland (1992), if the focus of the program is clear and the clients are invested in the outcome, significant change can occur. But, research studies are not necessary to confirm this subjective reality that one can be changed as a result of brief experiences. Most of us can point to profound changes we have made in our lives, based on experiences that were often short in duration. These experiences may have been initially positive or negative but they have left a lasting mark on who we became as individuals.

Acknowledging the potential value of short, one-day programs does not diminish the effectiveness of multi-day programs, it strengthens the underlying belief that experiences are transformative regardless of their duration. The actual length of the experience is less important than when the experience occurs in the developmental life of the learner, and how powerful the experience was to the learner. If the timing is right, and the learner is poised to gain from the experience, the amount of time spent in the experience will be somewhat irrelevant. Likewise, if the intensity of the experience is sufficiently powerful, the learner will be compelled to acknowledge the experience. Again, the number of days an experience takes place is only one ingredient that helps contribute to the ultimate power of the experience.

REFERENCES

Bacon, S. (1983). *The conscious use of metaphor in Outward Bound.* Denver, CO: Colorado Outward Bound School.

Bruner, J. (1960). *The process of education.* New York: Vantage Books.

Csikszentmihaly, M. (1975). *Beyond boredom and anxiety.* San Francisco, CA: Jossey-Bass.

Csikszentmihaly, M. & Csikszentmihaly, I.S. (1990). *Adventure and the flow experience,* in Miles, J. and Priest, S. (1990) Adventure education. State College, PA: Venture Publishing, Inc. (149–56).

Csikszentmihaly, M. & Csikszentmihaly, I.S. (1988). *Optimal experiences: Psychological studies of flow in conscious.* New York: Cambridge University Press.

Gass, M.A. (1985). Programming the transfer of learning in adventure education. *Journal of Experiential Education. 8,* (3), 18–24.

Maslow, A. (1970). *Religions, values and peak experiences.* Harmondsworth: Penguin.

Maslow, A. (1943). A Theory of Human Motivation. *Psychological Review, 50,* 370–96.

Priest, S., Kichar, R., Gibson, S. & Bronson, J. (1992). Evaluation of team development in corporate adventure training programs. *Journal of Experiential Education, 15,* (1).

Priest, S. & Lesperance, M.A. (1994). Time series trends in corporate team development. *Journal of Experiential Education, 17,* (1).

Thompson, B.L. (1991). Training in the great outdoors. *Training 28*, (5), 46–52.

Wagner, R, & Roland, C. (1992). *Does outdoor-based training really work?* An empirical study. Unpublished paper available from Roland and Diamond Associates Inc. Keene, NH. (p. 7).

Zelinski, M. (1991). *Outward Bound the inward odyssey*. Hillsboro, OR: Beyond Words Publishing.

Do One Day Adventure Programming Activities, Such as Challenge Courses, Provide Long Lasting Learning?

Tom Puk, Ph.D.

The question itself is problematic in that it could mean a number of different things. Does it imply that an individual would participate in one, one day adventure program or could it also mean that the individual would participate in a series of one day programs? If the latter, then the comparison really being made is between a sequence of one day programs compared to programs made up of a number of connected days and nights. The issue then would be whether or not packaging objectives and activities into one connected experience is more productive than separate, one day sessions.

The term "long lasting learning" is also problematic. What is long lasting learning? How long after the program are we talking about? How many days, months, years does long lasting imply? What would we accept as evidence of "learning"? Hattie, Marsh, Neill and Richards (1997) conducted a meta-analysis of 96 studies of adventure programs occurring over the past quarter century. The longest follow-up studies they found that claimed effects of adventure programs were 25 months subsequent to the program, although the mean length of follow-up stud-

ies was 5.5 months. They described 25 months as being a "considerable period" of time for effects to be maintained.

For the purposes of this discussion, I take this question to mean that an individual who participates in one, one day program may or may not benefit in terms of long lasting learning. Also for the purposes of this discussion, I would accept at a minimum that the term "long lasting" implies learning that lasts at least 25 months subsequent to the program. [However, personally I do not think 25 months is a considerable period of time to judge lasting effects. I consider long lasting learning to imply life-long learning and that positive effects would be maintained throughout the course of a life-time- after all, if positive effects changed dramatically after 25 months, what would be the point of rejoicing in claims of lasting effects that did not continue to positively assist participants throughout the majority of their subsequent years of life]? If the question also means to imply that an individual might participate in a number of one day programs, my answer to this question might be more qualified. However, either way, I do not feel the results would be optimum as compared to a program consisting of a number of consecutive days and nights.

Hattie et al. (1997) found in their meta-analysis that the common features of adventure programs are wilderness settings, small groups, a variety of mentally and/or physically challenging objectives, group problem solving and decision making requiring frequent and intense interactions, nonintrusive, trained leaders **and, most importantly for our purposes, a duration of 2 to 4 weeks.** Therefore, according to practice, adventure programs are in part defined by a sustained period of involvement.

The fact that this question would be contemplated at all is reminiscent of the findings of Hattie et al. (1997). In the conclusions of their meta-analysis of 12,000 participants in adventure based programs, they make the following statement: "The teachers of adventure based programs, however, have all too rarely used the research from their in-class counterparts to improve their programs, and they need to more fully appreciate that they are conducting an educational experience" (p.77–78). That is to say, that some basic understanding of research about teaching and learning would suggest that long lasting learning is challenging even with the assistance of sustained amounts of time and that speculative thinking that one day adventure programs will make a lasting difference is mostly wishful thinking. It may also be harmful thinking and may explain why in many jurisdictions, adventure education has never been fully embraced into regular classroom education. There is a lot of rhetoric in regard to the benefits of adventured based programs but Hattie et al. found that even in adventure based programs of sustained length there is, "...little evidence of the nature of cognitive changes that par-ticipants experience as they reconcile their conceptions of their selves, the adaptability of their prior coping strategies, and their cognitions as they confront the risks and adventures before, during, and after the program" (p.77). Therefore, in this discussion, it is important that we do treat adventure programs as educational experiences and apply basic principles of teaching and learning as well.

ANECDOTAL

First of all, let me make some personal observations. In 1971, a program for delinquent teenagers called Project D.A.R.E. (Development through Adventure, Responsibility and Education) was opened in Ontario under the auspices of the Ministry of Correctional Services. This was a very challenging, high-adventure, risk-taking program in which 14 to 16 year old boys (and eventually) girls participated. These students spent three months in this very intense program which attempted to change inappropriate behaviours that had developed over a life time of 14 years or more. After the first two years of this program, the results indicated that approximately 40% of these students ended up eventually being incarcerated in adult settings. Prior to D.A.R.E., approximately 80% of this type of delinquent ended up being incarcerated in adult settings. Considering the type of delinquents this program worked with (i.e., recidivist), the program was deemed to be a success. However, why was 40% of this population still not able to benefit more directly? Eventually, it became clear to us that we could do some wonderful things with these young people in the field, i.e., on the rock face or in the wilderness, and they could learn many different skills and their behaviour could be modified to some extent. However, the problem was helping the students transfer what they had learned about themselves and others in the field to their home environments. It was problematic for many to try to apply what they had learned in one setting to another completely different setting. Although it is taken for granted now (Brackenreg, Luckner & Pinch, 1994), what we learned from practice in the early 1970s was that transferring new learning to another setting, although more difficult to achieve, is equally as important as the instructional phase of this learning is to internalizing knowledge, skills and attitudes. Furthermore, we came to understand that a great deal of time is required working with students in their home environment after they leave the wilderness environment (an idea also confirmed by Rawson, 1973). One day adventure programs lack that kind of connection to the world that most people spend most of their time in. This connection and transference can't be accomplished in one day.

I use the DARE example to demonstrate that even in a very intense program of three months transference is still a moot objective. It can occur, but how knowledge is organized in the field is critical to a successful transfer experience (Gagne, 1985). In one day experiences, planners would have to be extremely cognizant of how the adventure activities were organized and instructors would need to be aware of specific teaching/learning strategies in order for transfer to work (Perkins, 1991; Rogers, 1997).

TEACHING AND LEARNING

Hattie et al. (1997) found 40 different outcomes of adventure education that have been studied over the past quarter century and proceeded to place these outcomes into six categories: academic, leadership, self-concept, personality, interpersonal, and adventuresome. Academic objectives are defined as reading and problem-solving and no doubt these lower order, less complex objectives such as acquiring knowledge and comprehension (Bloom, 1956) can be achieved in one day. Objectives such as learning the names of flora and fauna or parts of a canoe might be achieved in one day and have some lasting effect. No doubt memories will result that will have some lasting effect. However, attempting to modify character, to influence attitudes and change mindsets, which I suggest would be higher order goals of adventure programs, require a great deal of sustained time. This type of long lasting learning can not be achieved in one day. To suggest that it could would be to suggest that adventure education has some kind of magical powers. And although adventure education has advantages, such as the grandeur of the environment and the smell of pine that other modes of learning do not; adventure programs require domain knowledge, thoughtful planning and insight into human interactions and human growth, in order to deliver the full potential of their offerings.

I would suggest further that an additional category of conceptual understanding (Elmore, 1992; Puk, in press) should be an integral component of adventure education, that is, how things work. Each of us lives within multiple systems or organizations. Being in the outdoors at night, for example (something you probably wouldn't do in a one day program) reinforces the fact that we live in a universe (at least one), a galaxy, a solar system, etc. In order to make sense of one's place in the universe, which I would suggest is an important aspect of defining a self-concept, one needs to understand conceptually how it works. We also need to understand the universe within, that exists inside the billions of atoms that compose all things and that influence all things. These systems are for the most part, invisible to the naked eye and can only be understood conceptually. Trying to introduce conceptual understanding in one day would be superficial at best.

Another component of "long lasting learning" is that of reflection. Schon (1987) described two kinds of reflection: "reflection in practice" and "reflection on practice". Reflection in practice occurs during an event as the learner makes mental summaries of what is occurring and why it is occurring and how it relates to other things. Although theoretically possible in a one day event, again because so much is pressed into a short period of time, participants may not do much of this kind of reflection. Usually one day programs, because the organizers know they don't have a tomorrow to look to, pack a lot of activity into a short time period. It is doubtful that much time for reflection is provided because the participant might complain that he/she is not paying for "dead time". Thus, the student is kept busy until the very end.

However, what isn't possible in a one day event is for the participant to reflect after it is all over (reflection on practice) and then bring those reflections or mental summaries to the next event where learnings can be discussed, can be integrated further, can be challenged and/or reinforced, can be reapplied, and can be further expanded and internalized. This type of ongoing reflection can occur during activities that transpire over a period of time. A full understanding of what might be learned can only occur as the learner is able to continuously fill out the initial mental schema that has been developed. Impressions might result from one day programs but long lasting learning from which

the learner can benefit in the future is much more complex to achieve.

Another casualty of one day programs which tend to pack a lot of activity in a short period of time is self-directed learning. Again because of expectations perhaps of the participant, planners do not have as much flexibility to attempt to achieve objectives that take longer periods of sustained learning. In one day programs, participants are more apt to be following the schedule set out by the organizers rather than learning how to develop their own learning goals, developing plans for achieving those goals, being able to carry out those plans, and being able to monitor how well the plan is progressing (Puk, 1992). Adventure education should also be attempting to develop self-direction in participants so that they can develop their own goals once the organized session is over. Again, developing and achieving higher order objectives requires more time than one day.

Long lasting learning requires practice followed by feedback (Gagne, 1985). Just completing an activity once will not ensure internalization of the learning. As well, in order for transfer to take place, practice must also involve new examples of the same objective. However, one day programs do not usually allow for much practice, and certainly not with new examples of the same activity because there is no time, and again because not as many activities would be experienced if the time was spent on practice. The inherent limitation of one day programs is the perception by both organizers and participants that programs must be entertaining rather than educating. Providing feedback or in experiential education terms, "debriefing", also requires what might be perceived as "down-time", that is, non-activity time. However, feedback is crucial for long lasting learning (Brackenreg, Luckner & Pinch, 1994;

Hattie, 1987, 1992, 1993; Richards, 1976): "feedback is the most powerful single moderator that improves affective and achievement outcomes" (Hattie et al., 1997, p.75). Learners need to be able to express their own uncertainties, questions and observations in order that misunderstandings are clarified and alternate ways of doing things are identified. Feelings need to be shared so that sensitivity to others is fostered. Now certainly, adventure education contains a lot of ambiguity and uncertainty and this in fact is quite often deliberately planned in activities. Wonderment and mystery are integral to adventure education. The crucial balance that must be attended to is the amount of uncertainty and ambiguity with which participants are presented. There are degrees of stress inherent in uncertainty and ambiguity and the challenge of adventure learning is to control the amount of stress and to ensure that it has a positive, inspiring effect rather than a negative, debilitating effect on the learner. This is in part the crucial role of feedback. However, even some forms of feedback require reflective time in order to allow impressions to "age" and to mature over time.

One day challenge courses may sometimes be offered as a form of training for instructors. This would be similar to providing the traditional, short-termed, "one-shot" workshops that teachers often receive. There are considerable findings that suggest that this is an ineffective form of training (Shroyer, 1990; Slavin, 1989) and that long-term effects in the learner require a sequenced series of training sessions. Most often, new techniques learned during short, single experiences are not applied elsewhere because of the lack of follow-up supervision and support. Fox (1989) found that retention levels subsequent to one-time training sessions fall as low as 15% within 3 weeks of the training

session. Joyce and Showers (1988) found that new teaching techniques need to be practised minimally five times in the two weeks following the initial training in order for retention to occur. Again, internalizing new techniques takes time and external support.

RESEARCH STUDIES

What do research studies say about the relationship between the duration of the adventure program and the learning outcomes? Assessment of adventure programs has been problematic since the inception of this paradigm. Many of the claims have been based on testimonials or "statements of faith". Many claims have been made on the type of claim that "if Hahn (who developed the first Outward Bound school) said it, it must be true". In their meta-analysis of 96 studies, Hattie et al. (1997) admit to these problems. However, they do suggest that there are benefits of adventure programs that can be shown for some effects through quantitative analysis, for example in terms of improved self-concept, social skills and leadership competencies to name a few. However, what their analysis also clearly indicates is that duration does influence the outcomes of adventure programs. "Longer rather than shorter programs had the greatest effects" (p. 70). The longer the program, the greater the effect sizes found in these 96 studies. Therefore, the reverse of that would seem to indicate that the shorter the program, the lesser the effect sizes (to be fair, it should be acknowledged that this meta-analysis only examined two research studies of one day adventure programs). However, an additional finding is also of interest to this discussion. Programs with adults were more effective than programs with nonadults.

Thus, if we combine the two findings, it would appear that nonadults participating in one day programs would show the least benefit of adventure education.

A caution should be noted in regard to the Hattie et al. (1997) study. The authors excluded school-based outdoor education programs from their meta-analysis because they found them to be usually of shorter duration and because they "tended" to involve nonchallenging experiences. They excluded such activities as "tending the farm, building projects, bush walks, camping and natural science studies" (p. 51) as being nonchallenging, adventure experiences. This statement about the nature of adventure programs adds further to the complexity of our current discussion. I would certainly challenge their contention that the above mentioned activities may not be "challenging" and adventurous. I am of the belief that "Adventure is not in the guide book and beauty is not on the map. Seek and ye shall find" (Russell & Russell, 1973, p. 85). Adventure can be found in places other than just exotic, isolated locations.

Some further internal inconsistency can be found in the Hattie et al. (1997) position of what adventure programming is suppose to be. In their concluding comments, they make the curious statement that "outdoor, experiential, adventure-based education is not new" (p. 76). This statement seems to imply that indeed "outdoor education" is in fact synonymous with adventure education, which then leads one to wonder why they excluded examples of outdoor education programs from their study?

CONCLUSION

In this discussion, I have indicated the following: a) that in terms of making changes to character and personality, one day adventure programs are probably not very effective; b) that in terms of concepts such as transference of learning, reflection, conceptual understanding, practice and feedback, one day programs are not very conducive to achieving these objectives; and c) that some research findings indicate that longer is better in terms of having an influence on participants acquiring any lasting benefit. I have also reiterated that adventure educators should keep in mind that their programs are educational experiences foremost, thus the need to apply some of the same concepts of teaching and learning that regular classroom education does. When we do that, we start to understand the limitations of claims made for one day adventure programs. Yes, there are differences between classroom education and adventure education. There are also benefits unique to each paradigm. But claiming mystical powers simply on the basis of anecdote may be harmful to the long term viability of adventure education. Rather, we should attempt to ensure that the best quality learning experiences can be found in adventure programs.

In spite of the problem of the definition of adventure education that Hattie et al. (1997) used, there does appear to be some strong research evidence that the positive effects of adventure programs increase as the duration of the programs increases.

REFERENCES

Bloom, B.S. (Ed.). (1956). *Taxonomy of educational objectives: The classification of educational goals*. New York: David McKay Company, Inc.

Brackenreg, M., Luckner, J. & Pinch, K. (1994). Essential skills for processing adventure experiences. *The Journal of Experiential Education, 17* (3), 45–47.

Elmore, F.E. (1992). Why restructuring alone won't improve teaching. *Educational Leadership, 49* (7), 44–48.

Fox, N.V. (1989). Reading supervisors: Providing effective inservice education. *Journal of Reading, 33* (3), 214–215.

Gagne, E.D. (1985). *The cognitive psychology of school learning.* Toronto: Little, Brown and Company.

Hattie, J. (1987). Identifying the salient facets of a model of student learning: A synthesis of meta-analyses. *International Journal of Educational Research, 11,* 187–212.

Hattie, J. (1992). *Self-concept.* Hillsdale, NJ: Erlbaum.

Hattie, J. (1993). Measuring the effects of schooling. *SET, 2,* 1–4.

Hattie, J., Marsh, H.W., Neill, J.T. & Richards, G.E. (1997). Adventure education and outward bound: Out-of class experiences that make a lasting difference. *Review of Educational Research, 67* (1), 43–87.

Joyce, B. & Showers, B. (1988). *Student achievement through staff development.* New York, N.Y.: Longman.

Perkins, D. (1991). Educating for insight. *Educational Leadership, 49* (2), 4–8.

Puk, T.G. (1992). *Levels of aspiration for schooling: A pluralistic paradigm for restructuring education.* (Paper presented to the Canadian Society for the Study of Education, Canadian Association of Curriculum Studies, University of Prince Edward Island, Charlottetown).

Puk, T.G. (in press) Recurring phases of engaging life pursuits: Functionality, intuitive excellence, conceptual understanding and self-transcendence as they relate to teacher education. *Journal of Teacher Education.*

Rawson, M. (1973). Residential short-term camping for children with behaviour problems: A behaviour modification approach. *Child Welfare, 52,* 511–520.

Richards, G.E. (1976). *Some psychological bases and aspects of Outward Bound.* Canberra, Australia: National Outdoor Education and Leadership Services.

Rogers, B. (1997). Informing the shape of the curriculum: New views of knowledge and its representation in schooling. *Journal of Curriculum Studies, 29* (6), 683–710.

Russell, J. & Russell, R. (1973). *On the loose.* New York: Ballantine Books.

Schon, D. (1987). *Educating the reflective practitioner.* London, U.K: Jossey-Bass.

Shroyer, G.M. (1990). Effective staff development for effective organization development. *Journal of Staff Development, 11* (1), 2–6.

Slavin, R. (1989). PET and the pendulum: Faddism in education and how to stop it. *Phi Delta Kappan, 70* (10), 752–758.

CHAPTER 7

Should Articles on Special Wilderness Places Be Published?

YES PERSPECTIVE: Glen Bishop, Ph.D.
NO PERSPECTIVE: Christian Bisson, Ed.D.

Glen Bishop teaches part-time at Ferris State University in the Recreation Leadership and Management Program. He tends his garden in Rodney, Michigan with his daughter and wife. He has a Ph.D. from Michigan State University in Park and Recreation Resources.

Christian Bisson has been involved in outdoor experiential education since 1986. He received his Master's degree in Teacher Outdoor Education at Northern Illinois University and his Doctoral degree in Pedagogy from the University of Northern Colorado. He teaches adventure education at Northland College in northern Wisconsin and works seasonally for NOLS.

Should Articles on Special Wilderness Places Be Published?

YES

Glen Bishop, Ph.D.

Yes, articles should be published on special wilderness places. Publication of such articles should be encouraged and read by as wide an audience as possible. Although this chapter concentrates on the popular press, magazines such as *Time, Newsweek, Sierra, Audubon, Backpacker*, and *Outside*, the same arguments could also apply to film (including I-max format), television, and radio. For years CBS Sunday Morning has ended the show with a visit to a special wild place, no commentary, just the sounds and sights of nature. Not only has this been relaxing television viewing, but as a result I cannot help but think that in some small way people have been inspired to save such natural places from damage and destruction. The world is in short supply of special wilderness places, otherwise chapters like this would not be of interest, wilderness areas would not need special legislative protection, and there would be no need for national or state parks. And, we would have an abundance of special places a short distance from our homes, no matter where our homes might be, and have no concern for the future existence and quality of wilderness areas.

What is a special wilderness place? Places designated under the Wilderness Act of 1964 and related legislation are by definition special or they would not have been selected for special protection provided by the act. The Wilderness Act of 1964 defines wilderness as:

> A wilderness, in contrast with those areas where man and his own works dominate the landscape, is hereby recognized as an area where the earth and its community of life are untrammeled by man, where man himself is a visitor who does not remain. An area of undeveloped federal land retailing its primeval character and influence, without permanent improvements or habitation, and which (1) generally appears to have been affected primarily by the forces of nature, with man's imprint substantially unnoticeable; (2) has outstanding opportunities for solitude or a primitive and unconfined type of recreation; (3) has at least 5,000 acres of land or is of sufficient size to make practicable its preservation; and (4) may also contain ecological geological, or other features of scientific, educational, scenic, or historical value.

In addition to official federal wilderness areas designated by Congress, there are many other special wild places. Many units of the National Park Service have special wild qualities or they would not have been reserved, purchased, or donated, as the case may be. Many state parks are special or they would not have been preserved as parks. Wild and scenic rivers have at least one outstandingly remarkable resource value that makes them special (Doppelt et. al., 1993). On the other hand, all government lands are not necessarily special. Many military bases are not usually not thought of as special, although some may have special wild places within their boundaries. National Forests and BLM lands contain a mixture of areas which could be special or mostly valuable for the production of commodities, or a mix of special and commodity places. Specialness may be reduced when these special commodity lands are being used for commodity production. Meadows perhaps are not as special when they are being grazed by cattle; forests are not as special when the timber is being harvested; but these areas do grow back, cattle are rotated to a different pasture, and depending on timing, climate, soils, and other influences can reestablish most of their specialness given a long enough recovery period.

Of the areas that have no special designation and are open for commodity production of various sorts, such as timber, minerals, range, gas and oil, these lands may have special qualities which have not been recognized yet, and may be set aside for preservation in the future. Lands surrounding Corps of Engineers and Bureau of Reclamation reservoirs are often developed into parks managed by each agency itself or transferred to other federal agencies or state or local governments. These lands are often not recognized as special. They are valuable for water oriented recreation, perhaps, which is not special in the sense of this issue. How-

ever, tucked away in some of these park areas, there can be outstanding opportunities for experiencing the wild.

Special lands have some unique natural quality that is valued by people. Such a quality may be a rare form of life or a community of life. The quality may be outstandingly remarkable scenery or other truly magnificent opportunities for recreation. The special quality may be an outstanding geologic outcropping or evidence of human activity, perhaps very old. These qualities may provide opportunities for recreation, education or research.

Specialness is a status granted by society. When enough people with enough influence and power agree that a place has a special quality, then that place, at least in the United States, can be given special protection through the political process as a national or state park, a wilderness area or other special classification. The only way to maintain designation or to obtain designation in the first place is through the political arena. To be successful in the political arena, a critical mass of people must support protection. The popular press can be instrumental in developing this critical mass of people (Forestra, 1984; National Parks and Conservation Association, 1994; Runte, 1987).

Once a special place has received special designation there is no guarantee that the designation or protection will remain in place. Every 20 years or so, a member of Congress will propose selling large portions of the federal lands to private companies and individuals. Several early units of the National Park System were expunged from the system, such as Mackinac Island National Park, Michigan (Zaslowsky and Watkins, 1994; Zinser, 1995). A few years ago when the Bureau of Reclamation was developing plans for dams that would flood portions of the

Grand Canyon, advertisements and articles in the popular press protected this special wilderness place from inundation that would have greatly changed its character (Gilliam, 1979; Reisner, 1993). The articles and advertisements developed the mass of Grand Canyon supporters who by contacting members of Congress put an end to flooding a place that has been compared in grandeur to the large old cathedrals of Europe.

The Grand Canyon is obviously a special place; are all special places obvious? How are they determined? What kinds of special places are we asking about in considering whether or not articles should be published about special wilderness places? The question at hand specifies wilderness special places. Wilderness has two types of meaning. One type of meaning is the legal definition found in the Wilderness Act of 1964 which states that inside the wilderness boundary only a few selected activities may legally take place. Even some of these limited activities can be reduced, restricted, or managed if the wilderness managers perceive that the activities are causing environmental or social changes beyond those that have been deemed acceptable either in the wilderness management plan or by the wilderness act. The legal definition of wilderness applies to those areas that are formally designated as wilderness by Congress. Under the legal definition, wilderness is only wilderness if it is designated by Congress. The legal definition is related to a second type of wilderness definition in that a critical number of influential people have to agree that an area is, in fact, wilderness and fits the guidelines of the Wilderness Act if it is to be designated as wilderness.

The second type of wilderness meaning is what has been termed social or psychological wilderness. Wilderness is what people think it is and can include special wild places that would not fit the guidelines for legal wilderness found in the Wilderness Act as well as designated wilderness. My parents describe the region in east central Ontario where they have a summer lake cottage as wilderness. Their wilderness includes motorboats from small fishing skiffs to large cruisers, snowmobiles, float-planes, hydro electricity that provides light in their cottage, telephone service, lodges, grocery stores, and marinas. Should our question apply equally to my parents' social/psychological wilderness, legally Congressionally designated wilderness or both? Any relatively wild place can be, for some people, a special wilderness place. How special should a special place be? Who decides the degree of specialness? Should the question also apply to special cultural resources, such as Pompeii, which may be experiencing damage from hordes of tourists?

What is the purpose of restricting articles and restricting the press? Wilderness is for people and therefore, special wilderness places are for people. The Wilderness Act of 1964 states that "wilderness areas...shall be administered for...the gathering and dissemination of information regarding their use and enjoyment as wilderness..." If publication of articles is to be reduced or eliminated then the Wilderness Act will have to be amended. Perhaps the authors of the Wilderness Act included this section with good reason. Perhaps they anticipated this controversy, realizing that people would make the obvious assumption that magazine articles result in increased use and increased impact while at the same time knowing that without public knowledge, special wilderness places would be impossible to preserve. There is a danger of overuse of certain areas to the point that the often stated concern of "being loved to death" becomes true. Recreational impact can reach the point that the wild quality of special wilderness places is replaced by something that resembles the old hobo jungle along a popular rail line.

However, the link between the impacts of overuse and the publishing of articles is an assumed link, certainly one that has not received a lot of discussion in park and wilderness literature. Even if such a link exists, it is not a direct link. Magazine articles do not cause damage to special wild places unless the paper they are printed on comes from trees harvested from such places. It is the visitors who cause the environmental damage and the subsequent decline in wild qualities of natural areas. The indirect link between articles and damage provides wilderness managers with the opportunity to intervene and mitigate any potential damage "caused" by magazine articles by changing the behavior of visitors (the actual cause of the damage) through facility design, transportation access, fees, and permits (Jubenville and Twight, 1993).

Articles can be an important tool in visitor management. Many parks publish their own newspapers to educate visitors in order to protect park resources and protect visitors who might otherwise injure themselves while carrying out inappropriate activities. This knowledge would be more effective if received while the visitor was planning the trip. Models of recreation behavior often divide the recreational experience into several stages. One stage is the planning of the trip, another stage is travel to the site, a third stage is onsite activity, a fourth stage is travel back home, and the final stage is to reflect upon and relive the activity through the telling of tales about the adventure to friends and relatives, perhaps including pictures and using or wearing various souvenir items (Clawson

and Knetsch, 1966). One of the best ways recreation managers can influence recreation behavior to reduce impact is to contact recreation users in the planning stage (Jubenville and Twight, 1993). Once people have left for their chosen destination it is much more difficult for them to change their plans. If articles supply information during the planning stage of the trip, the knowledge is likely to have the most impact because potential visitors can prepare by acquiring proper skill, equipment, or even changing their destination. Articles may call on outdoor enthusiasts to avoid particular special wild places while suggesting alternatives which may absorb their activities with less damage to the environment. Articles read during the planning stage may suggest techniques and equipment to reduce environmental impact of visits to special areas resulting from normal activities involving cooking or personal hygiene. A party would feel much more secure having prepared to use backpacking stoves before arrival than having to switch at the last minute when the backcountry ranger informs them that campfires are prohibited. Articles read during the planning stage may increase awareness of and compliance rules and regulations designed to protect the milieu of the special wild place. Perhaps the uproar created by the protests of a well-known race car driver who received a ticket for riding a snowmobile in a wilderness area during the winter of 1997–1998 could have been avoided if the individual had better understood the reasons behind the ban on motor vehicles in the protected area. Prohibitions work best when the reasons behind the rules are understood.

Some managers would say that they have not observed much of an increase in visitation following magazine article publication, or that the increase is short-lived.

Some managers would conclude that any link between articles published and recreational impacts and damage is weak at best. Many managers would perhaps also conclude that it is their job to provide management of people and resources, rather than to restrict the freedom of the press.

Wilderness management should follow a biocentric philosophy in allowing human use. Biocentric philosophy means that the environment comes first. Wilderness is in short supply. Any amount of development, any amount of use reduces the wild of wilderness. Managing within a biocentric framework directs management to keep construction and development to the minimum needed to protect the resource (Hendee, Stankey, and Lucas, 1990). With a biocentric philosophy, no trails are constructed and no toilets are built unless the destruction caused by improper use demands it. Even then a biocentric manager would likely think first of ways to reduce use and rehabilitate damaged areas. Articles are important in order for the public to understand the biocentric philosophy and accept special wild places in their natural state without the addition of human comforts such as flush toilets and showers. Even among college recreation students, there are a fair number who would turn down a chance to visit a wilderness area, or would be disappointed should they visit, because they would not be able to find a plug for their hair dryer. They would not understand the lack of flush toilets, showers, tables, or other facilities. Without biocentrism, development, such as that in Yosemite Valley and in the geyser basin at Yellowstone, takes place. Such development is not necessarily bad, but it does reduce the wild aspects of these special wild places. Some people would argue that such development is good and should be expanded. Through the use of technology, people with disabilities, and others who lack the ability to participate in wilderness travel could visit special places and expand the benefits gained by society through preserving these special places . What is really wrong with an aerial tram to the bottom of the Grand Canyon? The tram itself would affect only a small portion of this Grand Cathedral. Wilderness is for people and, therefore, special wilderness places are for people. If wilderness held no human value, wilderness would not exist. It would be logged, mined, or developed into condominiums. What could the imagineers from Disney do with a back drop so grand? Only through articles in the press which explain the human spiritual benefits of preservation can special place "enhancement" be avoided.

People can value wilderness in a number of different ways (Walsh, 1986). Most of the ways do not require an actual visit by everyone receiving benefits, but they do require knowledge of the existence of special places. Popular articles are one major avenue of knowledge about these places. People can value special places simply by knowing of their existence. They derive pleasure by knowing that special places are around. Perhaps, but not in every case, greater value can be achieved if people can think that they one day may visit such a special place or one like it. A special place can be valued because people know they have the option of a visit in the future. Some people value special places because they like the idea that these special places will be around for the next generation to appreciate, visit, or derive lessons from (Hendee, Stankey, and Lucas, 1990). Articles contribute to all of these values.

Articles also contribute to values obtained by an actual onsite recreational visit or consumption value. Consumption value is the value derived from actually being there, breathing the pure air, enjoying the aroma of the wild, or using products derived from the special place. It is this type of value which can have adverse impact on the quality of the special place. People who value special places solely through articles do not impact the special place, except only through the impact of the journalist writing the articles. If the reporter did not write the article and create knowledge, then would the special place be valued? If the special place were not valued, would it be more vulnerable to destruction? The impact of one person visiting a special place to write an article is small, providing they are knowledgeable and skillful in outdoor techniques. Their impact is small compared to the hundreds of people who could visit the site. If visitation causes too much impact, then the visitation should be controlled and managed, not the publication of articles.

If there were no articles and no visitation, then there would be no value in preservation. The values and benefits derived from preservation are human values. Humans can value only what they know. Humans can know only through their own experience or the experience of others shared through in-person story telling or the press. In-person story telling takes time and is more expensive per person receiving the message than published articles. Because of the increased time and expense required, fewer people would know about and derive benefits from preservation. With less knowledge and fewer derived benefits, the value of special wild places without articles would be much smaller. With a lower value derived from preservation of special wild places, more people would be tempted to derive economic benefits through development or resource harvest from these places. As more people become tempted to develop for economic return, the more likely development will be chosen as a manage-

ment strategy in comparison to preservation. Without articles, the smaller the value of preservation; the smaller the value of preservation, the more the values and benefits of preservation would lose in a comparison with the benefits and values of development and resource harvest.

Most special places need some base level of visitation and use to justify their existence. Only through awareness can visitation take place. Articles are one means of creating awareness. Mather understood this when he undertook to develop portions of American national parks to stimulate tourism (Runte, 1987). He realized that without public support, the National Park Service would not survive long, and without public support, special places may someday in the future be sold to the highest bidder. In the future? It happens today! A forest of redwoods changes hands in a corporate take-over. The harvest scheme switches from sustained yield to "cut-out-get-out" to pay off the bonds which were used for the buy out. A forest in New York is saved from tract home development only at the last moment when enough support is achieved for the government to appropriate enough funds to save it. Special places disappear every day. Some are saved. What would be the outcome if no articles were published to raise awareness, knowledge, and value of preservation?

If articles about special places are not published, few people will know or care that they are damaged in the search for riches. Vandals hunt for ancient Native American artifacts, frequently destroying the archaeologic value of special places, logging occasionally encroaches across property lines from the not so special regenerated timber site to the site with old trees, sites may be grazed to the point that their specialness is lost; oil development can occur using methods that create more damage than necessary. If there are no published articles on these special places, few people will understand their value and the special places will be lost or degraded.

This chapter tries to make the point that it is the people and the resources that should be managed and controlled, restricted and rationed when necessary; the press should not be restricted. Some people reading this chapter may be thinking, yes that's right, in a perfect world where resource agencies, non-profit organizations, and even corporations have the resources and personnel to mount effective management efforts and all visitors act responsibly, there is no need for restrictions on the press. But, that is not the situation in our imperfect world. Natural resource managing organizations have historically been underfunded. In the press, the U. S. National Park Service has claimed to have a maintenance backlog of several billion dollars. The mantra of park and recreation agencies over the past 20 years or so has been "to do more with less" (Crompton, 1987). Public agencies have been told to find ways to provide more service, take care of more visitors and the impacts of visitation with fewer dollars. Many agencies are at the point where less is impossible. Some may see controlling the press as an inexpensive and easy way to reduce visitation pressures, reduce the need for maintenance and reduce the need for refurbishment and erosion control. Others have envisioned the press as a tool to use to encourage appropriate behavior that has minimal impact. Others have envisioned the press as a means of stretching scarce management dollars, doing more with less. The press can be and has been used to publicize opportunities for volunteers to work both in the private sector and with government agencies in maintaining special places, performing re-

search about special places, and helping other members of society to understand the human values of wild places.

Additional aid to management trying to do more with less are those articles which try to expand the lesser portion of the equation by stating the case for additional funding from government sources through rallying public support. Other writing efforts can contribute to campaigns designed to garner needed supplies, equipment, and support from the private sector. Private contributions often result in additional press to cover the good deeds which may encourage additional good deeds and improved public relations for the benefactor.

Publicity generated by articles builds support for special wilderness places. More articles describing the benefits of special wild places need to be published and read, not fewer. Articles can help garner funding, volunteers, and equipment. It is not the articles causing the damage it is the people visiting the sites, or the people making use of the resources contained on the sites, some of whom, out of ignorance, cause greater impact than necessary. Articles can educate, reduce ignorance, and be an effective management tool. In some cases articles should present the case for use reduction or elimination. When used for this purpose, those people whose opportunities for recreation experience or economic welfare are reduced may be better able to accept and understand a particular management action proposed or taken. The logical place to make these arguments are in articles about special wild places. Articles create knowledge; knowledge instills value; what is valued is conserved.

Much of the support for the continued publishing of articles on special wilderness places is contingent upon responsible writing which promotes the informed, responsible use of wilderness. Most of the articles the author of this chapter reads about wilderness are just that, responsible. So it is difficult to imagine irresponsible articles, those that promote use without concern for technique, crowding, trampling, erosion, pollution, and collection of artifacts or rare species. They probably do exist, but not in the material the author usually reads. Not long ago there was a television show that promoted gold mining. The techniques advocated started with the relatively innocuous panning of the gravel in the bottom of a stream, if that proved unsatisfactory viewers were encouraged to use a shovel to dig into the stream banks where gold may have been deposited during long ago floods, for those miners who were still not satisfied with the wait of their poke, more environmentally damaging placer and hydraulic mining techniques were demonstrated. Much of this activity appeared to be taking place on public lands, some of which undoubtedly could be considered special. This television show could be and perhaps should be considered irresponsible from an environmental viewpoint. But, as such, should the producers be prevented from trying to distribute and market the show? Should articles promoting stream hydraulic mining be prohibited? These articles are irresponsible from an environmental standpoint. The answer is, no, they should not be prohibited or prevented. Other shows and articles need to be published about special places and the damage caused by mining. The answer is to convince those that buy and produce the pro-mining products that preservation has a higher value. Who is to judge what is responsible? Is resource extraction less responsible than preservation? Some people would argue that preservation is the locking up of resources to create an expensive playground for a small group of rich, elite citizens and that it is far more responsible to use

resources to create wealth in which everyone will eventually have a share. Some would argue that attempts to limit use of special wilderness places is just another example of elitism, an attempt to keep out the majority so that a few with the right connections can enjoy a relatively private domain at public expense.

Any amount of use causes some environmental damage except to the most tolerant, sturdy, robust site (Hendee, Stankey, and Lucas 1990). To completely avoid impact, people should not visit special wild places. Instead, they could stay home and work to restore special wild place qualities to the cities and towns where people live (Riley, 1998; Sauer, 1998) . If cities and towns were more wild, perhaps some of the pressure on designated special wild areas would be relieved. However, if people should decide not to visit special wild places and to garden for restoration in their home communities, special wild places will lose some of their existence value. Commodity consumption value may then become the predominant consideration in the process of deciding management policy for these special places. Should this happen, special wild places will be more likely to produce oil, timber, and grazing for domestic animals, and less likely to produce values associated with wild land recreational experiences. Articles can add existence value to special wild places. By increasing the stock of values society harvests by preserving wild places, articles contribute greatly to their protection and preservation. Keep the articles coming. We need them. The lives of many readers would be duller without them. Imagine having to read a cheap mystery thriller instead of an account of the breathtaking beauty of some distant canyon, mountain, river, or the woodlot two miles from home. Besides isn't there something in the U.S. Constitution about freedom of the press?

REFERENCES

Clawson, M., & Knetsch, J. L. (1966). *Economics of outdoor recreation.* Baltimore: The Johns Hopkins University Press.

Crompton, J. J. (1987). *Doing more with less in the delivery of recreation and park services: A book of case studies.* State College, PA: Venture Publishing.

Doppelt, B., Scurlock, M., Frissell, C., & Karr, J. (1993). *Entering the watershed: A new approach to save America's river ecosystems.* Washington: Island Press.

Foresta, R. A. (1984). *America's national parks and their keepers.* Washington: Resources for the Future.

Gilliam, A. (Ed.). (1979). *Voices for the earth: A treasury of the Sierra Club Bulletin, 1893–1977.* San Francisco: Sierra Club Books.

Hendee, J. C., Stankey, G. H., & Lucas, R. C. (1990). *Wilderness management.* Golden, Colorado: Fulcrum Publishing.

Jubenville, A. & Twight, B. W. (1993). *Outdoor recreation management: Theory and application* (3rd. ed.). State College, Pennsylvania: Venture Publishing.

National Parks and Conservation Association. (1994). *Our endangered parks.* San Francisco: Foghorn Press.

Reisner, M. (1993). *Cadillac desert: The American west and its disappearing water,* (Rev. ed.) New York: Penguin Books.

Riley, A. L. (1998). *Restoring streams in cities: A guide for planners, policymakers, and citizens.* Washington: Island Press.

Runte, A. (1987). *National parks: The American experience.* Lincoln: University of Nebraska Press.

Sauer, L. J. (1998). *The once and future forest: A guide to forest restoration strategies.* Washington: Island Press.

Walsh, R. G. (1986). *Recreation economic decisions: Comparing benefits and costs.* State College, PA. Venture Publishing.

Zaslowsky, D., & Watkings, T. H. (1994). *These American lands: Parks, wilderness, and the public lands.* Washington: Island Press.

Zinser, C. I. (1995). *Outdoor recreation: United States national parks, forests, and public lands.* New York: John Wiley.

Should Articles on Special Wilderness Places Be Published?

Christian Bisson, Ed.D.

"But all conservation of wilderness is self-defeating, for to cherish we must see and fondle, and when enough have seen and fondled, there is no wilderness left to cherish."

(Aldo Leopold, A Sand County Almanac, 1949, p. 108.)

BEING LOVED TO DEATH

Devoted to the protection of our natural heritage, the pioneering work of Thoreau, Muir, Leopold, and Olson has, for well over a century, attracted the attention of the North-American public to the pristine and forgotten wild lands of Canada and the United States. Their quest for conservation led them to justify the protection of the land not only for itself but also for its recreational use. Influenced by this philosophy, the U.S. National Park Service Organic Act of 1916 declared that its mission was to "...conserve the scenery and the natural and historic objects and wildlife therein and to provide for the enjoyment of same in such manner...as will leave them unimpaired for the enjoyment of

future generations" (p. 64). This mind set led Roderick Nash (1982) to conclude that saving America's wildest land "...seemed dependent on building a clientele for it" (p. 316). Today, that "clientele" has swelled to a massive flux of people visiting our national parks annually. In 1997 alone an estimated 273 million people visited the U.S. National Parks[1] while 24 million visited the Canadian National Parks[2]. These numbers correspond respectively to 102%[3] and 79%[4] of each country's population.

It is ill-fated that by attracting people's attention to the beauty, pleasure, and need to recreate in the wilderness, the wilderness itself was doomed to be literally "loved to death" (Nash, 1982, p. 316).

NATURE'S CARRYING CAPACITY

The "boomerang effect" experienced by the wilderness conservation movement became a concern for environmentalists as early as 1936 when Lowell Sumner, a wildlife technician with the National Park Service, asked the fundamental question, "how large a crowd can be turned loose in a wilderness without destroying its essential qualities?" (Nash, 1982). Sumner's observation quickly led conservationists to borrow the concept of "carrying capacity" from the well established ranching industry and apply it to the now rapidly growing outdoor recreation industry (Nash, 1982).

Just as the ranchers had to determine how many head of sheep or cattle could graze in a specific area without permanently destroying it, so too did the national forest and park rangers have to ask themselves how many visitors could a certain environment absorb and still retain its wildness? (Nash, 1982). It is important to note that even in 1942, Lowell's concept of "carrying capacity" did not refer to any kind of recreational use, but specifically to the most careful traveling and camping practices of the time. Still today, "carrying capacity" implies the use of the best "leave-no-trace" or minimal impact traveling and camping practices promoted by the public land management agencies and the outdoor recreation industry. This means that a wilderness area visited by even the most careful outdoor enthusiasts can still be at risk if its specific "carrying capacity" is overrun by the sheer number of visitors.

Nash (1982) refined the concept of "carrying capacity" by identifying three main subcategories. The *biological carrying capacity* relates to the impact visitors have on other living species. The voluntarily or involuntarily feeding of wild animals by wilderness visitors is a prime example of actions that can eventually transgress an area's biological carrying capacity by modifying natural feeding behaviors. Second, the *physical carrying capacity*, which is perhaps the most easily observable in a short period of time, refers to the impact outdoor travelers have on the environment. An example of this impact is the destructive erosion process that too many travelers cause on fragile terrain. Finally, the *psychological carrying capacity* pertains to the effect users have on the experience of other users. By definition, wilderness areas should be a contrast to our "urban way of life," thus implying that solitude can be found in the wilderness. The overcrowding of popular wild areas can easily deter the most tolerant nature lover. This leads us to Nash's (1982) conclusion that any popular area runs the risk to be biologically, physically, and fundamentally impacted by well intended users.

FOUR CAUSAL REVOLUTIONS

According to Nash (1982), our overbearing love affair with the natural world is the result of four distinct revolutions. First in the mid 1800s, an *intellectual revolution* was initiated by the writings of Thoreau, Muir, and Leopold as well as the rapidly growing popularity of environmental organizations, such as the Audubon Society and the Sierra Club. The wilderness was once perceived as land remaining to be conquered, was now perceived as our last hope for social and environmental salvation. Second, an *equipment revolution* brought lighter and more specialized equipment designed to offer more comfort in the outdoors. In the 1930s, outdoor equipment was bulky and often required the use of pack horses. After World War II, the availability of nylon fabric considerably lightened basic camping gear, which made wilderness travel more convenient. Third, by the 1960s the *transportation revolution* brought a considerable increase in the quality of the road systems, paralleled by the growth of the North American automobile industry. With faster road networks and better automobiles, more people could plan vacations to far and exotic wilderness areas. Lastly, to establish this new passion for the natural world, a forth and crucial revolution had to take place; Nash (1982) called it the *information revolution*. According to Nash (1982), it is the massive amount of information delivered through outdoor magazines, guide books, and "how-to" books that finally compromised the fate of the North American wilderness. Before the existence of magazines like *Backpacker, Outside, Wilderness Camping, Explore Magazine*, or the publication of classic books like *The Complete Walker* (1968) by Colin Fletcher, one had to seek information by word-of-mouth, or by embracing the true spirit of the wilderness and venturing into it with little more than a map and compass. Nash (1982) bluntly explained this point when he wrote: "What took John Muir, Brower, and John Wesley Powell a lifetime to acquire is available today for $2.95" (p. 319).

WRITING A SENTENCE OF "DEATH BY LOVE"

Colin Fletcher himself, "the high priest of America backpackers," (Schueler, 1981, p. 119) declared that "The woods are overrun and sons of bitches like me are half the problem."[5] In a short article titled *Wronging by Writing*, published in Backpacker (1992), Fletcher directly addressed the issue of writing about pristine, unspoiled, and still unknown special wilderness areas. In it, Fletcher argued that the solution to the propagation of "where-to-go stories" is in the hands of both the writers and the readers. Fletcher included both parties in his solution since he believes that the personal needs of writers and readers are at the heart of the problem.

On one hand, the problem resides in the fact that professional outdoor writers write about "secluded" and "secret places" because they themselves like to find, explore, and enjoy these rare natural havens. After all, many are in this business because first and foremost they are inveterate outdoor lovers. And, like many of us, they have decided to make a living by doing what they love. Therefore, being paid to write about one's personal adventures in the wilderness becomes very appealing. However, the real question is, since professional outdoor writers write to earn a living, do they also ponder the consequences of their writings?

On the other hand, the problem also resides within the circle of readers who are demanding and expecting these "where-to-go-stories." Ironically, since they already know about the crowding of our best known North American National Parks, these readers are seeking information about lesser known paradises. After all, wilderness is best experienced alone, or at most, with only a few friends. Unfortunately, our modern way-of-life, offering merely two to four weeks of annual vacation time, does not allow us room to head out in the wild without a good idea of what we will find. We want nothing but the best and we want it quickly, ready to wear, ready to eat, and ready to explore. "Most people feel they can't afford... to make mistakes about the places into which they backpack" (Fletcher, 1992, p. 64). Hence, they ask for more "where-to-go-stories."

To support his argument, Fletcher (1992) recalls a conversation he had 35 years ago with Backpacker Magazine's founder, Bill Kemsley. During the early years of the magazine, Kemsley used to say to his writers, "run no stories describing specific places to go" (Fletcher, 1992, p. 69). Unfortunately, soon after, the magazine began to feature its first "where-to-go-stories." Fletcher, who was writing for the young magazine, approached

Kemsley and asked why he had changed his mind on "where-to-go-stories." Kemsley allegedly answered: "Yes, I know. I'm not happy about it either. But readers seem to demand it. Otherwise they won't buy the magazine and it'll fold" (Fletcher, 1992, p. 69).

Consequently, recreating in the outdoors has increased in popularity (The Outdoor Recreation Coalition of America, 1995), and the demand for "where-to-go-stories" is also increasing. In response to the demand, it is now easy to find articles bearing attractive, inspiring, and promising titles such as: "*Take the Plunge—Eight hidden spots to dive into this season*" (Outside Magazine, Vol. 22, No. 8, 1997); "*Pocket of Paradise*" (Sierra Magazine, Vol. 82, September/October, 1997); "*Big Parks, No Crowds*" (Backpacker Magazine, Vol. 24, No. 6, 1996); "*Lose the Crowds—Ten pieces of eden are waiting for you*" (Backpacker Magazine, Vol. 20, No. 4, 1992); "*Eight Top Hawaiian Sea Kayak Trips*" (Paddler Magazine, Vol. 18, No. 3, 1998). These are only a few of the most popular magazines, but each of them claims to reach a few hundred thousand readers each month.

Fletcher (1992) believes that, in the end, everyone is losing. The readers are cheated in their quest for a special place by seeking it the easy way. "The 'where-to-go-stories' do not provide what they promise. By their very nature, they blight the real values that wilderness, or any unspoiled green place has to offer" (Fletcher, 1982, p. 64). The ethical writers are left with troubled consciences, haunted by the potential consequence of their writing. Fletcher (1992) himself ponders: "If we write and publish stories about such places, what are we gaining, other than money? And, what are we destroying?" (p. 68). Ultimately, the real losers in this vicious *méénage-á-trois*, are the pristine mountain meadows, the small no-name lakes, the quiet sandy river banks, the fragile balanced rocks, and the bears and the chipmunks.

WRITING WITH GOOD INTENTIONS

Rennicke (1992) wrote a counter argument to Fletcher's titled *Giving the Land a Voice*. In this article, he suggests that keeping secrets is dangerous, selfish, and illusional. He believes that "publicizing public lands helps build a constituency for protection" (Rennicke, 1992, p. 66). His rational holds value, the more we know about a special and fragile natural environment, the greater likelihood it will be protected. Public opinion has already saved priceless and unique environments, like Yosemite Valley and the Grand Canyon to name only two. By giving a voice to the land, it is possible for the land to protect itself from mining, flooding, or clear cutting.

Interestingly, Rennicke (1992) and Nash (1982) used the example of the controversial 1963 damming of Glen Canyon in Arizona to support opposing points of view. While Rennicke (1962) explained that Glen Crayon was lost forever to the damming project because it was "one of the best-kept secrets in the Southwest" (p. 66), Nash (1982) explained that after the loss of Glen Canyon, the Sierra Club vowed not to make the same mistake with the inner gorge of the Grand Canyon. The club's response was to lead a national campaign to save the canyon by producing books, articles, and a film about it. Eventually, the Grand Canyon was saved from the damming project, but ironically, the canyon is now facing a new problem as a result of solving an old one. "Having been saved from the dam builders, the canyon's wilderness became threatened by the saviors themselves" (Nash, 1982, p. 332). Receiving the largest number of visitors annually in the U.S. National Park System, the Grand Canyon faces an increasing popularity that endangers the *physical, biological, and psychological* carrying capacity of the canyon's fragile environment.

Coincidentally, Fletcher (1992) himself admitted that he is partly responsible for the public fate of the Grand Canyon. After walking through the Grand Canyon in the mid 60s, Fletcher wrote *The Man Who Walked Through Time* (1968), which quickly became popular among canyon explorers. Concerned about writing this book, Fletcher first consulted a friend about the potential impact it could have on the number of visitors hiking the canyon. His friend, a geologist, assured him that the risk of attracting too many hikers to the Grand Canyon was very low. Today, Fletcher admits that they were both wrong, *The Man Who Walked Through Time* (1968) is still a best-seller and the Grand Canyon is still visited by an increasing number of hikers.

A QUESTION OF PERSONAL LAND ETHIC

In the end, the underlying issue of publishing articles about special wilderness areas brings us back to the philosophical debate between anthropocentrism and biocentrism. The question, which is still collectively unanswered, is simple: is the motivating factor for protecting wilderness areas based on human interests or natural interests? It is only by acknowledging this controversy that outdoor writers and readers can evaluate their impact on pristine environments.

For Nash and Fletcher, there are no easy solutions. Nash (1982) reminds us that managing human presence in our most popular wilderness areas with quotas, permits, and lotteries will only desecrate the meaning of wilderness; Fletcher (1992) argues that promoting newly discovered, remote, or foreign pristine areas will only transfer the problem from one place to another. The reality is that the solution to this dilemma lies much deeper within our relationship with nature. As Fletcher (1992) suggested, the problem in promoting special wilderness areas through writing is an interrelated one for which both the writers and the readers must take responsibility. As consumers of "where-to-go-stories", readers are as responsible for "loving nature to death" as the writers themselves. Unfortunately, neither group seems to understand the profound consequences and direct long term implications of their quest.

Perhaps, what Fletcher and Nash expound is that we have not yet achieved the "land ethic" suggested by Aldo Leopold. A "land ethic" that alerts us against our own protective actions, since, according to Leopold (1962), "all conservation of wilderness is self-defeating, for to cherish we must see and fondle, and when enough have seen and fondled, there is no wilderness left to cherish" (p. 108).

Since writing about secret and pristine wilderness areas, even for conservational purposes, can clearly contribute to the diminishing of wild places; it is once again important to ask ourselves, "should articles on special wilderness places be published?" As an outdoor lover and educator, I say, no. I believe that outdoor magazine writers and readers should aspire to a different type of promotional article. It is perhaps time to shift from "where-to-go" stories to "why-to-go" stories. Let us emphasize the benefits of discovering the natural world instead of emphasizing where we should go to find it. Instead of giving details on specific locations, perhaps offer stories of personal trips and the value they hold. Instead of listing all of the beautiful hidden places we should visit, perhaps list the positive benefits of finding one's own special wilderness.

To help us complete this "paradigm shift" let us ask ourselves this question. To remain pristine, wild, and healthy, do special wilderness places really need to be promoted through publications, or should special wilderness places be designated to be visited lightly by few and far between?

REFERENCES

Fletcher, C. (1992, June). Wronging by writing. *Backpacker, 20,* pp. 64, 67–69 & 87.

Fletcher, C. (1968). *The complete walker.* New York, NY: Knoph.

Leopold, A. (1949). *A sand county almanac: And sketches here and there.* New York, NY: Oxford University Press.

Nash, R. (1982). *Wilderness and the American mind* (3rd ed.). Binghamton, NY: Yale University Press.

The Outdoor Recreation Coalition of America. (1995). *Human powered outdoor recreation: State of the industry report.* Boulder, CO: The Outdoor Recreation Coalition of America.

Rennicke, J. (1992, June). *Giving the land a voice.* Backpacker, 20, 65–66.

Schueler, D. G. (1981). *The strange quest of the man who walked through time.* Smithsonian, *11,* 119–132.

ENDNOTES

1. US National Park System Annual Report, 1998, Interior Department of National Park Service.

2. State of the Parks 1997 Report, 1998, Minister of Public Works and Government Services Canada

3. The U.S. Census Bureau estimated the 1997 U.S. population at 267,636,061.

4. Statistics Canada estimated the 1997 Canadian population at 30,286,600.

5. As quoted in Roderick Nash (1982), Wilderness and the American Mind, p. 316.

CHAPTER 8

Have Adventure Programs Eliminated Too Much Risk?

YES PERSPECTIVE: Karl Rohnke

NO PERSPECTIVE: Camille J. Bunting, Ph.D.

Karl has an undergraduate degree from Washington and Lee University in Virginia and an honorable doctorate from Unity College in Maine. Karl has been an important "player" in the field of adventure education for over 30 years. He was a watch officer at Hurricane Island Outward Bound in 1967 and chief instructor at NCOBS until 1971. He left Outward Bound to become one of the founders of the Project Adventure (PA) program in Hamilton, MA, and has worked there continuously since that time. During his tenure at PA he served as director and president of the company. Karl has written over 10 books that relate to the field of adventure education.

Camille is the Director of the Texas A & M University's Outdoor Education Institute, and an associate professor in the Department of Health and Kinesiology. She has been an active professional in the field of adventure education for the past 25 years. In addition to administering the programs of the Outdoor Education Institute and teaching and facilitating adventure education experiences, she has maintained a research agenda focusing on the physiological and psychological responses to adventure activities.

Have Adventure Programs Eliminated Too Much Risk?

YES

Karl Rohnke

Contenser v. Fear Factor

Take a risk. Go For It! Risky Business. You can do it.

Is there enough of IT in your program? Risk I mean? Depends mostly on what you're defining, and how you define it.

Risk—"Possibility of loss or injury; danger; peril."

Danger? Peril? INJURY? Cancel the risk factor, I can't afford risk in my adventure program.

Consequence—"Logical result of an action or process; outcome, effect."

Well, that's not so bad, as long as it's not negative consequence. You can pick your challenges, but you don't get to pick your consequences? Hold the consequence!

Adventure—"An activity of uncertain outcome characterized by risk and consequence."

Risk and consequence? What have you got in the area of arts and crafts or star study? Maybe some native American stuff?

Dictionary definitions? Obviously. Tongue in cheek? Definitely. Real-life adventure (with associated hard-copy risk and pay back consequence) runs the spectrum from unrealistic Mountain Dew TV spectaculars to any "uncertain outcome" activity.

It's reader participation time. What are two activities you consider to be adventurous, or risky? Since I'm here and you're there, this Q&A scenario is obviously rhetorical, but think about it, and, did your "adventures" involve fear, and maybe some danger?

To continue this writer/reader query, I'll ask a few experiential questions prefaced by the three words, Have you ever...? This is meant to be revealing, so look in the mirror and raise your hand if the answer is yes.

Have you ever sky dived?, ...white water rafted?, ...pedaled a bicycle over one-hundred miles in a day?, ...trekked to a mountain top over 14,000 feet? ...walked through an antique shop? Antique shop? Of course, uncertain outcome, risk, excitement, consequence, it's all there. Adventure is largely in the eyes of the beholder.

Considering your responses to the above, two types of potential adventure need to be recognized: pure and programmed. An example of pure adventure would be an attempt to climb Mt. Everest, i.e. trying something that has risk and end-of-the-road consequences involved, and where the outcome is not predictable.

Pure

Programmed adventure? Those recreational activities that exhibit high perceived risk but which are statistically not risky. Well known examples are: white water rafting, horse back riding, and rock climbing, i.e. recreation for hire where the proprietors can't afford to let the clientele be injured or not often, anyway. So what about the antique shop, is it pure or programmed?

Points to ponder:
1. Personal adventure need not be life threatening or physically demanding.
2. Statistics don't preclude injury (accidents happen).
3. Statistics predictably indicate that life is for living.

A more pertinent and topical example of programmed adventure is participation on a challenge ropes course, in which case the participant deals with a high level of anxiety and fear, but where the actual risk of physical harm is minimal. The instructors know the risk is minimal, the participants do not.

Here's an example of what I mean, programmatically out of sequence perhaps, but dramatically clear. Scenario: A participant commits to trying an activity where the chance of performance failure is up-front and imminent, with the perceived chance of physical harm not far behind.

The activity (high ropes course element) is called a Pamper Pole, a 30–50' long utility (telephone) pole plopped in the ground vertically and solidly, well…, kind of solidly. The performance objective is to climb to the top of that pole using compassionately sequenced metal steps, maneuver into a hands-free standing position on top of the ridiculously small platform (about 10' × 10'), then dive to a cable supported trapeze that dangles approximately 6–7' away. Let me assuredly add, while attempting this "high wire" act the climber is securely connected to a belay protection rope. Adventure proprietors wouldn't remain in business very long if they allowed participants to make definitive, high speed contact with the ground.

This dramatic ropes course element has been extant since 1975 and has been *successfully attempted by literally tens of thousands of "gripped" participants. The Pamper Pole is an example of programmed adventure, i.e. a statistically predictable adventure experience.

A participant about to dislodge from the known of the wobbling platform to the unknown of suspended (belayed) flight is making an attempt that he/she perceives as being very risky. Am I going to be safe? Am I going to be injured? Will I fail in front of my peers and embarrass myself? Definitive and often therapeutic answers to these largely non-verbalized questions are soon revealed via experience, i.e. a large dose of very personal experiential risk. During this often emotionally intense process, the instructor can be confident in the safety of the system, thus being able to concentrate on facilitating the experience for the student without worrying about physical or legal consequence.

OK, thanks for the sales job, I'll give the Pamper Pole a try someday, but what's the point other than recognizing the programmatic value of perceived risk?

Pamper Pole use is an example of how safety, over time, has escalated within the industry to a point where the event has, at a few venues, become too safe. Too safe? Can you be too safe? There are any number of acronym organizations and agencies that would disagree.

At some point in the evolution of trapeze jumping some individual or committee decided that a second separate rope and belayer would make the event safer. Within the last couple of years I have heard that a third belay rope, a total of three separate ropes, and three separate belayers, is being used. How about four ropes? Why not six? Six belay ropes certainly provide more participant involvement, and the rope manufacturers would love it.

At least a couple dozen vertical poles used in the 70s and early 80s were regularly belayed with a single length of goldline rope connected to the climber (flyer) by a single secured turn of that rope around the participant's waist. Risky? No. Uncomfortable? Definitely.

I must confess to occasionally demonstrating the use of this basic and uncomfortable tie-in (my body) to shake up sacrosanct standards and tweak safety concepts of those who have only experienced or observed body harness protection. In doing so I'm not advocating a return to the single bowline tie-in, rather, I'm trying to historically and dramatically point out that for over five years the single bowline around the waist was THE rope connection of choice.

Is the use of a full body harness and three ropes necessary? Has the real risk and/or perceived risk been diminished by making the event safer? Indeed, has the event become conceptually "too safe?"

If a participant's experience while standing on top of the subtly moving platform, anticipating the jump, is unchanged as the result of the extra protective gear, the scenario is not too safe; the perceived risk is intact.

If the experience has been diminished by a plethora of attachments and gear, obviously reducing the perceived risk, the event has become too safe for some participants. Perception of risk must remain or the experience degrades to a carnival ride, no more than a cheap thrill.

Why risk at all? Didn't your Mom tell you, "It's better to be safe than sorry?"

Reasonable risk feels good, and reasonable risk ordinarily results in reasonable consequence, i.e. not catastrophic. An attempt to skateboard down Pikes Peak is unreasonably risky and the painful, perhaps final, consequences of crashing are in keeping with the unreasonableness of the attempt. Reasonable risk usually produces reasonable results. By purposefully risking either physically or emotionally, you are pushing your personal envelope to improve. You'll never get to second base without taking your foot off first. Without risk, expect little or no success.

How much should you risk?

If I could answer that question definitively I'd be in Reno right now, that's what makes risk risky. The question more appropriately should be, how much can you afford to risk? Or more poignantly, how much can you afford to lose?

Skiing double diamond trails feels good, crashing on steep terrain doesn't. Considering your skill level, how much can you afford to risk? What are you bringing to the table that allows you to responsibly take personal risks? (skills, experience, local knowledge, honesty, responsibility to self). How much do you want to gain? How much can you afford to lose?

As time goes by, you can count on safety standards and procedures escalating, (administrative safety seldom retrogrades) so, do what you can without getting reprimanded by operating within parameters that you know are truly safe with as much perceived risk as can be responsibly generated.

Finally, a bit of common sense fluff to temper the seriousness and gravity of this controversial topic. Too safe? Too dangerous? Too risky? No challenge? Elusively between exists the Goldilock's Adventure Flow State *(GAFS): first established as pertains to chairs, porridge and beds—not too safe, not too risky, but just right.

* successfully—Success in this context refers to a conscientious attempt rather than adhering to a performance standard.
* GAFS—Sorry about the cavalier use of the "flow state", it was just too apropos to pass up.

Have Adventure Programs Eliminated Too Much Risk?

Camille J. Bunting, Ph.D.

My answer is "no" for the following reasons:

1. The process of increasing safety has not eliminated *all* risk from adventure programs.
2. Human judgement remains a significant risk factor in adventure programs.
3. The outdoor environment offers risks beyond the control of 21st century technology and the most educated and experienced decision-makers.

The thoughts that follow are an explanation of why I do not believe that too much risk has been eliminated from adventure programs.

There has been ample documentation of our need for some level of risk or stress. It provides motivation and a sense of accomplishment (Csikszentmihalyi, 1975; Leuba, 1955; Selye, 1950, 1974) and at appropriate levels it enhances ability to perform physical skills at an optimum level. In 1908, Yerkes & Dodson published their findings regarding the relation of stimulus strength to rate of learning in mice. They found that while learning a skill, over arousal inhibited skill acquisition, but after significant competence had been acquired arousal enhanced performance.

However, it was also found that over stimulation could result in performance below the demonstrated competence level (Freeman, 1940). This general line of research has been followed throughout the 20th century, especially in terms of psychological arousal and its effects upon an individual's developing sense of self. Duffy (1932, 1957) revealed the same type of results, and was the first to discuss the concept of an inverted U shaped curve in the arousal—benefit relationship. Her research also pertained to performance types of outcomes and revealed that if arousal/stress continued to increase, the outcomes would begin to decrease in their positive nature. Adaptations of this concept were pursued by White, 1959; Harter, 1978; Csikentmihalyi, 1975; and others as it related to efficacy and competence. These theories have been modified over the years, but research has continued to find that risk and/or challenge can act as a positive motivator and elicit positive benefits. Due to this positive potential, they serve as cornerstones of adventure programming philosophy.

In the mid to late 1970s, Outward Bound type programs (growth through stress) began to be modified for a wider range of clientele, e.g. schools, corporations, mental health facilities, etc. As this occurred, an increasing number of measures were taken to reduce the *real risks* that were inherent in the programs. The intent was to decrease the *real risks* while maintaining and capitalizing on the *perceived risks*. Real risks could be identified as:

a) Doing high ropes course types of activities without a belay rope

b) Sending a novice group on a wilderness expedition without much training and/or a shadow instructor

c) Not making participants aware of the risks inherent in certain activities.

Perceived risks could be identified as:
a) Being 20–30 feet above ground clipped into a rope only 11 mm in diameter with a small aluminum device (carabiner)

b) The perception of becoming hopelessly lost in an unfamiliar and "uncivilized" wilderness environment, or

c) The anticipation of being physically uncomfortable and not knowing what to expect.

There is a significant perception discrepancy between a novice and an experienced outdoor leader. An 11-mm rope and carabiner for example, is perceived quite differently by a novice and an outdoor leader. The leader has prior experience that has allowed him or her to develop knowledge and trust in the strength of such equipment, whereas the novice has a limited frame of reference. Therefore, what may seem to be without risk (very limited *real risk*) to the instructor, may seem very risky (high *perceived risk*) to the participant. On the other hand, the opposite can also be true. For example, a novice canoeist can be unaware of the dangers inherent in paddling a fast moving river, because his/her frame of reference includes only successful fun and play on rivers and does not include any mishaps in that type of environment. As a result of the participant's prior experience but lack of education regarding the potential dangers associated with river sports, his/her *perception* of risk for canoeing is low, even when the *real risk* can be quite high. In a situation such as this, an inaccurate risk perception on the part of a participant can become a *real risk* in an adventure program, especially if the participant cannot be convinced of the risk potential.

As a professional in the field of adventure education, I believe the instructor's responsibility is to the client. That does not mean instructors can or should be able to guarantee safety. However, it does mean that instructors should have a clear understanding of their responsibilities and how to fulfill them. Likewise, clients should be made aware of their responsibilities, the types of risks associated with the experiences being provided, and what responsibilities they have for the safety of the activities. In the event of an accident, which of the following responses would you rather provide to a client's relatives? "There was nothing more I could have done to foresee this situation and to prevent it or to have improved my response to it." Or "If I had done (or hadn't done) "this or that", the outcome would probably have been different." Granted, you probably would not verbalize either statement, but one of the two would be ringing in your head.

I cannot imagine being in a position of leadership and choosing to put students/clients in a situation with a level of risk over which I could have exercised some control, and CHOOSING not to do so. Yet even as I am writing these words, images of myself doing this very thing come storming into my head. For example, I am a believer in having a group do the 14' Wall challenge course initiative without a belay rope. There are also rapids on rivers that I have allowed students to paddle, believing that they have not yet perfected the skills that are needed to complete the rapid without capsizing. Why have I done this and continue to do so? Because I, as an adventure educator, believe their experience will be enhanced or a greater level of learning will result than if such experiences are bypassed (as in portaging a rapid), or modified to essentially remove all risk (as in the 14' Wall with a belay rope). There are many times in our lives when taking a significant risk is necessary *if we are to move beyond a certain level of achievement* (i.e., monetary risks to expand a business, or emotional risks in verbally expressing our feelings for someone). As an adventure educator, I make risk related decisions based on observations of the maturity and skill of the group/individuals, knowledge of the environmental conditions, my professional assessment for risk of injury, and on an assessment of what will best facilitate the objectives. For example, I typically do not use the 14' Wall initiative with a group that has not been together long enough to establish and demonstrate caring interpersonal bonds which lead to attentive aggressive spotting. Additionally, I require everyone to wear a seat harness so secure handholds are available on each person. By making such decisions, the risk of the 14' Wall initiative is limited but certainly not eliminated.

When allowing students to paddle a rapid that is potentially beyond their current skill level, I do so as a result of assessing the danger to be low in the event of a capsize, and the potential for learning to be high. To further limit the risk, specific safety procedures would be reviewed and throw-rope stations set up. However, occasionally the objectives are best accomplished by portaging. This option may be best if:

a) The group has been having problems at other rapids and the present rapid is more difficult with a greater chance of bodily injury or wrapping a canoe around a rock.

b) Fatigue has become a factor increasing the chance for mishaps.

c) Some students have made it through previous rapids without capsizing by sheer luck rather than the use of correct skills, etc.

A critical lesson for outdoor adventurers is that *not* doing something, e.g., portaging a rapid or turning back in bad weather before summiting a peak, <u>can</u> be a sign of maturity and educated decision-making. It should not automatically be viewed as "wimping out." This is a difficult lesson to learn. We cannot look back at situations and determine that an accident would have happened if a different decision had been made. Unfortunately, we generally get feedback on our decisions only when accidents occur.

<u>Instructor judgement is a key factor in the level of risk associated</u> with adventure <u>activities and is critical for designing the appropriately structured and sequenced experiences.</u> To achieve educational objectives with the methods of adventure/challenge, there must be a progressive increase of motivating consequences. Typically these motivating consequences are unknown outcomes

[handwritten margin note: "not 'risk' at all costs."]

resulting from challenging tasks or even the possibility of negative outcomes. So our issue becomes: the level of risk or definition of *negative outcomes* that we are willing to accept in the exercise of our methods, without compromising the potential for accomplishing the objectives. In considering the level of risk we are each willing to accept, another question must be addressed. Are we interested in accomplishing the objectives most appropriate for our students/clients, or our own personal objectives? Are we who claim to be adventure educators actually adventure junkies, in pursuit of our own gratification? Since many of us seem to require a high degree of challenge in order to achieve our perception of positive outcomes, we may have difficulty believing that others could legitimately have different needs.

As stated earlier, there is ample evidence of humans' need for some level of challenge or stress. The difficulty comes in identifying the appropriate level for different people. Extremely high levels of physiological stress have been documented by heart rates, blood pressure, and catecholamine responses for a variety of adventure activities (Bunting, et.al, 1986, 1995; Schedlowski & Tewes, 1992; Williams, Taggart & Carruthers, 1978). From such empirical studies we know adventure activities are perceived as challenging. We also know that experience reduces the physiological responses (Epstein & Fenz, 1965; Schedlowski & Tewes, 1992), thus the possibility that the challenge might need to be increased for those with more experience. However, how do we determine what is "going too far?" Can we identify where an individual is on the Optimal Arousal graph (Figure 1)? Can we know how to increase the challenge for person "X" from level three to five without first going to six? Is it true that because person "X" is at a positive outcome

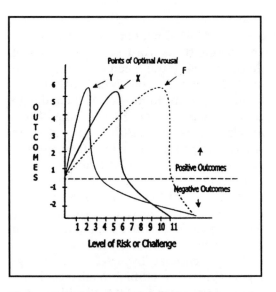

Figure 8.1 *Graphic illustration of how the Theory of Optimal Arousal may apply to three different individuals. Y = Client Y; X = Client X; F = Facilitator/Leader/Instructor.*

level at challenge three, that person "Y" will also accrue positive outcomes from the same challenge?

For some individuals in adventure programs, the level of challenge may not seem high enough and may need to be intensified for those individuals. On the other hand, the activity that most effectively moves them out of their comfort zone may be in a different realm, i.e. challenging interpersonal experiences with different age groups or in unfamiliar settings. An appropriate response to this situation is not necessarily to increase the level of risk in the same activity, because in doing so, we might be:

1. Putting the individual in a situation that could be detrimental to the person, our institution, or agency, and our profession.

2. Putting others in the group in a situation of seeming "less than" because they were posed a lower level of challenge.

3. Encouraging other group members to go beyond their optimal level of challenge, and thereby experiencing negative outcomes.

A challenge for adventure educators is to expand our repertoire beyond merely increasing the level of risk in our typical activities.

Even with the measures that have been taken to decrease the possibility of injury in adventure programs, there is ample risk remaining to provide a sense of accomplishment and positive (as well as negative) outcomes. Why would we hesitate to limit the risk of tragedy? Undoubtedly, my perspective has been influenced by a tragedy that I experienced as an adventure educator.

In 1986, I was returning from a field trip with a class of Backcountry Leadership students. At that time in our program, all of our field trips were accomplished by traveling in a caravan of private vehicles. All standard preparations had been followed, appropriate pre-trip instruction had been given, including safe driving practices for a caravan; risk-management procedures were followed; and the trip had gone well. However, on the drive home one of the cars carrying six students missed a turn. After missing the turn, the driver made a U-turn in the middle of the four-lane highway. The car was hit broadside by an eighteen-wheel truck. Four students were killed on impact, one never regained consciousness and died three months later, and one student survived extensive internal injuries. Devastating tragedies such as this do not happen often, but when they occur it is evident that risk is ever present and often beyond our control. Why then would we not limit the risks of those things over which we can exercise some level of control?

I personally do not like to be told that I have to do "such and such" OR that I can't do "such and such" for my own safety. I have an aversion to government dictates such as required motorcycle helmets, or the Association for Challenge Course Technology's 5,000 lb. minimum breaking strength rule for all life supporting equipment on a challenge course (ACCT Standards Booklet, 1998). Such an aversion is especially true when multi-pitch rock climbers regularly lead-climb with 4,000 lb. breaking strength dynamic rope clipped into one carabiner. However, when it comes to making a decision about the level of risk to provide my students/clients, I believe there is ample risk available to accomplish educational goals through adventure experiences while taking steps to limit the real risks involved. If I personally choose to participate in an adventure that has an extremely high level of risk (50% or greater chance of severe injury), that is a different situation than my providing such opportunities to people with less experience and less training. I am knowledgeable of the risks and possible consequences to myself, my students/clients however are paying for my professional judgement and experience.

My responsibility as an adventure educator, is to use the vehicle of challenging adventure with its varying degrees of consequences to provide opportunities for learning and growth. Just as a traditional classroom teacher has a responsibility to present material and assignments that will provide positive learning experiences, and a medical doctor has the responsibility to diagnose and treat for restoring health while doing no harm, an adventure educator has the responsibility to provide positive learning and growing experiences while doing no harm.

Let's take a look at a hypothetical situation. What if you were being treated for a serious illness and the doctor had just told you that the first treatment regimen was not working. Because of this, she prescribed an increased dose of the medicine you had been taking. That would seem to be appropriate. However, she did not tell you that the higher dosage has an equally high chance of destroying your kidneys as it does of curing the disease and making you even healthier than you have ever been. In addition, she did not mention that there were other possible cures, although those treatments took twice as long to obtain results, involved very bad tasting liquid medications, and their capability of providing extremely high health had not been proven. Why would you want to risk your kidneys when other means could produce similar results? Would you want your doctor to make her decision based on what she personally got the biggest payback (money or fame) from, or on what would be best for you?

For me, the decision is not a difficult one. I would not want to risk losing my kidneys, even for the 50% chance of gaining an extremely high level of health. But, if one of the doctor's main personal goals was to have an extremely high level of health for her patients, a 50% chance for that outcome might be viewed as an acceptable level of risk. After all, if it didn't work there could probably be a kidney transplant! Would it be appropriate for the doctor's personal goal, to influence the treatment decision for the patient? And would it be the doctor's responsibility to objectively present other alternatives?

Twenty-five years ago, helmets were not required for horseback riding programs as they are today. In 1995, Christopher Reeve was wearing a riding helmet and a protective vest in an equestrian competition. In the process of navigating a two-mile course that included 15 jumps, his horse suddenly stopped after initiating the third jump and Christopher was thrown to the ground. Even with the helmet and vest, enough risk remained that his neck was broken and he was left a quadriplegic. While adventure programs have eliminated many of the risks that were present in programs 10 to 25 years ago, I believe most of the changes have been positive and not excessive. The challenges and risks of uncertain outcomes continue to be cornerstones of adventure programming, and adventure educators have multiple options for structuring effective programs that meet learning objectives without increasing the risk of injuries.

REFERENCES

Association for Challenge Course Technology Challenge Course Standards (1998). ACCT.

Bunting, C. J., Little, M. J., Tolson, H., & Jessup, G. (1986). Physical fitness and eustress in the adventure activities of rock climbing and rappelling. The Journal of Sports Medicine and Physical Fitness, 26, 11–20.

Bunting, C. J. (1995). Physiological measurements of stress during outdoor adventure activities. The Journal of Experiential Education, 18, 5–11.

Csikszentmihalyi, M. (1975). Beyond boredom and anxiety. San Francisco: Jossey-Bass.

Duffy, E. (1932). The relationship between muscular tension and quality of performance. American Journal of Psychology, 44, 535–546.

Duffy, E. (1957). The psychological significance of the concept of "arousal" or "activation." The Psychological Review, 64, 265–275.

Epstein, S., & Fenz, E. D. (1965). Steepness of approach and avoidance gradients in humans as a function of experience: Theory and experiment. Journal of Experimental Psychology, 70, 1–12.

Freeman, G. L. (1940). The relationship between performance level and bodily activity level. Journal of Experimental Psychology, 26, 602–608.

Harter, S. (1982). The perceived competence scale for children. Child Development, 53, 87–97.

Leuba, C. (1955). Toward some integration of learning theories: The concept of optimal stimulation. Psychological Reports, 27–33.

Schedlowski, M. & Tewes, U. (1992). Physiological arousal and perception of bodily state during parachute jumping. Psychophysiology, 29, 95–103.

Selye, H. (1950). The physiology and pathology of exposure to stress. Montreal: ACTA Inc., Medical Publishers.

Selye, H. (1974). Stress without distress. New York: NAL Penguin, Inc.

White, R. W. (1959). Motivation reconsidered: The concept of competence. Psychological Review, 66, 297–333.

Williams, E. S., Taggart, P., & Carruthers, M. (1978). Rock climbing: Observations on heart rate and plasma catecholamine concentrations and the influence of oxprenolol. British Journal of Sports Medicine, 12, 125–128.

Yerkes, R. M. & Dodson, J. D. (1908). The relation of strength of stimulus to rapidity of habit-formation. Journal of Comparative Neurology and Psychology, 18, 459–482.

CHAPTER 9

The Ultimate Goal of Adventure Education Should Be the Improvement of the Individual, Not the Group Within Which the Individual Resides

YES PERSPECTIVE: Deborah Sugerman, Ph.D.
NO PERSPECTIVE: Dan Garvey, Ph.D.

Deb Sugerman came to the University of New Hampshire in the fall of 1997 after teaching at Unity College for 16 years. She received her Ph.D. in Forest Resources from the University of Maine in 1990. Her teaching includes courses in backpacking and whitewater canoeing as well as outdoor leadership and teaching methods. Deb's areas of interest lie in working with older people and people with disabilities, group facilitation and sea kayaking. Deb is the Director of the undergraduate outdoor education option at UNH.

Dan Garvey is a faculty member in Outdoor Education at the University of New Hampshire. He is the former President and Executive Director of the Association for Experiential Education (AEE). He received his Ph.D. from the University of Colorado and has written and researched extensively in the fields of moral development, international experiential education, and educational reform. Before joining the faculty at UNH he had a twenty year career as an administrator and practitioner, ending as the Director of the Merrowvista Education Center and the Vice President of the American Youth Foundation. He has also served as Executive Director for the University of Pittsburgh, Semester Sea Program.

The Ultimate Goal of Adventure Education Should Be the Improvement of the Individual, Not the Group Within Which the Individual Resides

Deborah Sugerman, Ph.D.

ABSTRACT

In the field of adventure education we work with groups. Yet our goal is the improvement of each individual within those groups, not the group itself. This concept is supported through our philosophical and historical base and in current literature and research.

INTRODUCTION

Kayla was excited and terrified. She had signed up for the backpacking course required for her college major and was getting ready to go out on the first weekend trip. She had never backpacked before. She had never even camped out before. She was unsure of herself; she was afraid she would not be able to carry the heavy pack; she was worried that she wouldn't be able to keep up with the rest of the group; and she doubted her ability to push herself when the hiking became difficult.

My job, as instructor for the course, was to make sure that Kayla became comfortable with herself while backpacking. My goals were to help her learn the basic skills of backpacking, and more importantly, to help her develop self confidence concerning her abilities and inner strengths. The tricky part was the fact that I had twelve other students, each at different skill and developmental levels going on the trip as well. My goals for the rest of the group members were similar to my goals for Kayla to help each of them develop individually through the skills of backpacking. The full value contract of support, respect, honesty, and fun laid the foundation for the group members to help each other reach his/her goals.

The change in Kayla at the end of the trip was evident. She was confident in her abilities to camp and backpack and was more self assured. In the final debrief she talked about how she thought her new confidence might spread to her other classes where she was also unsure of herself. My goals had been reached. She had developed not only as an outdoorsperson, but also personally through increased self confidence, increased ability to communicate effectively with other group members, and recognition of her strengths and abilities.

As Adventure Educators, we work with individuals. We work with them in a group setting, yet the main focus of our profession revolves around the development of individuals within the group. As professionals, we believe in the power of the group, yet realize that strong groups result from having strong individual group members. We focus on the needs of each individual within the group. This concept is strongly embedded in our historical and philosophical roots and is supported in our current literature and research.

THE PHILOSOPHICAL AND HISTORICAL BASE

From the very beginnings of experiential education, philosophers have embraced the concept of individual development within the group setting. Socrates, Plato and Aristotle believed in the importance of youth developing the virtues of wisdom, bravery, temperance, and justice in order for them to assume adult leadership roles. The virtues were taught to young people through direct and purposeful experience, usually in group settings, by involving them in situations that impelled them into action (Hunt, 1990). The method used was to challenge students as individuals within a group setting. The group provided a sounding board, a place where individuals processed their experiences and discussed their learning. The final result of the experiences was individual development. The group played a part in that result, but group development was not the objective.

Other philosophers such as John Locke and Jean Jacques Rousseau believed in the importance of the education of the individual. Locke, a 17th century philosopher and writer, promoted natural teaching methods

in working with individuals to develop virtue, wisdom, and learning. He believed that individual education was key in developing rational thinking, moral dependability, social capability, and adequate reflection and action (Fierser, 1998). Rousseau, in writing the novel *Emile*, described education not as the imparting of knowledge, but as the drawing out of what was already in the child. He believed in educating the individual solely for the individual's own sake (McClintock, 1998). It follows that as the norm for that time period was educating groups of children, these philosophers believed in the power and importance of working with individuals rather than with groups.

In the 1930s, Kurt Hahn was dismayed by the decline in attitudes and abilities of youth. He founded Outward Bound to bring about the development of the individual. He used the group as a context through which the individual would receive support and feedback. The school was built on the concept of an "intense experience surmounting challenges in a natural setting, through which the individual builds his sense of self worth" (Miner, 1990, p. 60). We again see the idea that individual development is the ultimate goal and that the group is used as a medium through which the individual measures growth and change. The Outward Bound movement has grown tremendously since that first school, yet the goals of individual development and improvement within the group context still remain paramount in the organization's philosophy.

The concept of individual improvement using the methods that Kurt Hahn developed has spread worldwide. The concepts have been incorporated into various environments and are being used with many different populations. Individual improvement within the group context can be seen in school settings (Dyson, 1996; Gass, 1990; Herdman, 1994; Prouty, 1990); in therapeutic settings (Davis-Berman & Berman, 1994; Gass, 1993; Maguire & Priest, 1994; Schoel, Prouty & Radcliffe, 1988; Weider, 1990), and in corporate settings (Maxwell, 1997; Priest, 1998). It is used with a wide variety of individuals including youth at risk (Kimball, 1990; Laurence & Stuart, 1990), people with disabilities (Ellmo & Glasser, 1995; Havens, 1992; Schleien, McAvoy, Lais & Rynders, 1993; Whittaker & Shepherd, 1990), older adults (Garvey & Garvey, 1997; Sugerman, 1990) and women (Warren, 1990, 1996). In each of the above examples, the ultimate goal is the improvement of the individual, not of the group. The group is used as a frame of reference for the individual, an environment in which the individual moves while working on change and development.

SUPPORT FROM CURRENT LITERATURE

Arising from the historical base, the current field of Adventure Education defines itself in terms of the development of the individual. Contemporary authors discuss the importance of the individual in adventure education, and what he or she develops as a result of participating in group experiences. Miles and Priest (1990) state that "the defining characteristic of adventure education is that a conscious and overt goal of the adventure is to expand the self, to learn and grow and progress toward the realization of human potential" (p. 1). Priest and Gass (1997) echo this definition by defining adventure education as the branch of outdoor education concerned primarily with interpersonal and intrapersonal relationships; the development of the individual within the

group context. Other writers in the field (Ewert, 1989; Miles, 1987; Zook, 1987) describe the goals of adventure education as personal growth, development of self concept, individual self understanding and self exploration. The goals are accomplished through the use of the group setting and through the support and structure of the group, yet it is the individual's development that is of utmost importance.

In addition to defining adventure education based on individual improvement, the process and product also reflect the importance of the individual within the group setting. One of the earliest models developed by Walsh and Golins (1976) describes adventure education as a process in which the individual is placed in a unique physical and social environment, presented with challenging problem solving tasks which create a state of adaptive dissonance. The individual adapts to the dissonance through mastery of the tasks, then transfers lessons learned back to his or her everyday life. The individual is at the center of the process, the group is the support structure which allows for mastery and transfer of learning. Priest and Gass (1997) describe the potential product of adventure education programs as "people who understand themselves more fully and relate to others more effectively" (p. 20).

SUPPORT FROM RESEARCH IN ADVENTURE EDUCATION

Research reflects what is important to professionals in a field. In adventure education, the majority of research has been conducted to identify the extent and impact of experiences on the individual. Since the early 1950s studies have been made on the social, individual, and therapeutic benefits of adventure education: the concept of the individual and what he or she gains from the experience. Very little research has been done which looks at the development of the group as opposed to the individual. According to Klint (1990) and Ewert (1989), research has been conducted in the areas of self confidence, motivation levels, deviant behavior and substance abuse, among others. Titles such as "The influence of an Outward Bound program on the self-concept of the participants" (Nye, 1976), "Adolescent sex-role stereotyping: Change through wilderness courses" (Pate, 1997) and "The effect of two different debriefing approaches on developing self confidence" (Priest, 1996) convey the breadth of research done on individual improvement through adventure education.

CONCLUSION

The idea is conveyed from the historical and philosophical roots, from the literature and from research in the field that the ultimate goal of adventure education is the improvement of the individual. The historical and theoretical base of adventure education support our responsibility to the individual. Yet we do not work with individuals in a vacuum; we work with individuals in a group. It would seem as if the purpose of the group in adventure education is as a context for individual development and improvement. Personal growth results from feedback and support from other group members. In order to facilitate individual improvement, the group must be kept intact and moving through the orderly stages of group development. It is our role as Adventure Educators to help individuals translate the experiences that happen in a group setting into opportunities for personal growth.

REFERENCES

Davis-Berman, J. & Berman, D.S. (1994). *Wilderness therapy: Foundations, theory and research*. Dubuque, IA: Kendall/Hunt Publishing Company.

Dyson, B. (1996). Two physical education teachers' experience of Project Adventure. *Journal of Experiential Education, 19*(2), 90–97.

Ellmo, W. & Graser J. (1995). *Adapted adventure activities: A rehabilitation model for adventure programming and group initiatives*. Dubuque, IA: Kendall/Hunt Publishing Company.

Ewert, A.W. (1989). *Outdoor adventure pursuits: Foundations, models and theories*. Columbus, OH: Publishing Horizons, Inc.

Fierser, J. (1998). *Internet Encyclopedia of Philosophy* [On-line]. Available Internet: http://www.utm.edu/research/iep/l/locke.htm.

Garvey, D. & Garvey, D. (1997). Facilitating learning with older adults. *Journal of Experiential Education, 20*(2), 80–85.

Gass, M.A. (1990). Adventure programs in higher education. In J. Miles & S. Priest (Eds.), *Adventure education* (pp. 385–401). State College, PA: Venture Publishing Co., Inc.

Gass, M. A. (1993). *Adventure therapy: Therapeutic applications of adventure programming*. Dubuque, IA: Kendall/Hunt Publishing Company.

Havens, M. (1992). *Bridges to accessibility*. Dubuque, IA: Kendall/Hunt Publishing Company.

Herdman, P. (1994). Adventure in the Classroom. *Journal of Experiential Education, 17*(2), 18–25.

Hunt, J.S. (1990). Philosophy of adventure education. In J. C. Miles & S. Priest (Eds.), *Adventure education* (pp. 119–128). State College, PA: Venture Publishing Co. Inc.

Kimball, R. (1990). The Sante Fe Mountain Center. In J.C. Miles & S. Priest (Eds.), *Adventure education* (pp. 11–16). State College, PA: Venture Publishing Co., Inc.

Klint, K.A. (1990). New directions for inquiry into self-concept and adventure experiences. In J.C. Miles & S. Priest (Eds.), *Adventure education* (pp. 163–172). State College, PA: Venture Publishing Co., Inc.

Laurence, M. & Stuart T. (1990). The use of adventure in reducing and preventing socially deviant youth behavior. In J.C. Miles & S. Priest (Eds.), *Adventure education* (pp. 379–384). State College, PA: Venture Publishing Co. Inc.

Maguire, R. & Priest, S. (1994). The treatment of Bulimia Nervosa through adventure therapy. *Journal of Experiential Education, 17*(2), 44–48.

Maxwell, J. (1997). Increasing work group effectiveness: Combining corporate adventure training with traditional team building methods. *Journal of Experiential Education, 20*(1), 26–33.

McClintock, R. (1998). *Institute for Learning Technology* [On-line]. Available Internet: http://www.ilt.columbia.edu/academic/digitexts/rousseau/bio_rousseau.html.

Miles, J. (1987). The value of high adventure activities. In J. Meier, T.W. Morash & G.E. Welton (Eds.), *High-adventure outdoor pursuits: Organization and leadership* (pp. 4–7). Columbus, OH: Publishing Horizons, Inc.

Miles, J. & Priest, S (Eds.). (1990). *Adventure education*. State College, PA: Venture Publishing Co. Inc.

Miner, J. (1990). The creation of Outward Bound. In J. C. Miles & S. Priest (Eds.), *Adventure education* (pp. 55–66). State College, PA: Venture Publishing Co., Inc.

Nye, R. Jr. (1976). *The influence of an Outward Bound program on the self-concept of the participants*. Unpublished doctoral dissertation, Temple University.

Pate, L.J. (1997). Adolescent sex-role stereotyping: Change through wilderness courses. *Journal of Experiential Education, 20*(3), 161–165.

Priest, S. (1998). Physical challenge and the development of trust through corporate adventure training. *Journal of Experiential Education, 21*(1), 31–34.

Priest, S. (1996). The effect of two different debriefing approaches on developing self confidence. *Journal of Experiential Education, 19*(1), 40–42.

Priest, S. & Gass, M. A. (1997). An examination of "problem-solving" versus "solution-focused" facilitation styles in a corporate setting. *Journal of Experiential Education, 20*(1), 34–39.

Priest, S. & Gass, M. A. (1997). *Effective leadership in adventure programming*. Champaign, IL: Human Kinetics.

Prouty, D. (1990). Project Adventure: A brief history. In J. C. Miles & S. Priest (Eds.), *Adventure education* (pp. 97–110). State College, PA: Venture Publishing Co., Inc.

Schleien, S., McAvoy, L., Lais, G. & Rynders, J. (1993). *Integrated outdoor education and adventure programs*. Champaign, IL: Sagamore Publishing.

Schoel, J., Prouty, D., & Radcliffe, P. (1988). *Islands of healing: A guide to adventure-based counseling.* Hamilton, MA: Project Adventure.

Sugerman, D. (1990). Programming adventure education for older adults. In J.C. Miles & S. Priest (Eds.), *Adventure education* (pp. 403–410). State College, PA: Venture Publishing Co., Inc.

Walsh, V. & Golins, G. (1976). *The exploration of the Outward Bound process.* Denver: Colorado Outward Bound School.

Warren, K. (Ed.). (1996). *Women's voices in experiential education.* Dubuque, IA: Kendall/Hunt Publishing Company.

Warren, K. (1990). Women's outdoor adventures. In J. Miles & S. Priest (Eds.), *Adventure education* (pp. 411–418). State College, PA: Venture Publishing Co., Inc.

Weider, R. (1990). Experiential therapy: An adventure in self-discovery enters the psychiatric hospital. In J.C. Miles & S. Priest (Eds.), *Adventure education* (pp. 35–44). State College, PA: Venture Publishing Co., Inc.

Whittaker, T. & Shepherd, C.W. (1990). C.W. HOG: Pathways to understanding in the outdoors. In J.C. Miles & Priest, S. (Eds.), *Adventure education* (pp. 29–34). State College, PA: Venture Publishing Co., Inc.

Zook, L. (1987). Outdoor adventure programs build character five ways. In J. Meier, T.W. Morash & G.E. Welton (Eds.), *High-adventure outdoor pursuits: Organization and leadership* (pp. 8–17). Columbus, OH: Publishing Horizons, Inc.

The Ultimate Goal of Adventure Education Should Be the Improvement of the Individual, Not the Group Within Which the Individual Resides

Dan Garvey, Ph.D.

ABSTRACT

The primary goal of outdoor adventure activities should be the development of the group, rather than the development of each individual who is in the group. This belief will be supported by developing the following three theses:

1. Human development depends on groups.
2. Healthy groups can help ensure healthy people.
3. Most people join groups to accomplish their individual goals.

INTRODUCTION

In an ideal world, there would be no conflict between the needs of an individual and the needs of a group. In such a world, outdoor educators would be able to focus on the unique aspirations of individual group members, carefully designing experiences for each participant. If a person had difficulty reaching his/her potential, the leaders would have the time and resources to support the person through this period of personal development. In this ideal world, groups would be constituted to allow individual achievement and success to occur. The group would simply be a collection of people who are internally motivated and directed, and who happen to be conducting their singular activities together. The group would be organized and maintained solely to support members of the group as they attempt to attain their personal goals.

This ideal world rarely exists. In the real world, outdoor educators are often asked to choose between the needs of individuals and the needs of the group. In the real world of outdoor education, leaders are more often functioning as sociologists, managing the group, rather than psychologists, counseling each individual in the group. The leaders' desire to address the individual needs of participants creates a persistent tension as leaders attempt to balance personal attention to individuals within the larger goals of the group. The following scenarios are two examples of how this tension can become manifest in outdoor education programs:

vs.?

Mary and Tom are outdoor educators working with a group of high school students on a three-day adventure program. The goal of the program is for the students to learn to work as a group, so that they can make a positive impact on their school community. Most of the students are happy to have this time out of the classroom and eagerly participate in the initiative activities that are offered. They earnestly attempt to understand how the group is working and how their personal behavior contributes to the successes or difficulties faced by the group. But, one of the students is hostile and non-participative. He is unwilling to take part in most of the activities and shows little interest in being part of the group, or the program. This student's lack of participation is consistent throughout the entire first day. He is not actively hostile, but he passively demonstrates his contempt for being in this program. Tom and Mary have concerns about this student. They feel he is not taking advantage of the experience and that his lack of interest might be a sign of other problems this student might be having in other areas of his life. In addition, the leaders are very concerned about the negative effect that this particular student is having on the entire group, seriously limiting the progress the group could be making towards its goal. At the end of the first day, Mary and Tom reflect on their progress with the group, and wonder if the student should be asked to leave the program.

Elements of the above scenario have been experienced by many outdoor educators working with reluctant group members. There are a myriad of options Mary and Tom can consider. Perhaps, the student should stay in the group, since he may learn valuable lessons about his behavior and its impact on others. Or, the student could be asked to leave because his behavior is interrupting the progress of the group. To a large extent, the way this problem is resolved depends on the orientation of the leaders. What do they see as their responsibility; is it to the individuals in the group, including this reluctant student, or is their responsibility to the group as a whole?

These are very difficult questions. If the student is allowed to stay, greater and greater energy and attention may need to be given to that student, at the expense of the group goal. The ultimate program goal: "to help the group learn to function better," should not be sacrificed because one individual is either unprepared or unwilling to participate. In the above scenario, both the reluctant individual and the group can learn valuable lessons about the manner in which personal needs and desires must be modified as one attempts to function within a social context. The leaders should make reasonable attempts to engage the reluctant student, but the choice of continued participation rests with this student. If the student remains non-participatory, action must be taken to remove the student from the program.

Another example of the potential tension between the goals of the group and the goals of individual participants is found when a client, intending to take part in extended outdoor adventure program, such as Outward Bound, NOLS or a summer camp trip program, attempts to begin the activities without an adequate level of physical fitness. Many outdoor leaders have faced the problem of trying to decide if a person who has signed-up for a program has the level of physical conditioning necessary for the trip. Despite the notices that may have been sent with the course materials about the importance of being in reasonable physical shape, clients often arrive in marginal physical condition to participate in demanding outdoor activities. If finances are a major concern of the program, the client may be allowed to begin the course so that the tuition revenue is not lost. Setting aside the financial concerns, (which involves a whole different set of tensions regarding the client's participation), leaders are often required to choose between taking the individual on the trip, thus modifying how strenuous the trip will be, or telling the person to come back when he/she has met the minimum physical conditioning requirements, thus allowing the trip to meet the goals of the program as advertised.

In both of these examples, real tension exists between the desires of an individual and the needs/goals of the group. When such a choice has to be made, between the needs of an individual or the needs of the group, the best decision is usually to favor the needs of the group. Using the scenarios above as examples, the non-participatory student would be asked to either become involved or go home, and the client who lacks adequate levels of physical fitness would be encouraged to return when they have met the minimum physical conditioning requirements for the course. These recommendations may at first reading appear harsh, but they are based on the following assumptions.

HUMAN DEVELOPMENT DEPENDS ON GROUPS

We are born into this world as one of the most helpless of all animals, neither able to feed nor defend ourselves. We are totally dependent on the attention of others for our very survival. We are born with a certain genetic blueprint, but it is through our social interactions that we begin to develop and form our unique personalities and the sense of who we are. While there are very few examples of people who have existed with little or no social interaction, one of the most famous accounts of a person being raised in near isolation is the story of Anna.

Anna was born to a young unmarried farm girl. The father of the farm girl was greatly displeased with the new baby and the shame this baby brought upon the family. In an attempt to reduce the abuse the young mother received from her father she put the baby in a small room in the attic. For six years Anna received only enough food to keep her alive. When Anna was finally discovered, she could not sit-up, walk, or talk. She was noncommunicative and caused the doctors to initially believe that she was deaf, and brain damaged. After being placed in a special school, Anna began to progress very rapidly due to the social interaction she received. Eventually she learned to take care of herself and run and play with the other children (Davis, 1948).

This is a dramatic story that points to the need for social interaction as a basic requirement for human development. Since social interaction is such an essential ingredient for development, outdoor leaders need to pay much greater attention to the social units (groups) that people are in. People don't solely develop by themselves, they develop, in part, due to their relationships to others. Since most outdoor activities take place in groups, a natural setting exists for individual growth to occur because such growth is within the context of the group.

HEALTHY GROUPS CAN HELP ENSURE HEALTHY PEOPLE

There is a widespread belief, evidenced by the practice of many outdoor educators, that healthy individuals create healthy groups. While this is true to a degree, a more accurate statement would be, healthy groups help develop healthy people. The differences in these statements might be subtle, but they can be profound. The idea of individual improvement being accelerated through positive group interactions was described by Lawrence Kohlberg (1969) in his "Just Community" theory. Kohlberg believed that some groups create expectations and norms which help modify the individual and raise the performance and behavior of every group member. Anyone who has been a member of a highly effective team can remember the personal sacrifices that were made and the ultimate success achieved by the group. The group actually makes each person function at a higher, more productive level than he/she would have if he/she were working on his/her own. Just communities can be a part of what we offer in outdoor education; communities that help to create a group that will pull for the very best in its members. If the primary goal of outdoor activities is to help individual people grow and develop, the best way to do this is to make sure that the group the person participates in is as healthy as possible.

Much of the adventure education field has a decidedly United States flavor. Placing a higher value on the goals of a group rather than those of an individual is almost un-American. Many cultures throughout the world (ie: Canada, China, Japan, Sweden, to name a few) give greater value to the group than the individual. In these cultures personal wants are secondary to the best interests of the group. The U.S. culture is often defined by individual improvement and personal development. This support for the individual is one of the most distinguishing characteristics of the U.S. culture. If people from other countries were asked to describe "an American", they would surely mention a belief in individual rights and the freedom of the individual near the top of their list of American characteristics. U.S. History teaches that the United States is a country of individuals, a country founded on the concept of "rugged individualism". Great men and women explored the frontiers, cleared the land, and created a democratic government. In fact, some Americans believe so strongly in individualism that it's difficult for them to seriously consider that it is our social interactions that are primarily responsible for forming the individual. An individual, separate from a social context, can not adequately develop physically or psychologically. The stronger and more functional the social groups, the stronger and more functional the group members. Making the ultimate goal of adventure activities the development and maintenance of the group seems to be "un-American", but such a priority is in keeping with most of what we know about how people grow and develop.

MOST PEOPLE JOIN GROUPS IN ORDER TO ACCOMPLISH THEIR INDIVIDUAL GOALS

Perhaps the most compelling argument for placing the needs of the group ahead of the needs of the individual can be made by asking and answering the question: "Why do people join groups?" Although there are a wide variety of related reasons, the fundamental answer is that people join groups because they are able to achieve greater results than they would have achieved had they functioned as solo agents. People understand that they will be participating in a group when they attend an adventure program, there is no surprise that other people have signed-up for this same

activity. Individuals, by their very participation, are asking to be treated as a member of a group. In adventure education the group is necessary in order to accomplish the tasks. Therefore, the group has a very practical function. If outdoor leaders expect participants to learn how to function in groups once they leave the program, real life achievements and consequences should be available for group members while they are participating in an adventure program. Simply stated, the needs of the group are of greater value than the needs of any one individual. The individual goals that brought the group together can only be achieved within the group setting.

Returning to the scenario of the disinterested student. If we do not ask the student to make a commitment to the group or leave, we are sending a very important message to the other students in the group. The message being: "When a single person in a group is non-participatory, stop the group activity and devote substantial time to the needs of that individual." This may be an appropriate lesson if the goal of the program is personal development or therapy, but most groups are not assembled as personal growth activities for their members. They are formed so individuals can achieve their personal goals with the assistance of the other members.

We have all experienced the elation of working with a highly effective group to achieve a goal. As a member of a sports team, an expedition, or a group of staff, most of us have celebrated our accomplishments with a group that made it possible for certain personal goals to be realized. Usually there was a group leader, a coach, expedition leader, or a staff supervisor, who attended to the needs of the group and made the goals of the group evident to each of the members. Outdoor leaders need to play this type of role for their participants.

Even if the goal of an adventure program was to be personal development rather than group development, it would be very difficult to achieve success helping each individual person because personal development would be beyond the training of most staff. Most outdoor leaders are not professionally trained therapists. In addition to the problems presented by a lack of adequate training for staff, there is also the issue of not having adequate background information about most client groups. Personal development by outdoor leaders must assume some knowledge of the individual before he/she arrives. Without such prior knowledge, how would a leader know what type of trip and which activities are most appropriate for *this* individual? When the group is a true therapeutic adventure activity, a focus on the individual rather than the group may be appropriate, but only a small percentage of adventure activities are truly intended for personal therapy. Unfortunately, some outdoor leaders believe their primary role is as an individual therapist, attempting to meet the needs of each person. As laudable as this approach may be, most outdoor leaders have neither the formal training nor the background information on their clients that is necessary to attempt a therapeutic intervention. Adventure education leaders should see their role as group facilitators not therapists. Outdoor leaders are often very skilled in group process, they understand how and why groups work. This understanding has been gained through the experience of doing their jobs.

CONCLUSION

The broadest question we face in this section of controversial issues is the fundamental question about how our identity is formed and how our personality is changed. In many ways this is the same debate that was present between sociologists Cooley (1954) and Meade (1934) versus psychologist Freud (1949). Cooley and Meade suggested that it is our interactions with others that creates our sense of self. Cooley's "Theory of the Looking Glass Self" referred to the formation of the self as a process of learning who we are through the reflections of other people's reaction to us. Freud's idea of internal struggle between the id, ego, and super-ego is a much more individual process of self discovery. In Freud's theory, the person focuses attention inward to learn who he/she is. In Cooley's theory, the person focuses outward towards the group to gain personal identity.

In the intervening years since this debate first began, more credibility has been placed on the social aspects of individual development, rather than the more introspective and self-reflective theories of Freud (especially when one is interested in the development of well adjusted people as opposed to those who may be psychotic or neurotic). We have learned that other people help us to define ourselves. People change and improve, at least in part, because it is a necessary condition for their continued social interaction.

Positive behavior is developed because it helps us be accepted in our social world. Outdoor leaders can have the greatest positive impact on individuals by investing most of their time and energy focused upon the group. Good groups will usually help produce better people.

REFERENCES

Cooley, C.H. (1954). *Social organization: A study of the larger mind.* Glencoe, IL: Free Press.

Davis, K. (1948). *Human society.* New York: MacMillan.

Freud, S. (1949). *An outline of psychoanalysis.* New York: Norton.

Kohlberg, L. (1969). *Stages and sequence: The cognitive-developmental approach to socialization.* In D. Goslin (Ed.) Handbook of Socialization Theory and Research (pp. 347–480). Chicago: Rand McNally.

Meade , G. H. (1934). *Mind, self and society.* Chicago, IL: University of Chicago Press.

CHAPTER 10

Should Processing Techniques, Such as Framing and Debriefing, Be a Mandatory Part of Facilitation?

YES PERSPECTIVE: Clifford E. Knapp, Ph.D.
NO PERSPECTIVE: Mark Havens, Ed.D.

Clifford E. Knapp is a Professor of Curriculum and Instruction at Northern Illinois University's Lorado Taft Field Campus. He has had a long-time interest in community building, processing skills and group dynamics. He believes that the future of world depends upon humans increasing their human relations skills and desiring peace with others and the planet.

Mark Havens, Ed.D., is the President of Accessible Adventures, Inc., based in Grayslake, IL and Sisters, OR. For the past 15 years, Dr. Havens has worked with companies to develop high performing teams, clarify their mission, vision and values, and resolve conflict. Some of his clients include Arthur Andersen, LLP; Baxter Healthcare Corporation and Warner-Lambert. Mark has worked extensively in all regions of the United States, Europe and Asia. He has authored or co-authored five books and 25 articles on team development and experiential learning. He has also delivered numerous national and international presentations on team building and experience based learning. Mark received his B.S., Magna Cum Laude, from the University of Utah, and both his Ed.M. and Ed.D. from Boston University. Prior to founding Accessible Adventures, Inc., Mark coordinated graduate level teacher training programs at Indiana University, Boston University and Portland State University (1980–1989).

Should Processing Techniques, Such as Framing and Debriefing, Be a Mandatory Part of Facilitation?

Clifford E. Knapp, Ph.D.

Before outlining some of the reasons why my answer to this controversial question is an emphatic "YES", I would like to examine some of the key terms contained in the wording of the question. Only after doing so, will my response make more sense to the reader.

The first word, "should" immediately points to a values question. The Old English root, "sceolde" means owed or obliged to. As adventure educators, we need to examine what we owe to our participants and are obligated to do in our leadership roles. Many professionals would consider this question to be one of moral significance because the answer affects the lives of people entrusted to our care as group facilitators. When we conduct processing sessions, we are obligated to provide physical and emotional safety to the program participants. Skillfully executed processing techniques is one way to provide the safety we owe them.

What are "processing techniques"? I believe there are at least two meanings of the word "processing". Processing 1 occurs in healthy individuals as they internalize and analyze information through sensory input

in order to construct knowledge. Processing 1 takes place when an individual's brain searches for patterns of meaning to be applied in solving problems. When the brain sorts out meaningful input from the environment and connects it to past experiences for later use, we call this "learning". Because this construction of meaning is innate, it can be considered to be an automatic, self-directed human response. Knowledge acquisition can be channeled and focused by our immediate environment, but it cannot be stopped completely. A healthy human brain organizes and categorizes information by registering and retaining it. As facilitators of adventure education programs, we and the participants in a group, can influence how individuals process information, but we can't prevent them from learning on their own.

Processing 2 is the leadership act which is designed to help the participants acquire deeper understandings than those occurring during Processing 1 situations. Facilitators implement adventure-based activities so that participants can gain personal insights and use this new knowledge for solving future problems. According to Luckner and Nadler

(1997, p. 8) and many other professionals, "processing is...an activity that is structured to encourage individuals to plan, reflect, describe, analyze, and communicate about experiences." The underlying theory of learning is grounded in what is called "constructivism" which incorporates the tenet that individuals learn by constructing meanings from new and preceding experiences in a context of supportive social interactions (Luckner and Nadler, 1997, pp.13–14). Many educational researchers and leaders (e.g. Vygotsky, Dewey, and Piaget) recommend the facilitation of learning experiences as a way to encourage developmental change. The theories of cognition advanced by these thinkers involve learning in social settings. They believe the group provides a powerful vehicle for eliciting clarification, justification, and elaboration from the participants. Vygotsky argued that what students do with the assistance of others is "...even more indicative of their mental development than what they can do alone" (Knapp, 1992, p. 33).

Smith, Roland, Havens, and Hoyt (1992) believe that the processing phase of group adventure activities is a critical leadership ingredient. They state: "By merely facilitating a group through an activity and then immediately moving to another activity, [this] makes the program recreational and diversionary. Challenge Education facilitators concur that group discussion needs to follow most activities" (p.156).

In this chapter the term "processing" refers to the Processing 2 definition (facilitator-led group sessions), even though Processing 1 (self-directed meaning making) will usually occur at the same time.

Contained in the main controversial question are two examples of processing skills—framing and debriefing. In the professional literature, the terms "processing

and reflecting" are often used interchangeably. In fact, the term debriefing is often used as a synonym, but in this chapter it will have a more restricted meaning. Here, debriefing refers to the facilitator's attempts to help participants gain meaning from a particular experience *after* completing it.

Because adventure educators generally acknowledge the importance of the experiential learning cycle, let's define this cycle before elaborating on the meaning of process skills. According to Gaw (1979, p. 147) the learning cycle consists of a series of five phases. Each phase defines an objective designed to move the learner toward personal changes in various sensing, thinking, feeling, wanting, or acting dimensions. The phases and associated objectives are:

1. Experiencing—to generate individual and group data through structured activities

2. Sharing—to report the data generated from the experience

3. Interpreting—to make sense of the individual and group data

4. Generalizing—to develop testable hypotheses and abstractions from the data

5. Applying—to bridge the present and the future by planning how the generalizations can be tested in new situations (transfer)

Because adventure educators generally agree that numbers 2–5 make up the main elements of processing, these components are considered to be integral elements of the learning cycle. Even though some adventure educators disagree on the number of stages or use different terminology (see Knapp, 1992, pp. 36–38) for other experiential learning models, they usually use this learning cycle as a guide to implementing most program philosophies. Many professionals contend that merely experiencing activities (without the sharing, interpreting, generalizing, and applying stages) does not qualify as effective experiential education. According to Gaw (1979, p. 147), the use of techniques that enable the facilitators to progressively accomplish the objectives of each stage of the learning cycle is defined as processing.

Two of the techniques used to illustrate how facilitators attempt to guide participants toward the acquisition of new learnings are framing and debriefing. According to Luckner and Nadler (1997, p. 114), framing is defined as setting the stage for what is about to take place in the structured activity. It is also called a briefing session and could include providing information about safety issues, needed equipment, prerequisite skills instruction, explanations of activity rules and goals, or motivational or tone-setting messages. According to Priest and Gass (1997, p. 182) debriefing is the process of facilitating a group discussion concerning the details, analysis, and evaluation of the group's behavior following the completion of the activity.

Luckner and Nadler (1997, pp. 71–75) list twelve leader techniques or interventions commonly used to structure and process experiences: 1) introducing a content focus (framing), 2) examining the group process, 3) eliciting feelings, 4) exploring essential facts or individual thoughts and feelings, 5) seeking specific information, 6) deciding on the sequencing of events, 7) giving direct feedback, 8) offering relevant group dynamics theory, 9) analyzing task maintenance functions, 10) diagnosing possible reasons for group difficulty, 11) helping participants change the meaning they ascribe to events (reframing), 12) and intervening to protect emotional safety. If the facilitator implements any of the techniques (numbers 2–12 above) after a group activity, these are considered to be debriefing skills.

Processing, as it is used in this chapter, refers to a structured event that is usually conducted by the facilitator of a group. One purpose of processing is to assist the participants in making sense out of their planned and unplanned experiences. The leader encourages the verbal sharing of thoughts and feelings in considering emerging human relations dynamics and other issues. Another purpose of processing is for the participants to acquire new knowledge which can be applied later in their personal and/or professional settings back home. There are many techniques that leaders can employ to accomplish this aim, including framing and debriefing.

The word "mandatory" suggests a situation in which a value or rule is to be enforced, either by some external authority or by an internal, personal authority. External authorities in the adventure education field could be the professional organization's certification or accreditation guidelines or ethical conduct codes, the rules and policies of specific public or private organizations, or governmental laws. Internal authorities could be an individual's personal conscience, mental model, or values that guide behavior considered to be right and good. One reason that organizations and governments make certain behaviors mandatory is the belief that some leadership practices are more ethically sound and that all people in the professional community will benefit by following a recommended prescription for proper behavior.

Let's examine the last word in the controversial question—"facilitation." The facilitation role is the primary professional vehicle for helping participants achieve the goals of adventure education. The main purpose of facilitation is to assist the participants in developing their own personal meanings from individual or group experiences. In addition to implementing a variety of processing techniques, facilitators also should possess knowledge and skills in leadership areas such as: 1) helping participants learn more about each other, 2) diagnosing individual and group problems and issues, 3) supporting and maintaining physical and emotional safety, 4) developing supportive norms and guidelines, 5) designing and implementing effective experiences, 6) monitoring agreed-upon goals and objectives, 7) modeling productive behavior in the group, 8) observing, and evaluating group progress, 9) summarizing accomplishments, and 10) conducting group closure activities. Priest and Gass (1997, p. 186) condenses these facilitator roles and responsibilities by listing five "Ds" in sequential order: diagnosis, design, delivery, debriefing, and detachment. They believe these phases represent five important leadership roles for effective facilitators.

Now that the key words of the main question are defined and explained, the points supporting my argument can be more easily understood. Well-qualified facilitators should be required to conduct processing sessions when leading groups because most of their participants will achieve maximum benefits from applying these techniques. Priest and Gass (1997, pp. 178–186) outline the evolution of facilitation techniques in adventure programs since their inception. They describe "six generations" of historical approaches to facilitation. All six approaches are in use today, depending on the facilitators' qualifications and the type of program (therapeutic, educational, or recreational) in which they are employed. They can be used in isolation or combined in various ways to

accomplish the program goals. The first generation involves no debriefing at all after the activity because of the leader's assumption that the experience is powerful enough to "speak for itself". In this approach the participants are left "…to sort out their own personal insights" after the activity (p.181). Priest and Gass state: "This approach is fine as long as you're not concerned with achieving identified or prescriptive intrapersonal and interpersonal goals" (p.181). What responsible organization would choose to ignore these important program goals by not promoting processing sessions? The second generation of facilitation involves the facilitator telling the participants what they have learned from the experience. This is a questionable practice if the facilitator has limited knowledge of what the participants actually learned. Without listening carefully to the participants' expressed thoughts and feelings throughout the experience, the facilitator will not accurately be able to assess what they know. The third generation involves the facilitator guiding the processing only after the experience has been completed (debriefing). This is usually done by asking a series of carefully sequenced questions or by structuring other ways of eliciting feedback from the group. This is the most typical approach to processing used today. The supportive social setting in which processing usually takes place, allows a participant to express thoughts and feelings about what was learned and to also listen to what others have learned. The fourth, fifth, and sixth generations of facilitation involve specific facilitator interventions employed before or during the activity. For example, the facilitator may focus the participants' attention on possible key learnings before conducting the activity or might introduce the activity by using appropriate metaphors (framing) to help them understand the relevance of what they will be asked to do later. The more skilled the facilitators are, the more choices they have in selecting the most appropriate facilitation approaches. The only way that using the first generation approach (letting the experience speak for itself without facilitator intervention) can be justified is in the case of an inexperienced novice facilitator. However, most professionals would agree that unskilled novices should not be given responsibilities for facilitating adventure groups. Caution should be exercised in implementing the second generation approach (having facilitators tell the participants what they have learned) because facilitators may not be able to gather enough data without conducting adequate sharing sessions. The remaining four generations constitute the main tools of effective, well-prepared facilitators. The literature clearly supports the inclusion of these more complex forms of processing in the professional facilitators' repertoires.

Another reason to require that facilitators implement the various components of the experiential learning cycle (experiencing, sharing, interpreting, generalizing, and applying) is because of the important gender issues which sometimes arise in coed groups. Typically, women develop a moral reasoning framework based mostly on nurturing care and relationships in groups. Typically men develop a framework based mostly on justice and rules (Morse 1997, p. 127). When women and men engage in adventure activities together, they sometimes view the world differently. By avoiding a processing component in the learning cycle, gender conflicts and issues may not be satisfactorily resolved. Morse makes this point clearly: "In the absence of active facilitation of this aspect [group dynamics and relationship issues] ...shallow, careless, or even negative communications patterns can often result" (1997, p. 127). Issues of gender are not the only factors that may distort the communication process among individuals. Other issues, such as balancing leadership and followship, expressing thoughts and feelings, deciding when to lead and follow, making cooperative and authoritarian decisions, and defining individual commonalities and differences, can create barriers to community-building if they are not processed effectively.

In summary, processing techniques, such as framing and debriefing, should be a mandatory part of facilitation. If we believe in the validity and power of the experiential learning cycle, we should use it as our guide to facilitating groups. The components of this cycle can direct our practice. If we believe that facilitating activities in group settings will help participants capitalize on the learning potential of experiences and construct meaningful knowledge to help them live a more productive life, we will develop a full range of processing skills and techniques. If we believe that learning is primarily a social enterprise, we will use the power of the group to help participants learn more efficiently. If we believe that facilitators should employ many techniques, including processing skills, we will continue to expand our knowledge and improve how we implement them with participants. If we believe that we can help our participants by leading processing sessions far better than by letting the experience "speak for itself" or by telling them what we think they learned without receiving sufficient feedback, then we will make use of more complex processing strategies and adapt them to meet our specific program philosophies. If we believe that processing experiences will help the participants face and resolve more group communications issues and conflicts than by simply ignoring them, then we will use all of the processing knowledge available in the literature and demonstrated by skilled facilitators.

The challenge of creating a better world through effectively using processing skills in adventure education is ours to accept or reject. My hope is that we will accept the challenge and continue to grow as professionals.

REFERENCES

Gaw, B. A. (1979). Processing questions: An aid to completing the learning cycle. *The 1979 Annual Handbook for Group Facilitators*. La Jolla, CA: University Associates, Inc. 147–153.

Knapp, C. E. (1992). *Lasting Lessons: A Teacher's Guide to Reflecting on Experience*. Charleston, WVA: ERIC Clearinghouse on Rural Education and Small Schools.

Luckner, J. L. & Nadler, R. S. (1997). *Processing The Experience: Strategies to Enhance and Generalize Learning*. (2nd ed.). Dubuque, IA: Kendall/Hunt Publishing Company.

Morse, A. J. (1997). Gender conflict in adventure education: Three feminist perspectives. *The Journal of Experiential Education, 20* 124–129.

Priest, S. & Gass, M. A. (1997). *Effective Leadership in Adventure Programming*. Champaign, IL: Human Kinetics.

Smith, T. E., Roland, C. G. Havens, M. D. & Hoyt, J. A. (1992) *The Theory and Practice of Challenge Education*. Dubuque, IA: Kendall/Hunt Publishing Company.

Should Processing Techniques, Such as Framing and Debriefing, Be a Mandatory Part of Facilitation?

Mark Havens, Ed.D

My "gut" reaction to this question evoked several thoughts and additional questions, some of which include: Do facilitators of experienced based learning (EBL) actually think that participants are incapable of transferring the learning from these experiences to their everyday lives, on their own? While observing many facilitators frame and debrief EBL activities out of context, I thought it would have been better for the participants to process those experiences on their own. If we are obliged to bring closure to an experience, are we not then inhibiting the learning style of people who need more time for reflection?

Fortunately, my mind will take over my "gut" for the rest of this chapter. Mandatory use of framing and debriefing in experience based learning is not necessary and can be inappropriate in certain situations. When I provide an EBL program for a customer or client, I make sure that I "frame" and "debrief" myself first. Additionally, I make sure that I understand what the customer wants and then prepare myself by determining what is my responsibility for transferring learning and what is the participants. I determine and set the boundaries.

AN OVERVIEW

There are three types of EBL programs I offer my clients. These services direct me in how much, if any, I frame or debrief an experience. They include:

Networking—This service is used when the client wants participants to get to know each other better. Typical goals might be: (a) to help new team members get to know each other better, accelerate relationship building, (b) to reinforce a new "theme or strategy" in a company (e.g., encourage sales representatives to go from selling and being knowledgeable of one product to selling and understanding a portfolio of products), or (c) to help people who use English as a second language feel more comfortable speaking in large groups prior to an extended leadership training program.

These networking experiences are usually four to eight hours long with little or no follow-up. Only about 10% of the framing and debriefing is up to me and 90% is up to the participants. My primary responsibility is to provide a safe physical and emotional environment, and of course, reinforce the strategy or theme. I may not frame or debrief any of the activities and if I do, the focus is on the theme of the event.

Enrichment—Enrichment programs use experience based learning activities to reinforce skills, knowledge and attitudes required for effective teaming. Prior to an enrichment experience, a diagnostic process, usually a survey, is necessary to determine the current state of the team. For example, if a team does not have a results-driven structure (e.g., a lack of clear roles or accountabilities), then the EBL activity will highlight either the lack of this characteristic or reinforce this characteristic in the team. The frame and the debrief is centered around the characteristic of the team, not each individual.

Team characteristics, not personal issues, create the boundaries to which I hold the customer and myself when conducting these programs. My responsibility for framing and debriefing is around 50% and the same percentage holds for the participants. I choose activities that will reinforce the teaming skills or concepts based on the data collected from the diagnostic; thus I don't have to resolve specific issues between team members.

Intervention—Experience based learning activities can be used as an intervention process when interpersonal issues between team members are so dysfunctional that they get in the way of the team or group working effectively and efficiently. Typically, interventions are conducted with small working teams. A thorough diagnostic—interviews of everyone involved—is required to determine where to begin. Also, it is imperative that all participants, as well as the facilitator, understand the boundaries for the intervention process. In essence, once the data from the interviews are clarified and agreed upon with the group, the facilitator then chooses, frames and debriefs the EBL activities focusing on the issues raised.

The responsibility is 90% up to the facilitator to provide frames and debriefs that can potentially help the team members raise and resolve issues. Ten percent of the responsibility for frames or debriefs is up to the participants—remember, however, that everyone involved in an intervention needs to be 100% mentally present. Follow up is a requirement for implementing intervention programs or experiences. Issues are purposely raised through experience based learning, so it is imperative to have a method for maintaining a relationship with the group until there is some form of resolution.

Obviously, the boundaries between networking, enrichment and intervention programs are never black and white, the lines can blur. However, it is clear that after an EBL activity in a Networking program, the facilitator should not be focusing the debrief on whether "Joe" feels the same lack of support at work as he just experienced by being mishandled during a "Spider Web" activity. In fact, framing and debriefing can negatively impact the tempo of a Networking pro-

Table 1. A closer look at networking.

Before the Session	In the Moment	After It's Over
clarify customer needs by phone or letter	pay attention to physical, emotional and intellectual safety	follow up usually by letter or phone
clarify logistics		evaluate at the end of the session
meet with leader (if possible)	reframe or refocus around the theme or strategy	keep debriefs focused on concepts or the theme, not individuals
plan the program—usually focused on a theme	pay attention to the energy of the group	
frame activities around theme (if necessary)		do not be afraid to enforce the boundaries if participants want to discuss personal issues with team members in the large group
choose additional staff by appropriate technical and non-technical skills		

Adapted from "When The Bough Breaks...The Group Is Not Responding, Now What Do I Do?," by M.D. Havens & B.B. DeJovine (1987), a paper presented at the Association for Experiential Education, Heartland Regional Conference.

gram and keep the client from meeting his/her goals. It is important to identify what the customer wants, set boundaries around responsibilities, both yours and the customers, and then maintain those boundaries.

Table 1. represents a closer look at the service of Networking and challenges the reader to think about what to focus on *before the session, in the moment* and *after it's over*. More specifically, for the purposes of this Chapter, Table 1. gives direction as to how much framing and debriefing is required on the part of the facilitator. Before the session, make sure that you construct "frames" for the activities centered on the appropriate theme(s) of the session. Remember, however, that it is not necessary to frame each experience.

While the activity or process is happening, you refocus or reframe around the theme only. This is not the appropriate context nor have you been contracted to challenge people individually. Finally, if you debrief, keep

the boundaries intact, encourage the group to talk about the theme or whether they got to know each other better, not whether they feel let down by the group or feel that the leader lacks vision.

Table 2. focuses on the use of experience based learning as an enrichment process—you are enriching or enhancing teaming skills, knowledge or attitudes that are required for the team to work more efficiently and effectively. It is important to collect data to assure that you and the customer have clear objectives for the program. These data will provide you with direction for framing and debriefing the activities or experiences you choose to implement. Listed below are questions I ask participants of a team prior to planning a program (I collect the data using a survey that can be faxed to and from a client assuring confidentiality for each team member.):

1. Does your team understand your fundamental purpose/mission?

Table 2. A closer look at enrichment.

Before the Session	In the Moment	After It's Over
meet with leader to clarify specific goals and objectives	pay attention to physical, emotional and intellectual safety	follow up in person (if possible)
ask contracting questions (e.g. be specific about not resolving issues between team members as a part of this service)	reframe or focus on objectives or clarified data (e.g. the teams' ability to deliver effective feedback to one another)	evaluate with follow up in 2–6 weeks
understand the situation/business the group is in	pay attention to specific objectives	debrief should focus on specific objectives, agreed upon by you and the sponsor
use team effectiveness survey if possible	pay attention to task/maintenance processes	debrief yourself as the facilitator
plan program based on specific objectives and data collected from the survey		
frame activities around objectives (usually skills, knowledge and attitudes related to teaming)		
choose staff accordingly (e.g. knowledge of communication styles, the function of marketing or Total Quality Management)		

Adapted from "When The Bough Breaks...The Group Is Not Responding, Now What Do I Do?," by M.D. Havens & B.B. DeJovine (1987), a paper presented at the Association for Experiential Education, Heartland Regional Conference.

2. Does the team understand and support the direction in which you are heading for the next 3–5 years?

3. Is the structure effective for supporting your long-term goals?

4. Do team members have the technical skills and competence necessary to accomplish your mission?

5. Do team members have the interpersonal skills and competence to accomplish your mission?

6. Are the major processes you use to accomplish your tasks effective and efficient?

7. Are your team members committed to the team's success?

8. Are team member roles and responsibilities clear enough for you to function effectively?

9. Do team members support and collaborate with one another?

10. Does your team leader help you focus by establishing and sticking to a few key priorities?

11. Does your team leader help you develop so you can share in the leadership role?

12. Are team members rewarded for their contributions to the team?

13. Has the team discussed and agreed upon standards of excellence (behavior) to which they hold each other accountable?

14. Is there a high level of trust on your team?

15. Does your team manage conflict well by encouraging and considering all ideas, debating them on their own merit, and staying open to inquiry and influence?

16. Is your team able to continuously improve by sharing positive and constructive feedback on both the quality of your outcomes (task effectiveness) and your approach (process effectiveness)?

You can use this survey in just a yes/no format or have the respondent rate each question, 1 (low) to 5 (high), depending on the extent to which they think the team models the action. When the data is collected and clarified with the team, you can benchmark the data against characteristics of high performing teams. I use characteristics reported by Larson & LaFasto (1989), briefly outlined below:

A high performing team has:

1. A Clear, Elevating Goal

Clear understanding of its objective

A belief that the goal embodies a worthwhile or important result

2. Results-Driven Structure

Clear roles and accountabilities

An effective communication system

Monitoring individual performance and providing feedback

Fact-based judgment

3. Competent Team Members

The necessary technical skills and abilities to achieve the desired objective

The personal characteristics required to achieve excellence while working well with others

4. Unified Commitment

Commitment to team goals over personal goals

Sense of loyalty and dedication to the team

5. Collaborative Climate

Honesty—integrity, no lies, no exaggerations

Openness—a willingness to share and a receptivity to information, perceptions and ideas

6. Standards of Excellence

Establish a set of standards which embrace individual's commitment, motivation, self-esteem and performance

Hold each other accountable

7. External Support and Recognition

Resources needed to do the job

Support by individuals and agencies outside the team

Reward and incentives are clear

8. Principled Leadership

Sustain the vision

Catalyze alignment

Evolve policy and structure.

Once you have collected the data, clarified the results *with* the team and bench marked the data, then you have something concrete in which to plan activities, frames

Table 3. A closer look at intervention.

Before the Session	In the Moment	After It's Over
interview all participants	pay attention to physical, emotional and intellectual safety	mandatory follow up scheduled
stress anonymity of data		follow up with Human Resources Department or leader—better yet, partner with an internal HR professional
stress confidentiality	reframe on specific issues	
clarify data prior to planning agenda	surface behavioral patterns	
understand the situation/ business the group is in	ask group to clarify assumptions (e.g. task, purpose, approach)	debrief around specific issues agreed on by the team
pay attention to contracting	ask group to clarify purpose; "Towards what end?" "How will doing that help you achieve your task?"	debrief yourselves as the facilitators
contract to "adjust the approach"		ask, "so what"?
assess participation readiness of the group	try use of metaphors	
brief around specific issues that the group has agreed to address	it is okay to miss some things— they will come back	
co-facilitate with internal Human Resource Professional or psychologist	stick with issues at the expense of agenda	

Note. Adapted from "When The Bough Breaks…The Group Is Not Responding, Now What Do I Do?," by M.D. Havens & B.B. DeJovine (1987), a paper presented at the Association for Experiential Education, Heartland Regional Conference.

and debriefs around. While the EBL program is underway, your job is to refocus around the skills, knowledge or attitudes that you have targeted as developmental areas for the team, not highlight issues between team members in the group. The debriefs, as well, should focus on those teaming skills that are the focus of the session. During enrichment programs it is tempting, as a facilitator, to raise issues that you see inherent in the group.

However, you must have the discipline necessary to keep yourself and the group committed to the boundaries established and agreed upon prior to the program.

If critical issues arise and the client agrees to it, you can document the issues/ concerns and contract to focus on them during an intervention program.

Table 3. represents a closer look at using EBL as an intervention process. It is mandatory that you complete a diagnostic process prior to planning frames, debriefs and activities. I recommend interviewing all team members prior to the program. This provides a better chance at understanding the issues on the team and will give you assurance that everyone involved understands the boundaries and ground rules of the program. It is recommended that you partner with someone internally (e.g. Human Resource Professional for the team) to ensure that there is on-going follow-up after the initial EBL program is complete.

Once the interview data is collected, it is recommended that you review the data with the leader so there are no surprises. Then, clarify the data with the entire team and agree on what issues should be addressed. Now you have the necessary guide for planning frames, debriefs and activities. It is your responsibility to provide the opportunity for the team, through frames, debriefs and EBL activities to raise and resolve issues that are getting in the way of the team working effectively and efficiently day to day.

The challenge in doing interventions is keeping the group focused on the issues and having the courage to raise and resolve them. You must, however, keep physical and emotional safety in the forefront of everyone's mind. A plan for follow-up should be contracted for and planned up front so there is a guarantee that the team members will have long term support for resolving personal and team issues.

FINAL THOUGHTS

Medical technology has surpassed the level of moral discussion around what physicians should and should not do with it. Otherwise, physicians have the technology now to possibly clone human beings, but physicians and the public at large have not put enough energy into the ethical dialogue that would provide guidance for how far physicians can go in using the available technology.

Professionals who use experience based learning are in a similar situation. A great deal of energy goes into designing new challenge course elements, obtaining the latest in portable materials for indoor adventure use, and learning a more recent version of an EBL activity. On the other hand, we have limited discussions on the boundaries for framing and debriefing the experiences that result from the materials and activities we covet. We tend to be activity focused versus process focused.

Mandatory framing and debriefing, as a part of facilitating adventure or experiential learning, is premature if not dangerous. The model I outlined in this Chapter—Networking, Enrichment, Intervention—in itself is not scientific or researched. Quite frankly, it is a way to make sense out of all the services I offer customers and helps guide me and the client so we know the boundaries of the service. Until we put as much energy into the non-technical aspect of our work as we do the technical, we will find ourselves in the same boat as physicians—we have plenty of tools, we just don't agree or understand how far to go with them. Mandating the use of framing and debriefing in the use of adventure learning, would be the same as mandating potential disaster!

There is some evidence that people tend to remember interrupted tasks better than completed ones (Weisbord, 1987). This is important for us, as facilitators, as we have to have confidence that people are capable of and will continue to think about and debrief their unresolved issues—themselves. I think that we are insecure at times in the services we offer, which compels us to provide exquisite frames and serious debriefs in order to validate the effectiveness of our programs. I am just as proud of the Networking programs—sometimes called an event or recreation—I provide as I am the Intervention programs. Creating a safe environment for adults to be playful and get to know each other better is a valuable service.

Finally, I think that facilitators of adventure and experiential learning can be very judgmental of their clients. What I mean is that there seems to be an inherent need to impose personal philosophies such as (a) "I need to help these people who work too much and have their priorities misplaced," (b) "I need to rescue these people from the tyranny of big business," or (c) "I need lecture them on being less results oriented." This paradigm can cause facilitators to work too hard at creating the "right" frame or debrief and alienate the customer. Until we discuss, struggle with and agree on basic boundaries for this practice, mandatory use of framing and debriefing in facilitating adventure learning is a step in the wrong direction.

REFERENCES

Havens, M. D. & DeJovine, B. B. (1997, March). *When The Bough Breaks...The Group's Not Responding, Now What Do I Do?* Paper presented at the Association For Experiential Education Heartland Region Conference, Camp Tecumsah, IN.

Larson, C. E. & La Fasto, F. M. (1989). *TeamWork: What must go right/what can go wrong.* Newbury Park, CA: Sage.

Weisbord, M.R. (1987). *Productive workplaces: Organizing and managing for dignity, meaning, and community.* San Francisco: Jossey-Bass.

CHAPTER 11

Is the Process of Experiential Learning (Outside the Classroom) Practical in Higher Education Settings?

YES PERSPECTIVE: 1. Iain Stewart-Patterson, B.P.E., M.ED.

                        2. Tom Puk, Ph.D.

NO PERSPECTIVE: Scott Wurdinger, Ph.D.

This chapter provides two YES perspectives as well as a NO perspective. The second YES response offers a point of view specifically regarding teacher education programs.

Iain Stewart-Patterson, BPE (Calgary), MEd (Calgary) is a fully certified mountain guide (UIAGM) with the Association of Canadian Mountain Guides. He has over 20 years experience ski touring, mountaineering, ice and rock climbing. He has been on expeditions to Nepal, Peru, Mexico, and Alaska as a team member, guide, or leader. On technical rock and waterfall ice terrain, he has completed over 30 first ascents. Iain is currently the program coordinator of the Adventure Guide Diploma at the University College of the Cariboo, where he teaches a combination of theory and activity courses.

Dr. Puk is an Associate Professor in the Faculty of Education, Lakehead University, Thunder Bay, Ontario, Canada. He was one of the original developers of Project D.A.R.E (Development through Adventure, Responsibility, and Education), an outdoor program for delinquents started in 1971. He currently teaches (among other things) Outdoor Experiential Education programs as part of a teacher certification, Bachelor of Education program. He has conducted extensive research on self-directed learning and inquiry and is currently conducting research to link quantum theory with curriculum development and also the role of nurturing in teaching and learning.

 **Scott Wurdinger** is a Professor in the Department of Educational Leadership and Coordinator of the Experiential Graduate Program at Minnesota State University in Mankato, MN. He has been teaching adventure education since 1976, and has worked for a variety of organizations including adventure programs such as Outward Bound, corporate adventure training programs, psychiatric hospitals, and colleges and universities. Dr. Wurdinger is the author of *Philosophical Issues in Adventure Education* and is an active member of the Association for Experiential Education (AEE) and the Association for Challenge Course Technology (ACCT). He reviews articles for the *Journal of Experiential Education* and serves on the Professional Review Committee for the ACCT. He lives in Mankato, MN with his wife, Annette and daughters, Madeline and Lauren.

Is the Process of Experiential Learning (Outside the Classroom) Practical in Higher Education Settings?

Iain Stewart-Patterson, B.P.E., M.Ed.

INTRODUCTION

The answer to this question is most definitively "yes". The key word to examine is "practical". It is certainly desirable; so why not make it practical? The many benefits to experiential learning have been acknowledged over the years by a multitude of learned scholars. "In what I have said I have taken for granted the soundness of the principle that education in order to accomplish its ends both for the individual learner and for society must be based upon experience" (Dewey, 1938, p. 89). There are factors which on initial inquiry, seem to limit the practicality of conducting adventure education classes in an experiential manner. These factors include: instructor abilities, time, number of students, student—instructor ratio, the reality of role-playing, the level of control retained by the instructor, and the post-secondary grading process. There are ways to overcome all of these obstacles. However, it requires a rethinking of how we conduct business (Wurdinger, 1996).

A philosophical question as to the nature of schooling must first be considered. Should knowledge be acquired for the sake of knowledge, or should it be acquired for the ability to apply it in a real world situation? Are we nurturing the mind, or preparing it to deal with day to day challenges? (Jernstedt, 1986). This paper will focus on the development and education of outdoor leaders. There are both specific job skills and generic employment skills that need to be addressed in an outdoor leadership training program. Needless to say the majority of these skills will be applied in a job setting that is wilderness oriented. The use of an outdoor classroom is required to appropriately prepare students for these challenges. When the Adventure Guide Diploma at the University College of the Cariboo, in Kamloops, British Columbia was first proposed to an industry symposium, the response from a highly placed member of one of the foremost guide associations was summed up as, "You can't train guides inside the walls of a college. You have got to be outside!!" Although it seemed a very negative comment at the time, there is some truth to the matter. To produce the best outdoor leadership training possible in a higher education setting, an experiential based curriculum using both indoor and outdoor classroom sessions, must be employed.

DEFINITION

The Association for Experiential Education (AEE) has established the following definition of experiential education. "A process through which a learner constructs knowledge, skill, and value from direct experience" (Luckmann, 1996, p.7). Some of the key principles of experiential education practices that are applicable to this topic include:

- Experiential learning occurs when carefully chosen experiences are supported by reflection, critical analysis, and synthesis.

- Learners are engaged intellectually, emotionally, socially, soulfully, and/or physically. This involvement produces a perception that the learning task is authentic.

- The results of the learning are personal and form the basis for future experience and learning.

- Because the outcomes of experience cannot be totally predicted, the educator and the learner may experience success, failure, adventure, risk taking and uncertainty.

- The design of the learning experience includes the possibility to learn from natural consequences, mistakes, and successes (Luckmann, 1996, p.7).

Experiential learning can be considered both a process and an outcome. Carver (1996, p.9) describes experience as involving "any combination of senses, emotions, physical condition, and cognition." She cites four principles which can be considered essential to the experiential learning process. They are: authenticity, which refers to the real-life experiences that provide relevant meaningful learning; active learning, which refers to the level of participation the students have in constructing the learning process; drawing on student experiences; and providing mechanisms for connecting experience to future opportunity. Students are more than empty vessels. Each individual's experience both prior to the event and during it are used to create learning that is unique to that individual. The most common method of connecting these experiences to future events is critical reflection.

Wagner (1986, p. 218) proposes that "the more general tradition of learning from experience has found practical expression in three different models of formal instruction: group process, simulation games, and field experience". Groups and group dynamics are certainly a major part of the outdoor experience. From Outward Bound to Everest expeditions, the dynamics of group behaviour are ample breeding ground for learning to take place. Simulation-games are approximations of reality that use a peer group leadership setting in place of real clients. The intent is for the student to be able to transfer the learning that has occurred beyond the context of the simulation.

BENEFITS OF AN EXPERIENTIAL LEARNING PROCESS

In a study conducted by Jernstedt (1986), students who participated in optional experiential labs associated with an academic English course were found to perform better on later exams than those who did not participate. The students did not know any more facts, they just more fully understood the concepts. The lab component formed a bridge for the transfer of course content to real life experiences after the course. "Students who use information they are trying to learn, who challenge and grapple with their new knowledge, or who use it to solve new problems, tend to learn more effectively than students who passively read, memorize, or merely absorb that to which they have been exposed" (Jernstedt, 1986, p.110).

Experiential educators have, at times, been considered the equivalent of cult members. They are firm believers in a process that has not achieved universal acceptance. Some have been evangelical in their persuasion of others. Yet there is a distinct reluctance on the part of non-believers to embrace the process. Hendricks (1994) suggests that researchers have only recently developed the tools necessary to more fully measure the effectiveness of the experiential learning process. Perhaps these future research endeavors will persuade more educators to adopt experiential methods.

THE FACTORS THAT LIMIT THE PRACTICALITY OF AN EXPERIENTIAL LEARNING PROCESS.

There is no shortage of excuses for not employing experiential learning processes in the post-secondary arena. Given that the status quo is one of a didactic oriented, classroom-bound environment, it takes a motivated educator to go beyond the norm. However, all the following roadblocks to the practical implementation of outside the classroom experiential learning can be overcome.

Instructor Abilities

The ability of the instructor to create an environment that is conducive to learning ex-

perientially is key to the whole process of education. The personal practical knowledge of the instructor "is a particular way of reconstructing the past and the intentions for the future to deal with the exigencies of a present situation" (Connelly and Clandinin, 1988, p.25). Not all instructors have learned how to create an educational environment that permits experiential learning inside the classroom, let alone outside the classroom. This is particularly apparent in universities that hire faculty based on their content specific academic credentials and their research publications, rather than their ability to teach. There is a tendency among educators to teach in a style that is appropriate for their own personal learning style and to use teaching methods that they, themselves, have experienced as a learner. Good teachers have had good teachers as role models. The implication here is to break the cycle of ineffective teaching.

If the group process model is used, as described by Wagner (1986), the instructor's ability to handle group dynamics is critical. The problem becomes one of integrating the group dynamics with the experiential learning process, where the needs and desires of an evolving group process must be addressed. This usually requires the instructor to have an advanced level of facilitation skills to ensure participant safety, because the students' psychological well-being can be severely compromised when an instructor oversteps her ability to protect the students from each other, as emotions rise and conflicts emerge.

Time

Direct instruction, predominantly through the use of lectures, is a time honored favorite for the delivery of a large quantity of material in a short period of time. It simply takes longer to foster an environment that stimulates experiential learning, and to allow the process to evolve to its natural end point. Direct instruction is a time effective method of teaching; or is it? For three hours per week, for thirteen weeks the students diligently copy down notes. A week or so later they spew it all back in a three hour marathon of exam writing. The course is done; and they may have learned something. A month later, six months later, six years later, how much do they remember? What is the long term retention compared to the curriculum that integrates an experiential approach to learning? Dewey (1938) suggests that the problem is one of the subject matter being learned in isolation. "But it was segregated when it was acquired and hence is so disconnected from the rest of experience that it is not available under the actual conditions of life" (p. 48).

The Number of Students and Ratio of Students to Instructors

The sheer volume of students may limit the quality and quantity of learning opportunities. Classes that are too large will dilute the level of interaction with the instructor. The flipside to this scenario is that there can be a synergistic critical mass when dealing with advanced students who have significant levels of previous experience in outdoor activities. They not only learn from the instructor, but also from fellow students. For example, when the course objective is leadership, how many students can realistically get a chance to assume the mantle of leadership for a significant duration? Yet, those who do, benefit immensely.

The ratio of students to instructors is related to the numbers game. This ratio must be lowered in order to increase each individual's time on task. More instructors must be hired which results in an increase in cost.

There needs to be a balance achieved between cost and effective delivery of the course. Take the example of ski touring, a six to one student instructor ratio results in each student spending an average of one hour per day in the leadership position. This produces seven hours of leading time in a 45 hour course. Having a group of eight reduces the leading time to five hours; while a group of three doubles it to 14 hours.

Role Playing

A mock leadership role, with peers acting as clients is not the same as having real clients. Rotating the lead among a group of peers provides an opportunity for peer feedback at the leadership level. Although there is much to be said for observing and critiquing a fellow student, it does not allow the apprentice leader to get the feel for real client reactions to the proffered leadership style. The two most glaring examples are that of fitness and technical skill proficiency. The peer group is likely to be fairly homogenous in terms of fitness and skills. This contrasts sharply with real clients who may not have the opportunity to partake in outdoor activities on a frequent basis.

There is also the issue of peer group dynamics. Honesty, ego and the level of trust within the group play roles in the quality and credibility of peer feedback. For example, the question: "How is the pace? Is it too fast?" asks the student leader hopefully, as he/she breaks trail through knee deep snow and struggles with the route finding in the steep trees of Roger's Pass, deep in the Selkirk Range of British Columbia. The leadership role produces stress for the participant leaders who are less skilled or less fit than their peers. Their energy is being diverted into personal survival mode rather than into helping their "guests" have a quality outdoor experience. The verbal response from the peer group is a non-descript, "Fine". The underlying meaning, tone and body language are "Stop holding up my learning opportunity. Get your butt in gear. We will not complain about how slow you are going in front of the instructor. We will pretend to be good happy clients. Also, there is a better way to go, but it is your leading experience at the moment, so we will be quiet." In the event of a rest break being called by the tired leader, real guests would be appreciative of the break, while the peer group may be frustrated at the thought of its learning experience being compromised by the presence of a weaker peer and downgraded to the lowest common denominator.

The outdoor leader must develop a refined sense of the level of comfort that the client is experiencing. This can best be achieved through interaction with real clients. There are many subtle indicators of client satisfaction that a leader needs to pick up on. Are they upbeat and talking, or quiet and reserved? Are they sweating, breathing hard, pale, or flushed? Are they taking notice of their surroundings? Are they aware of the environmental hazards?

Control

The instructor must be willing to relinquish control of the curriculum to allow students the opportunity to construct their own meaning of the experience. The AEE definition of experiential education, refers to a lack of predictability in the outcome and the possibility to learn from mistakes. With regards to instructor control, there is a fine line to walk in an outdoor adventure setting. Given the severity of the natural consequences in many adventure pursuits, some errors may be too serious to relinquish control to the learner. Needless to say, the death or injury of a learner in an experiential education setting may be too high a price to pay. However, if we eliminate risk completely do we guarantee the death of the soul? (Unsoeld, 1985, p.112). The instructor needs to provide a safety net without appearing to do so. Nonetheless, a student attitude of, "If I do anything unsafe, the instructor will step in and take over" may develop. While this may be workable in the short term, it has major ramifications post-course, as it creates dependency and bad habits.

Grading

The greatest roadblock to creating an experiential learning environment in a post-secondary setting is the institution's need, and to some extent the students' needs, for grades. Traditional higher education settings inhibit the use of experiential education. "If knowledge is constructed by the learner, then how does the teacher evaluate this knowledge and place a letter grade on it, and what is the feasibility of providing direct experience for every student in a 50 minute class?" (Wurdinger, 1996, p.60). The summative marking process works against the process of experiential education. How many university courses have a class after the final exam to provide a further learning opportunity and to promote the continuity of experience?

Ongoing feedback from the instructor is instrumental to the coached learning process. End-of-course personal interviews provide an opportunity to summarize the learning that has occurred. A letter grade alone provides meagre feedback. Feedback through a personal interview, without applying a letter grade or mark breakdown does not satisfy the students' needs for the quantifiable end result that the previous twelve or more years of education has brought him or her to intrinsically desire. A combination of ongoing instructor feedback and end of course personal interviews can create a potent tool for learning.

Prescott College, in Prescott Arizona, has used a format called authentic assessment for many years (V. Savage, Personal Communication, March 29, 1998). A learning contract, which forms the basis for assessment, is created with each student. The final written evaluation is based on the student's "competency" in the subject matter. Perhaps this is a viable alternative solution to the conundrum of post-secondary grading of experiential learning.

PAVING THE ROAD TO SUCCESS— WAYS TO MAKE IT HAPPEN

The Development of Generic Problem Solving Skills

There are many things we should be doing to prepare the student for complex decision making in a constantly changing environment. By inextricably linking the acquisition of knowledge with its application, we are able to train leaders to adapt to changing conditions.

> The profession of guiding involves decision-making and application of techniques in circumstances where the number of variables and combination of factors produce an infinite number of potential scenarios. There are seldom right or wrong answers in guiding. Guides must be prepared to modify techniques, change approach, and make judgments based on what is required, to the best of their knowledge, at a given time and place (Klassen, 1996, p. iii).

There is a need to focus on a generic problem solving process, rather than a specific action-reaction oriented event. "The most effective learning comes when the student, during the original learning, engages in the behavior which will later be used as a test or example of the success of that learning" (Jernstedt, 1986 p.110). Behaviors which have been successful in the past will provide templates for future decisions, but cannot be blindly applied in the hope that there is sufficient similarity between the two events.

Application time is critical. On a seven day long rock climbing course, the instructor is hard pressed to: explain and demonstrate, allow for practice time, and then evaluate the learning of each new technique. In the big picture, more application time is needed. Logged activity days are one way to achieve it. A further two week practice session with ongoing coaching and feedback from an instructor will effectively help the students internalize and consolidate the skills to become part of their personal practical knowledge.

Getting Inside the Students' Heads

If we believe that the learning occurs because the students are able to construct knowledge, skill and value from direct experience, then we must develop an understanding of what the students' perceptions of the experience have been. We must adapt our teaching style to the ongoing and changing needs of our learners. To do this we need formative feedback from our class. Brookfield (1996) offers us a format for achieving this; he calls it the critical incident questionnaire (CIQ). Here students fill out a form at the end of each week or session in which they describe the most poignant aspects of the day's or week's events. The initial submission is anonymous, due to the perceived power differential between students and instructors, as it is important for the students to have an anonymous method of communicating their feedback. But a course-end summary from each student, which includes his/her identity, provides a means of ascertaining student participation.

Letter writing to the instructor is a variation on the above exercise, which provides an opportunity for the students to reflect on the course material and engage in a professional discourse at a personal level. This is an interactive process, which can lead to growth for both the students and the instructor. The objective is to involve the students more fully, both in the specific subject matter and the way the course fits into the program and it helps the instructor to better understand the issues from a student's perspective. Having the letters as a graded component of the course is a double-edged sword. On the positive side, the instructor is able to respond to each individual's queries. The flip side is that it may not be the emancipating exercise that it should be; the anonymous entry allows for a more open expression of student feedback.

Instructor Modeling of the Desired Outcomes

The instructor demonstrates behaviors, such as the decision making process, in a real setting (i.e. route selection in hazardous terrain). Should we cross the avalanche slope? Where shall we cross it? How do we manage the group as we cross it? An important part of the process is that the instructor is able to communicate the thought process (Clement, 1997). "This is what I am thinking here...These are the factors that I am considering..." This verbal thinking provides a "concrete expression of what it means to grapple intellectually with a

difficult concept" (Jernstedt, 1986, p.112). The most difficult aspect to communicate is the intuitive, sixth sense of danger. "This slope does not feel right. It might avalanche. Let's get off it now!" How do we know, let alone communicate this to our students?

Storytelling can also be used to illuminate the instructor's prior learning. The explanation and analysis of events previously dealt with by the instructor can form the basis for vicarious learning of risk avoidance and management strategies. A previously dealt with crisis or emergency can be posed as a question to students. "This is the scene. What would you do?" This is followed by a discussion of the actual events. It is important to differentiate between what actually happened and what would have been the "best" or ideal solution.

Instructors not only need to model the desired outcomes, but they must also have the required training and experience to facilitate the ongoing group dynamics. This may mean taking additional training courses.

Integration of Courses

The creation of a holistic program will address a greater breadth of student needs. The team teaching of a number of course titles as an integrated unit would bring together the skills and teaching styles of a number of instructors in a collaborative effort, which would provide linkage between related program aspects. By establishing links between related theory and practical aspects of the program, the students can see the interrelation of the various courses within the program of study. For example: a. First aid scenarios can be used for leadership practice. b. Risk management plans can be developed for activity courses. c. Food training can be integrated into trip planning and client care in the field. An entire integrative package could be developed where the students would design an instructional session, develop a budget, put together a business plan, lesson plans, a risk management plan, and a marketing plan; after which, they would deliver the package and reap the rewards.

Design the Program Around the Process.

Budgeting for an outside the classroom experiential process is essential because competition for higher education government and private funds is intense. Providing a rationale for expensive experiential programs requires a well thought out and persuasive proposal. It is all too easy to blame the budget for our instructional and program related shortcomings. Scheduling the appropriate time frames for the experiential events to take place is just as important. The standard university format of five or six semester length courses per term does not allow much latitude in the non-traditional delivery of learning events. All the courses within the program need to be scheduled together. If all the courses are taught in a block format, then the experiential learning format can be an integral part of the process. In most cases the problem then becomes one of creating options for the students. If everyone takes every course, scheduling is easy.

Prior Learning Assessment

Prior Learning Assessment (PLA), or advanced placement, is a relatively recent tool to be integrated into post secondary education. A natural extension of experiential learning within the confines of the educational institution; credit can be given for life experiences that have led to demonstrable learning. This truly is experiential learning that has oc-

curred outside of the classroom. However, there is a vast difference between experience and learning. There is an oft repeated quote that "Good judgment is the result of experience. And experience is the result of poor judgment" (Unknown), but not all experiences result in learning and growth. For example, negative-event feedback occurs when a decision that is made results in a non event. A slope is assessed as having a stable snowpack. It is crossed and it does not slide. Therefore, the right decision was made, or was it? "The belief that all genuine education comes about through experience does not mean that all experiences are genuinely or equally educative. Experience and education cannot be directly equated to each other. For some experiences are mis-educative" (Dewey, 1938, p.25). The widespread implementation and utilization of PLA is still in its infancy, but it certainly provokes thought as to what and how experiential learning can take place.

CONCLUSION

"What we must do is increase the number and quality of ways in which the developing mind can encounter and grapple with the worldly embodiment of its expanding knowledge"(Jernstedt, 1986, p.111). Not only is the process of experiential learning practical in higher education settings; it is highly recommended due to its emphasis on the integration of complex decision-making skills with the application of technical outdoor skills. Clearly, we can celebrate a diversity of educational approaches and still create a program of study that provides the students with a learning opportunity which encompasses a complex multitude of skills. All too often a scarcity of the almighty dollar prevents programs from including experiential learning components in the curriculum. The program must be initially designed with the intent of including experiential learning. The obstacles are more easily overcome when they are anticipated, rather than reacted to. It is a rare educator who has the foresight to envision the difficulties to be surmounted and the foresight to do something about it.

REFERENCES

Brookfield, S. (1996). Experiential pedagogy: Grounding teaching in students' learning. *The Journal of Experiential Education, 19*(2), 62–68.

Carver, R. (1996). Theory for practice: A framework for thinking about experiential education. *The Journal of Experiential Education, 19*(1), 8–13.

Clement, K. (1997). The Psychology of Judgment for Outdoor Leaders. *Proceedings of the 1996 International Conference on Outdoor Recreation and Education (ICORE)*, 45–51.

Connelly, E. M. & Clandinin, D. J. (1988). *Teachers as Curriculum Planners*. New York, NY. Teachers College Press.

Dewey, J. (1938). *Experience and Education*. New York, NY: MacMillan.

Hendricks, B. (1994). *Improving evaluation in experiential education* ERIC Clearinghouse on Rural Education and Small Schools. (ERIC Document Reproduction Service No. ED 376 998).

Jernstedt, G. C. (1986). Experiential components in academic courses. In R. Kraft & J. Kielsmeier (Eds.), *Experiential Education and the Schools* (pp. 109–117).

Klassen, K. (Ed.). (1996). *Technical and professional guidelines*. Banff, AB. Association of Canadian Mountain Guides.

Luckmann, C. (1996). Defining experiential education. *The Journal of Experiential Education, 19*(1) 6–7.

Unsoeld, J. (1985). Education at its peak. In R. Kraft & M. Sakofs (Eds.), *The Theory of Experiential Education, 2nd ed* (pp. 108–122).

Wagner, J. (1986). Integrating the traditions of experiential learning in internship education. In R. Kraft & J. Kielsmeier (Eds.), *Experiential Education and the Schools* (pp. 218–225).

Wurdinger, S. (1996). The theory and pedagogy of experiential education: A critical look at teaching practices. *The Journal of Experiential Education, 19*(2) 60–61.

Is the Process of Experiential Learning (Outside the Classroom) Practical in Higher Education Settings?

Tom Puk, Ph.D.

This article proceeds from the following perspective: I am referring to teacher education programs that are part of a university degree program. I also at times differentiate between experiential learning in general and outdoor experiential education programs. Wurdinger (1997) describes experiential education as a "learning process" (p.37) and as such can be used within traditional school subjects, either inside the classroom or outside. I use the term outdoor experiential education to describe this problem-solving learning process when it is applied in natural settings (rather than for example a school yard or an urbanized setting) and when it utilizes interdisciplinary subject-matter. I also describe outdoor experiential education as having distinct educational goals, such as being able to deal with ambiguity and uncertainty that are inherently found in natural settings. [Although the term "wilderness-based" experiential education (Hunt, 1994, p. 3) might be used in place of "outdoor" experiential education, the degree of "wilderness" would still be problematic]. Due to the parameters of the question, I do not refer to experiential education conducted within the

regular classroom (for example, Simmons, 1995; Warren, 1988), nor constructivist learning in general (DeLay, 1996).

The first task required to debate the issue of practicality is to find examples of such programs in teacher education programs. Raffan (1995) suggests that there are "very few teacher training institutions that offer specific programs for preparing experiential educators" and suggests the Association for Experiential Education Schools and Colleges Directory (1995) as a source for his claim. A current review of the literature would also seem to confirm this assertion. There are a limited number of references in the literature to teacher training programs that involve experiential education and/or outdoor experiential education. This paucity of programs (at least described in the literature) may provide some indication that there are practical challenges involved in developing such courses. As Raffan points out, "experiential education…is almost never elevated to the status of a statutory subject, like mathematics, or reading" (p.117). Some journal articles describe experiences that are a portion of a course rather than a course devoted entirely to experiential and/or outdoor experiential learning. For example, Mungo (1983) describes a pre-service field experience program in which students locate in diverse cultural/ethnic communities in order to experience cultural diversity prior to their first practice teaching. Hastie (1994) describes a weekend adventure experience that third year pre-service students engaged in as part of their physical education teacher training program. Still others (for example, Gilsdorf, 1995) describe workshops that either pre-service or in-service teachers participate in.

I would go further than Raffan's assertion (1995) to suggest that there are even fewer institutions that offer specific programs for preparing academics (i.e., teachers of the teachers) to develop and teach experiential education and/or outdoor experiential education in teacher training programs. Part of the problem, as he points out, is that the institutional infrastructure required to train teachers in experiential education is relatively young. One problem with this situation is that the few teacher training programs that offer experiential education depend upon the energies of a few people. There is an ebb and flow nature to such programs as these few people come and go, as their energies wax and wane. This has to be a practical consideration for any administrator in creating such a program. You can always find many qualified people to teach English or physical education, etc., in a tenure track position in a teacher training program. It is not as easy to find people to teach in outdoor experiential programs with the same level of qualifications (the assumption being made is that the teacher training program is being operated in a university and that therefore the tenure track position would normally require a doctorate). Once these key people leave, the administration is left with a program that

requires that they find a person with unique experiences and qualifications. It is understandable that administrators might be hesitant to make those initial forays into such a program.

Ironically, it would seem that although Dewey (1969) first spoke of experiential education in terms of using it in the school curriculum (Plato first spoke of learning through experience in philosophical terms, Wurdinger, 1997), it has for some time been associated with adventure and challenge, usually associated with the wilderness, and has only recently begun to come full circle as experiential education returns to its origin, that is, the school curriculum. One determinant of whether something (experiential education) is "practical" or not is its suitability to be used in a specific context (in the curriculum of a teacher training program). That is, does it "work" and what do the people involved think about its usefulness?

Two of the courses I teach as part of a Bachelor of Education, preservice teacher education program at Lakehead University, Ontario, involve curriculum and instruction in geography. Most students are at least 22 years of age or older. Many are in their 30's, some are in their 40's. Some are in a consecutive, one year program and some are in the fourth year of a concurrent program. Many have been out of school for awhile, either working or traveling. A few either have a master's degree or are working on one. In other words, these students are for the most part mature adults in a program beyond the undergraduate level. Both of these courses emphasize both a constructivist and experiential philosophy and practice of education. During the very first class of the year in each of these courses (both fall and winter), without any prior warning, students are immediately sent outside in pairs in order to gather certain geographical information at different sites around campus. Lakehead University is fortunate in having a river, lake, dam and hiking trails right on campus. Students plan their own route for this tour and move at their own pace as they visit predetermined sites marked on a map. They acquire information such as how fast the river is flowing or how deep the ice is, the high water mark of the river and the elevation of certain land marks (estimations), compass directions, the purpose of the dam, etc. They are also asked to imagine what they would find different about the various sites they visit if they had made this tour in 1900. Few of these students know the campus very well; for some it is their first day on campus. This is their first course experience with the concept of place, that is, where they are and how they fit into their local environment and more generally in life. Once all the students have left the classroom, I then go out on the "route" and meet the various pairings as they are gathering their data. I also ask them ambiguous questions that help them to start to reflect on knowledge that they might have previously thought could only be found in books or that I might have provided for them, such as what geography is.

At the end of the year, many students remark in their personal narratives on the positive impression this first session had on them. Overwhelmingly, students say they value learning about and experiencing experiential education during their teacher training. They are pleasantly shocked out of their otherwise blase understanding that learning is not about going from class to class, sitting and listening/recording what the professor says is worth knowing about, or even what knowledge is. It reminds them that geography is not something theoretical that is found in books and on the blackboard or that comes

from the mouths of "experts". Geography is real and is beyond the classroom. The experience also begins a process whereby they come to understand that knowledge about geography is constructed on a daily basis through their own experiences. There are no universal truths found in textbooks. They construct their own understanding of geography. These two courses are examples of experiential learning (out of classroom) within a regular course offering.

> From the moment I first stepped into this geography class the underlying theme has been that geography is indeed "out there". I remember my very first day in this class, feeling lost and confused when I was immediately thrust into a situation where I had no idea what was going on...I knew right away that this course was going to be something special and I was indeed going to learn a lot (1998, student course summary).

> From day one we were introduced to a different type of learning. At first I didn't like the activity, I wanted more instruction and I wanted to know the outline of the course. I wanted to know the assignments and tests I had to do to complete the course, to get my "A". I realize now that I felt that way because all of my undergraduate years were about knowing what hoops I had to jump through to achieve my degree. Our outside activity on the first day showed me that geography can be about taking your students outside of the confines of the classroom and letting them practice the discipline rather than just hear about it (1998, student course summary).

> The experiential aspect of this course made it different from all of my other courses. The first day really set the tone for that experience. Exploring a strange new campus, with a new person [students were paired with another person they did not know] was a powerful way to interact with both the human and physical parts of geography. The tone

was then followed up by [the instructor] saying "geography is out there". "Geography is out there" was then the underlying theme that was carried throughout the course (1998, student course summary).

The practical issues that the instructor has to deal with in such an experience is that students have to be back in 90 minutes for their next class and that they don't get lost. Also, as with any program such as this, it takes more energy on the part of the instructor to organize the lesson and then actually go out of the building into the outdoors. It is not as convenient as staying indoors, going from classroom to office to classroom, especially at -35 degrees F (however I suspect most outdoor educators thrive on this). The practical consideration is that the instructor has to have had a life-time of such experiences in order to have developed a comfortableness, ability and willingness to spend the amount of extra energy it requires to take student-teachers outside the classroom.

Faculties of education are in the business of trying to teach people how to teach. Quite often, however, this is done by examining the theory of how to teach as an entirely mental exercise. What better place to teach about experiential education than in a faculty/school of education and what better way to do so than in an experiential manner! Utilizing the outdoors requires some flexibility in terms of the time involved and getting back on time, in order that students can attend other courses. Quite often this kind of scheduling requirement can be built into the timetable.

One of the oldest Canadian teacher education programs involving outdoor experiential education (as described in the literature) has been offered by Queen's University, Faculty of Education, Ontario, Canada. This quality program has been embedded in a Bachelor of Education program for the

past three decades (Raffan & Horwood, 1988). However, it has changed over time, changes I would suggest that mostly have to do with financial pressures, personnel and safety issues. The program at one point was a Co-operative Program in Outdoor and Experiential Education (Horwood, 1985) lasting approximately 16 months, well beyond the usual 8 month teacher education program offered elsewhere in Ontario. Today the program has diminished in length and scope while trying to maintain a quality program. One of the defining components of the program has been the night hike. In the early 1980's, the night hike lasted until 2–3 a.m., travelling across some very rugged and potentially dangerous terrain. By 1988, this had been scaled back so that students usually finished by 9 p.m. (Raffan & Horwood, 1988). One of the reasons given by the authors for this change in the nature of the night hike was safety considerations.

Safety is certainly an issue in terms of the practicality of outdoor experiential programs in teacher education. In regular classroom education, students are safely attached to their desks. By the very nature of outdoor experiential education, there are times when students must experience separation from instructors in order that the students develop their own sense of self-dependence, leadership, sensory awareness and aesthetic appreciation. Having instructors, most of whom are very high energy people who tend to have a gravitational effect on students, with the students all the time during their explorations often distorts the learning experience for the student. Given this need for separation, the instructor at times only knows that the students are out there "somewhere" and will only know where, either at certain times along the way or not until the very end of the experience.

It only takes one serious injury to place an entire outdoor experiential program in jeopardy. Classroom instructors do not have to face these aforementioned issues. It takes a certain type of person, who has experienced these kinds of situations him/herself to be able to handle similar experiences as the instructor. Whereas in the regular classroom, instructors can wax and wane about theoretical issues from a safe, abstract distance; in outdoor experiential education there is no place for instructors who have not experienced the kind of reality in which they are about to place their students.

It is at this point I would like to disagree with Coleman's assertion (1995) that "[t]hose of us who attempt to analyze, to dissect, to generalize about experiential learning are as parasites, gaining our life blood from the vitality of those who do it" (p.123). In my opinion, the best researcher is both practitioner and theoretician. It is only when you attempt to dichotomize the two that problems arise. Instructors in higher education settings need to be good researchers as well as practitioners. Those who do it should also be those who research it and vice versa. Again, the individuals involved are the key to the practicality of such programs.

We have recently developed an Outdoor Experiential Education Program in the preservice program at Lakehead University. Students can choose to major in an Outdoor Experiential Education, intermediate/senior teachable or enroll in a less intensive elective on Teaching Outdoor Experiential Education. Some programs select students who are " already predisposed to learning experientially" (Raffan, 1995, p.118). The primary prerequisite in the Faculty of Education program at Lakehead is "a sincere interest in and a love for, learning and living in the outdoors" (Puk, 1997). Students select themselves based on what they read and from conversations they may have with the instructor or former students. Most of them don't really know what experiential education is all about when they begin the course. Most start out by equating outdoor education or outdoor recreation with outdoor experiential education. Hopefully, it is by the end of the course that they will have become predisposed to experiential education. The following, taken from a personal narrative assignment that all students must complete at the end of the course, exemplifies this change of perspective that we hope all students will come to realize for themselves:

> What is outdoor experiential education? Before this course, I would have said that it was the same as regular outdoor education. I think now, as a result of this course, that I have a greater understanding of the distinction between the two philosophies. Right from the first class, when I arrived at the science lab only to find that the group would be meeting on the other side of the campus, I was learning about experiential education firsthand. Rather than statically sitting in a classroom acting as a passive receptor to the information being presented by a professor, my classmates and I were immediately given a task to complete. This routine was repeated in all of our subsequent classes. The first tenet of experiential education therefore, is that students must be actively involved in their own learning. In other words, experiential education is not a spectator sport!

> As we approached the date for our first residential weekend at Kingfisher Lake, the first cooking group met with [the instructor] to plan the menu for the weekend. [The instructor's] only directions were that we had a set amount of money to spend in order to feed our group for the weekend. Although he would answer specific questions when asked, he did not offer any additional information

even when it was obvious to him that we might be overlooking something essential. This theme was to be repeated throughout our two weekends at Kingfisher; only the most basic information and directions were given at the outset of any activity. [The instructor] didn't want us to blindly follow his directions but rather, as a group, determine our goal and plan how we would reach it. The second tenet of outdoor experiential education therefore is that students shouldn't be given too many directions at the outset of a task, but instead, should be encouraged to develop their group problem solving skills. Put simply, experiential education doesn't come with a set of directions —and batteries are not included!

[As a result of working in groups], the members of the class quickly got to know each other and as a result were very supportive of each other when we were working towards the completion of a task. This constant nurturing among the members of our class helped to reduce the chance of anyone feeling excluded and ensured that within our smaller groups, everyone participated equally. The third tenet of experiential education, therefore is that the members of a group must look out for each other because, as a group, they have not completed any activity until all members of their group have completed it. In a nutshell, no group is stronger than its weakest member!

Through this course I have come to see the difference between outdoor experiential education and regular outdoor education. Whereas regular outdoor education emphasizes the acquirement of technical skills and knowledge, experiential education puts more emphasis on less tangible skills; skills in the areas of hands-on learning, problem solving and group dynamics (Allan, 1998).

During the first year and subsequent years of offering the Outdoor Experiential Education Program at Lakehead University,

we could not keep up with the demand for these courses. Whereas, originally we were looking for 25 students, we ended up with approximately 150 students applying to take the course. These students were willing to pay an extra activity fee over and above high university tuition fees, to cover the costs of transportation, accommodation, equipment and food. After three to four years of undergraduate courses, students said they were looking for an alternative to the regular type of course offering. However, it is so ingrained in university students that learning takes place indoors, that even with access to descriptions of the course, including the warning that "the course is adventurous, and students will be getting wet and bumped around", students still come to the first few classes ill-prepared in terms of clothing. A common comment is "I never thought we would actually be going outside!" Many students come to the first class in January in running shoes, without mitts and a hat. "On a cold day in January, class began. We were told to meet the instructor outside by the field house. Who would have thought, outdoor education classes outside?" (1998, student course summary). However, students soon buy into the practice and philosophy that no matter what the weather, rain, snow, or 30 degrees below zero, the course activities proceed.

Breaking this mindset is like the snap of a frozen butterfly knot: assumptions, lethargy, and reticence are shattered like bursting ice particles. This first session is like a watershed. Many students later explained that they deliberated after the first session whether, in fact, they could complete the course. "The next twenty-four hours were spent thinking and analyzing. Should I get out while I'm still alive or should I try to stick it out?" (1998, student course summary). Waddling through deep snow in the middle of the regular school day, or wading across a river, or falling off ropes can be quite a shock to most. All but a few return the next day. "As I was walking to school the next morning, I started thinking about the course. I feel that this course taught me a lot about myself and others and most importantly, the value of teamwork. I think that if I had dropped this course, I would have missed out on a very valuable experience" (1998, student course summary). The first tastes of outdoor experiential education are tantalizing.

However, the high numbers also create a practical consideration. As Raffan (1995) pointed out earlier, experiential education does not usually enjoy the elevated status of what are considered "core" subjects, such as language arts and mathematics. A small university, with limited resources, may not be able to provide extra faculty for such a program, which once again means that all the work falls on a few shoulders and once again we are talking about the energy levels of those few faculty involved. Due to administrative pressures, class sizes start to creep up and the quality of the program may begin to suffer.

Another practical consideration that looms largely when offering an experiential education course to students who have already had four years of traditional undergraduate education is the paradigm shift that students must suffer. This shift involves accepting and understanding the unique philosophy of experiential education—in particular, those elements that involve ambiguity and uncertainty. Students are so accustomed to having everything laid out for them, they sometimes find it a challenge to make the mental adjustment of learning by experiencing. Some students might perceive the paucity of instructions by

the instructor as being a deliberate plan to withhold information for the sake of retaining power and control, rather than it being a component of the course philosophy. Hunt (1994) would describe this as an ethical consideration: how much information or to what degree are "secrets" withheld? Certainly, students may be more reassured when everything is explained to them before the experience and when they are asked for their informed consent. As Hunt says, "why not simply inform students what these differences are [between experiential and traditional education] before they begin the experiential process?" (p. 65) and that it "is a rather simple matter to inform students before the fact that secrets may be kept [during the course] in order to facilitate learning" (p. 65).

I have found, in fact, that to provide university graduates with an understanding of what experiential education is, and **to do this in an experiential manner**, is anything but a simple matter. One of the tenets of experiential education is for the learner to acquire knowledge by being immersed in the situation and by subsequently reflecting on the situation in order to construct meaning. To even explain that there are differences that they are going to experience in the course and that "secrets" (i.e., pertinent information) are going to be withheld is to erode to some degree the self-discovery that is essential to experiential education. Each and every intervention by the instructor detracts to some degree from this essential tenet. As in

> quantum theory, observation by a second party (e.g., the teacher or a peer) will have a significant effect on the path of the [learner]. This possibility might give us pause for thought in all teaching acts. Even the slightest intervention by the teacher with the learner...will have some kind of effect (Puk, 1995, p.262).

Thus, the disclosure of information is a dilemma and a component of the complexity of experiential education that must be dealt with in an on-going basis. The practicality challenge is that most students have received most of their schooling through traditional means where they can put very little energy and self-learning into asking a question, and yet, receive a bounty of decontexualized information automatically. Press a button, ask the instructor, find the page number, and all will be revealed. They are conditioned to expect simple answers and to have the content of a course provided in a straight-lined, unambiguous manner. Certainly there may be some problem-solving involved in the traditional setting but seldom does the student actually have to identify and grapple with the very parameters that define a course or an experience. These are usually implicit.

Part of the answer to this dilemma, I would suggest, involves timing (when to share information and when to withhold). Part involves the style of delivery. It is exceedingly important not to give the impression that withholding information is a game of one-upmanship and mind control by the instructor, but rather that the shortfall of information is a sincere attempt to allow each and every student as close to a "no trace camping" experience as possible (in this instance, minimum trace of the instructor's knowledge, beliefs and biases). Bare-bones directions allow each student to derive unspoiled meaning from his or her own experiences and not from the trace meaning they believe they observe from the mannerisms, directions, and experiences of others. Bare-bones directions, if given in this vein, actually represent a higher degree of respect for the learning experience of the student rather than the perceived intent to control other people's

lives. However, it is a very fine line that the instructor has to negotiate!

CONCLUSION

Experiential education programs are certainly practical in a faculty of education. The first step requires a willingness on the part of faculty to adapt its existing courses. However, instructors must be prepared for the struggle that many students will undergo, as the students shift from dependency on the system to indicate what should be valued in terms of knowledge, to a degree of dependency on themselves to derive meaning. Outdoor experiential education programs have some additional challenges. We need more graduate programs that offer training in outdoor experiential education so that these programs are not so dependent upon the energies of a few; or are they are successful in the first place, because they are unique and not everyone can offer them?

REFERENCES

Allan, N. (1998). *Personal narrative for ED 4438 Teaching Outdoor Experiential Education*. (Course assignment, Faculty of Education, Lakehead University, Thunder Bay, Canada).

Association for Experiential Education (1995). *Schools and colleges directory*. Boulder, CO.

Coleman, J.S. (1995). Experiential learning and information assimilation: Towards an appropriate mix. In K. Warren, M. Sakofs, & J.S. Hunt (Eds.), *The theory of experiential education* (pp. 123–129). Dubuque, Iowa: Kendall/Hunt.

DeLay, R. (1996). Forming knowledge: Constructivist learning and experiential education. *The Journal of Experiential Education, 19* (2), 76–81.

Dewey, J. (1969). *Experience and education.* New York: MacMillan/Collier Books. (Originally published in 1938).

Gilsdorf, R. (1995). A workshop sequence in adventure education for German educators. *The Journal of Experiential Education, 18* (3), 145–149.

Hastie, P.A. (1994). Redefining "enjoyment": Prospective physical education teachers' appraisal of "enjoyment" following an outdoor adventure camp. *The Journal of Experiential Education, 17* (3), 29–33.

Horwood, B. (1985). Are good teachers born or made? A Canadian attempt at teacher midwifery. *The Journal of Experiential Education, 8* (1), 30–32.

Hunt, J.S. (1994). *Ethical issues in experiential education.* Dubuque, Iowa: Kendall/Hunt.

Mungo, S. J. (1983). Stress, burnout, and culture shock: An experiential, preservice approach. *The Journal of Experiential Education, 6* (2), 27–31.

Puk, T. (1995). Creating a quantum design schema: Integrating extra-rational and rational learning processes. *International Journal of Technology and Design Education, 5* (3), 255–266.

Puk, T. (1997). *Letter to students interested in taking the intermediate/senior outdoor experiential education course.* Thunder Bay, ON: Lakehead University, Faculty of Education.

Raffan, J. (1995). Experiential education and teacher education. *The Journal of Experiential Education, 18* (3), 117–119.

Raffan, J. & Horwood, B. (1988). Reflection on action: The evolution of a program component. *The Journal of Experiential Education, 11* (2), 9–13.

Simmons, S. (1995). The teacher education program consortium: A new network for professional development in experiential education. *The Journal of Experiential Education, 18* (3), 120–127.

Warren, K. (1988). The student directed classroom: A model for teaching experiential education theory. *The Journal of Experiential Education, 11* (2), 4–9.

Wurdinger, S. (1997). *Philosophical issues in adventure education.* Dubuque, Iowa: Kendall/Hunt.

Is the Process of Experiential Learning (Outside the Classroom) Practical in Higher Education Settings?

Scott Wurdinger, Ph.D.

When Dr. Tom Potter and I were soliciting authors for this book we found that numerous individuals wanted to write the YES side to this question, but no one wanted the NO side. My assumption is that most people in the field of adventure education are avid supporters of experiential learning, and therefore wanted to write in favor of its use. But, this question is not about whether one supports the use of experiential learning; it's about whether or not it is practical in higher education settings. I, too, am a firm believer in the effectiveness of experiential learning, but in many situations this method is impractical in higher education classrooms.

Before I explain my side of this question however, it would be beneficial to define the term "experiential learning." One way it has been defined, is as a spectrum of teaching techniques used in the college classroom (Wurdinger, 1998).

As one moves along the spectrum from left to right, the amount of experiential learning increases. Lectures are the least experiential, where students sit passively and receive information by listening to teachers. Application of information is not included with

this technique, but students may choose to apply information on their own. Individual presentations, also on the left side, are short presentations given by students. This technique is similar to lecture except that students are presenting the lectures rather than the teachers.

Group presentations, role plays, debates, and group projects occur when groups of students plan, prepare, and present ideas and activities to the class. Presentations vary in length and are dependent upon such things as the nature of the assignment and group size. These techniques require students to work together in small groups, which in turn, help them develop thinking, communication, and interpersonal skills. Smith and MacGregor (1992) would argue that these techniques fall under the umbrella of collaborative learning, which they define as, "a variety of educational approaches involving joint intellectual effort by students, or students and teachers together. In most collaborative learning situations students are working in groups of two or more, mutually searching for understanding, or meanings, or creating a product" (p.10). And although

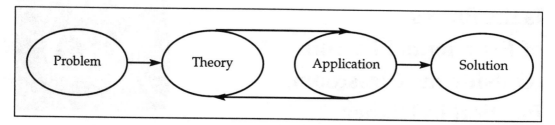

Figure 11.1 *Proactive experiential learning model.*

collaborative approaches to learning appear to be more effective than lectures (Astin, 1993), they do not provide direct experience in real life settings.

Field experiences and internships, found on the right side of the spectrum, however do provide students with direct experience that allow them to acquire the necessary skills of their profession. Such off campus experiences typically require a certain number of hours to complete and are set up in conjunction with organizations that provide supervisors for student interns. These techniques are highly experiential and provide students with opportunities to explore their chosen profession for extended periods of time.

Another way experiential learning has been defined, according to Henry (1993), is through a sequential step-by-step process. For instance, Dewey (1916), Coleman (1976), and Kolb et.al (1991), have developed learning sequences with various components, that, when completed, result in experiential learning. After examining these sequences, Wurdinger and Priest (1999) developed the Proactive Experiential Learning Model (PELM) that includes four components: a problem, a theory, an application, and a solution.

The PELM is proactive rather than reactive because students initiate the learning process. The job of the educator is to design problems that are meaningful to students so that they become interested and motivated to solve the problems on their own. In this model, the learning process is initiated with a problem, and in order to discover a solution, learners must apply information in real life settings. Discovering a solution, however, may require learners to go back and forth between theory and application several times. The application phase occurs when learners take information and test it against reality. It is the application phase of this cycle that makes the learning experiential. For instance, if a college student is studying to become an adventure education instructor, he or she must take what is learned in an academic setting and apply it by teaching adventure education skills to groups of participants.

McKeachie's (1994) definition of experiential learning also focuses on learning that occurs outside the classroom. He suggests that it is a "broad spectrum of educational experiences, such as community service activities, field work, sensitivity training groups, internships, or cooperative education involving work in business or industry" (p. 140). These definitions imply that experiential learning is more than just hands-on learning. It is hands-on learning that allows students to explore the requirements and intricacies of a particular

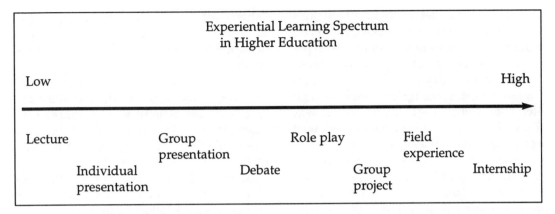

Figure 11.2 *The degree of experiential learning increases as one moves to the right.*

profession. It is learning that requires learners to be practitioners at different times during their college/university experience. It has purpose and meaning because students apply their learning in settings that have immediate consequences. Therefore, for the purpose of this chapter, experiential learning will be defined as application of information in real life settings that allows students opportunities to practice their professions.

How often are students allowed to explore and practice their profession during their undergraduate experience? If they are lucky, they will have enrolled in a program that has an internship and/or field experience as part of their graduation requirement. Unfortunately however, undergraduate college students spend a majority of their formal academic experience in the classroom, which is not a conducive setting for experiential learning. Obstacles such as time constraints, supervision, evaluation, and class size make it difficult for teachers to integrate experiential learning into their curriculums, and are reasons why experiential learning is impractical in higher education.

Universities and colleges structure many of their academic courses to meet for 50 to 80 minutes, one to three times a week. This structure is often extremely inflexible. It presents a time constraint for teachers wishing to integrate experiential methods and severely limits what the teacher can accomplish; which is probably one of the main reasons why 70–90 percent of professors use the traditional lecture format as their primary teaching technique (Blackburn et.al.,1980). Structuring college/university courses to include longer class periods would allow teachers to employ experiential methods, resulting in more effective learning environments.

To illustrate my point I will use a college course I teach, called Ropes Course Facilitation Skills, as an example. The first time I taught this course it was scheduled for a full semester on Tuesdays and Thursdays from 2:00–3:50 p.m. Even though this class was one hour and 50 minutes long, it was still too short to provide meaningful experiential learning opportunities. My primary goals for the course were to teach technical safety skills, processing techniques, and provide opportunities to practice these skills with actual clients. At the outset, four class periods were set aside for students to experience a progression of activities that could be used in a one day ropes course program (e.g. stretching, spotting, low elements, high elements, debriefing). My thinking was these four classes, which were to be viewed as the equivalent of a one day ropes course program, would allow students to experience the activities through the eyes of a participant. I thought this would help them become more effective facilitators because they would gain an understanding of how programs utilize designed progressions. This, however, was not the case. Students had a difficult time remembering the sequence of activities and mentioned that the experience was disjointed because of the long time lapses between the classes (it took a total of ten days). If the class had been four hours in length, it would have taken only two classes (three days) to finish the progression. Many jobs, including those in adventure education, involve completing tasks and projects that require substantial blocks of time, and if college/university courses were structured for longer amounts of time, then teachers could include experiential activities that more accurately reflected a student's chosen profession.

Another problem with the ropes course class that resulted due to lack of time, was the difficulty I encountered while trying to administer a skills test. It is much easier to administer a written exam in a 50 minute class period than it is to test for skill competency. One part of the test I administered asked students to demonstrate how to attach a cable pulley to a belay cable; an important skill for instructors to learn. Due to the lack of time I tied a climbing rope between two telephone poles waist high and asked stu-

dents to attach the pulley to the rope. This simulated exercise allowed me to test 20 students in one class session, but it did not accurately measure their ability.

The next time I taught the course however, was in the summer which enabled me to change the structure. The course was scheduled for four hours a day for two weeks, which significantly changed the way I taught the course. During the skills test for example, students actually climbed the telephone poles, wrapped the poles with their lobster claws, and attached the pulleys to the belay cables. This skills test was significantly superior to the one I designed in the first course. Here, students learned how to free their hands by hanging from their lobster claws, and if they dropped one of the devices to the ground during the test, they had to climb back down, retrieve the device, and climb back up to attach it. They learned from their mistakes which helped solidify their learning. Longer class periods would allow teachers an opportunity to utilize more extensive and meaningful methods of student evaluation.

During the course it was also difficult to arrange times for students to practice their facilitation skills with actual clients. Students had opportunities to observe one day ropes course programs, but for most students this was possible only on the weekends when it didn't interfere with their other classes. Longer class sessions would have allowed students valuable opportunities to observe and gain first hand experience facilitating groups of participants. Longer blocks of time would permit teachers to include off campus experiences during their scheduled class periods. Experiential learning would be much more practical if colleges and universities structured their academic semesters to include three and four hour class periods as opposed to the usual one and two hour time blocks.

Another reason why experiential learning is impractical in higher education is because it is difficult to find supervisors willing to commit the time to train students engaged in off campus experiences. For example, in the field of education there is little incentive for teachers to take on the added responsibility of supervising student teachers if there is little or no compensation. Tasks such as preparing lessons, explaining curriculum content, and demonstrating teaching and discipline techniques require large amounts of time from supervising teachers. From my own experience working with teaching assistants, I discovered that in many cases, it would have been easier to teach the course myself than to train the assistant to teach the course. In the field of adventure education, interns are often viewed as cheap labor and are given menial tasks that do not challenge their skill level. Good supervisors will challenge students and allow them to experience skills that are necessary to acquire to become professionals. In some situations this may require supervisors to take risks. For example, a student intern who has a weak performance while facilitating corporate team building activities may result in a loss of business for the supervisor. But, if the student is never allowed to facilitate, then how will he or she learn necessary skills? Supervisors need to take on the role of a teacher and explain, demonstrate, and provide constructive feedback which may require large amounts of time, energy, and commitment.

Evaluating students who are engaged in off campus experiences is also a difficult task. In the past I had the responsibility of supervising physical education student teachers as part of my teaching load. This entailed driving to the school site, observing the student

for 40–50 minutes, writing up an evaluation, and then discussing the evaluation with the student. Sites were as far as 30 miles from the university, and each student had to be evaluated twice during the semester; this procedure was extremely time consuming. During this process I discovered that two evaluations per student were hardly adequate for a 320 hour student teaching practicum. I have also taught college courses where students were required to teach activities to elementary and middle school students. I could not evaluate their performance because they were all doing their activities during the same time period at several different schools. Furthermore, school supervisors were remiss in filling out evaluation forms, so even though their activities may have been exciting and enjoyable for students, they did not provide student teachers with meaningful feedback.

Larger classes also create a problem for experiential teachers. How can a teacher provide meaningful experiences for an individual student who is in a class with 200 other students? It appears that the value of many academic programs is based on the number of student credit hours generated. Faculty who generate large numbers of student credit hours not only have better job security, but often receive more privileges, such as release time, technological resources, and larger budgets than other faculty. Unfortunately, larger classes make it difficult for teachers to provide and supervise experiential learning opportunities for each individual student. Experiential learning is not practical for large lecture classes, but large lecture classes generate substantial revenue.

In the ideal world of experiential learning, professors would teach fewer courses with greater intensity. They would have smaller classes and spend more time outside the classroom in the real world teaching students valuable occupational and life skills. The classroom would serve as a meeting place to reflect on previous experiences, discuss relevant readings, and plan future activities. There would be minimal time constraints, and evaluations would be easy because teachers would accompany students in the field. This however, is not the dominant paradigm. More likely, students take four–six courses per semester and run from one building to the next taking notes that are to be recalled for midterm and final exams. Obviously, removing barriers such as short class periods and large classes would help to make experiential learning more possible, but the biggest problem facing experiential educators is that the field is obscure and the philosophy is often misunderstood. There are very few institutions that offer undergraduate degrees in experiential education, and even fewer at the graduate level. Motivated teachers who understand the philosophy of experiential education will find ways to implement it regardless of obstacles. Experiential educators need to educate colleagues and administrators about this philosophy and its benefits, which may help remove some of the barriers. The more individuals in higher education who understand the philosophy, the more likely the barriers will begin to disappear.

REFERENCES

Astin, A. W. (1993). *What matters in college? Four critical years revisited.* San Francisco: Jossey Bass.

Blackburn, R. T., Pellino, G.R., Boberg, A. & O'Connell, C. (1980). Are instruction improvement programs off target? *Current Issues in Higher Education*, 2 (1). 32–48.

Coleman, J. S. (1976). Differences between experiential and classroom learning. In M.T. Keeton (Ed.), *Experiential learning: Rationale, characteristics, and assessment.* San Francisco: Jossey Bass.

Dewey, J. (1916). *Democracy and education.* New York: The Free Press.

Henry, J. (1993) Meaning and practice in experiential learning. In S. Weill & I. McGill (Eds.), *Making sense of experiential learning: Diversity in theory and practice.* Buckingham: Open University Press.

Kolb, D., Rubin, I. & Osland, J. (1991). *The Organizational Behavior Reader.* (5th ed.). Englewood, NJ: Prentice Hall.

Mckeachie, W. J. (1994). *Teaching tips: Strategies, research, and theory for college and university teachers.* (9th ed.). Lexington, MA: D.C. Heath.

Smith, B. & McGregor, J. (1992). What is collaborative learning. In A.S. Goodsell et.al. (Eds.), *Collaborative learning: A sourcebook for higher education.* University Park, PA: National Center On Postsecondary Teaching, Learning and Assessment.

Wurdinger, S. & Priest, S. (In press). Experiential learning: A new model for integrating theory and application in the learning sequence. In J. Miles & S. Priest (Eds.), *Adventure education.* (2nd ed.). State College, PA: Venture Publishing.

Wurdinger, S. (1998). "Experiential techniques for the college classroom." Association for Experiential Education Heartland Conference Presentation. Kalamazoo, Michigan.

CHAPTER 12

Do Contrived Adventure Experiences, Such as Ropes Courses, Hinder Participants from Developing a Connnection to the Natural World?

YES PERSPECTIVE: Nicky Duenkel, Ph.D.
NO PERSPECTIVE: Stephen Streufert

Nicky has worked extensively in various educational settings, in attempt to further understand the development of ecological consciousness and nurture the exploration of, and connection to, a greater sense of Self. Her journeys have enabled her to become grounded in a deeply felt and profoundly experienced sense of relationship with the earth. Through her practice she encourages all those around her to question deeply, think critically and act intentionally. Her latest journey has led her to the Gulf of Maine Bioregion, where she joins students and co-faculty of the Audubon Expedition Institute in seeking to co-create a more environmentally and socially just world. Nicky has a passion for learning and loves to play!

Stephen Streufert has been leading experiential wilderness courses since 1983, including instructional work for the National Outdoor Leadership School (NOLS) and the North Carolina Outward Bound School (NCOBS). Recent forays from behind a desk include serving as the Director of Staffing and Staff Development for NCOBS and the pursuit of a Masters Degree from Minnesota State University, Mankato. He currently resides with his sweetie in Eugene, Oregon.

Do Contrived Adventure Experiences, Such as Ropes Courses, Hinder Participants from Developing a Connection to the Natural World?

Nicky Duenkel, Ph.D.

This will be a fantastic summit attempt, I thought to myself, as I steadily continued climbing in front of the others. Conditions were excellent and the good firm snow was allowing us to ascend efficiently. We were making incredible time and thoroughly enjoying the spectacular, exposed views. With Everest, however, you are always facing the unknown. Time passed and soon enough, the snow conditions began to change and the beautiful day quickly deteriorated. We trod our way slowly and carefully now, through the cracked and heavily drifted snow, as we rose toward the South Summit. Clouds were moving in and the wind started blowing stiffly across our faces. Within minutes, it seemed, we were virtually in white-out conditions. With ice axe in hand, postholing our way through knee deep snow, I carried the awareness of traversing the very thin knife-like edge of an incredibly steep slope, with Tibet dropping off thousands of feet below us on one side and the southwest face of Everest on the other. Climbing into the amassing storm, one error in judgement could mean severe injury, or even death. My glasses were fogging up and I could barely

see a few feet in front of me. Concerned about the lost strength and demoralization from the aborted summit attempt the day before, I decided it would be safest to turn the team around and abandon the climb. Everest's summit would once again elude us.

Maybe I'll succeed tomorrow, I thought to myself as I gingerly removed the helmet-like apparatus containing the tiny computer screens, one in front of each eye giving slightly different views so as to mimic stereoscopic vision. Then I removed the specialized gloves and footwear which passed on my actions to the computer, changing the graphics accordingly and giving me the feeling of movement through the blustery winter scene. I recalled some of the computer-generated sounds and odors which further enhanced and reinforced my virtual visual illusion. What could be better, I asked myself, than to transmit the sights, sounds, and sensations of a natural world adventure in a safe and controlled simulated computer environment, while remaining thousands of miles away from the real thing?

The above scene may not quite be reality yet (or perhaps it is?), nonetheless, there is little doubt as to whether complex and elaborate virtual adventure experiences are within our technological grasp. The question that comes to mind for me is this: How fundamentally different is this virtual adventure experience from that of spending an afternoon paddling in a wave pool, climbing on an indoor climbing wall, or ascending the pamper pole on a high ropes course? All have the potential of hindering participants from deepening their connection to the natural world. Indeed, contrived adventure experiences offer a delusional substitute for a rich, sensory, first hand experience with the actual rhythms and textures of the more-than-human world. Much like a television nature series, they serve primarily to contribute to our emotional and spiritual distancing from intimate interaction with both inner and outer 'nature'. As we become increasingly distanced, in both physical interaction and cultural perspectives, we continue to distort human-natural world relationships. Contrived adventure experiences serve as merely one more way of muting the natural world in our daily existence on this planet.

THE WHAT: CLARIFYING THE QUESTION

Prior to delving further into this issue, it would seem necessary, and important, to clarify a couple of underlying assumptions inherent in this chapter's guiding question in order to properly set the stage for what is to follow. The first of these assumptions is the definition of a 'contrived adventure experience'. The second assumption pertains to identifying the type of human-natural world relationships that we should ideally be seeking to develop.

What is the definition of 'contrived'? Based on the Webster's New World Dictionary (1980), contrived is thought to mean: "1. To think up; devise, scheme; plan, 2. To construct skillfully or ingeniously; fabricate, 3. To bring about, as by a scheme; manage" (p. 309). There is little doubt that adventure activities such as high and low ropes courses, indoor climbing walls, wave pools, and virtual reality simulations all fall quite clearly within the definition as having been 'thought up' or 'constructed skillfully; fabricated'. I would also argue, however, that on a deeper level a much larger realm of adventure experiences could be deemed as contrived, than one would initially consider. Could it not be said, for example, that the underlying intentions of the majority of adventure education programs (i.e. therapeutic, corporate, challenge, etc.) is "to bring about" particular learning objectives and/or to "manage" or manipulate participants' experiences toward certain pre-determined outcomes? This being the case then, and barring any negative connotations which may have become associated with the notion of contrived, the thesis held in this paper is that the field of adventure education is predominantly composed of contrived experiences.

"Developing a relationship with the natural world" can also connote various truths. My personal belief, which I propose as an underlying tenet for this paper, is that there is a need for a fundamental shift in North America's culturally dominant way of perceiving our relationship with the natural world (and with each other for that matter, but that is another issue, or is it?). Rather than viewing ourselves as separate and superior to the natural world, we need to come to a deeply held understanding of our synchrony with other beings and the dynamic of life, awakening to our interconnected realities and drawing upon our instinctive resonance with the earth. Gaining this depth of consciousness entails thoroughly questioning and examining the patterns and conditions of our thoughts and actions toward the natural world in order to create cultural beliefs and practices that will enable non-commodified and sustainable forms of relationships (Bowers, 1993). Consequently, the essence of my argument is that not only do contrived adventure experiences often serve to physically distance and separate us from the natural world; more importantly they fail to actually bring into question our deepest cultural assumptions which are hindering and impeding the unfolding of meaningful human-natural world relationships. Continuing to project our cultural prejudices and misconceptions, results in supporting the status quo and prolonging the delusion that we are disconnected from the ecological web. Meanwhile, maintaining our current worldviews and lifestyles is sustaining the condemnation of other beings to extinction.

THE SO WHAT: CHALLENGING CULTURAL ASSUMPTIONS

So what are the cultural assumptions underlying, and acting as foundations for, contrived adventure experiences that are yearning to be identified and challenged? First and foremost is the perpetuation of a mechanistic worldview. Stemming from Descartes' renowned method of analytic thinking, introduced in the 17th century, the traditional Western worldview is one of reducing complex phenomena to a small number of simple pieces that are easily understood. The world is, therefore, seen as a collection of objects with relationships between them remaining secondary.

Simulating the natural world through the construction of indoor climbing walls and wave pools directly involves this breaking down and analyzing, focusing our attention on the parts while obscuring the workings of the system as a whole. The inherent assumption, of course, is that the whole is too complex and we must, therefore, simplify and cut down on the number of variables in order to succeed or understand. So let us remove from the picture the influence of, and our interaction with, varying weather patterns, rock disintegration, river bank erosion, unexpected strainers and sweepers, wildlife, and a whole host of other potentially unforeseen natural processes which could affect our levels of success. In doing so, real life complications are either avoided or portrayed simplistically.

The simplification of contrived experiences is misleading, however. The result of taking apart a living system, such as the natural world, is quite simply to kill it. The natural world is complex, relational, and ever-changing. Contrived experiences are simplistic, objectified, and static. As machines continue to serve as the analogue for understanding life processes, we keep on distancing ourselves from the buzzing complexities and realities of the natural world. While mechanistic reasoning is firmly ingrained in our Western culture, it clearly has inherent and elemental limitations. As Senge (1990) illustrates:

> We are taught to break apart problems, to fragment the world. This apparently makes complex tasks and subjects more manageable, but we pay a hidden, enormous price. We can no longer see the consequences of our actions: we lose our intrinsic sense of connection to a larger whole. We then...try to reassemble the fragments in our minds, to list and organize all the pieces....The task is futile—similar to trying to reassemble the fragments of a broken mirror to see a true reflection (p. 1).

Henderson (1998) thoughtfully illustrates the shortcomings of this mechanistic worldview in relation to contrived adventure experiences:

> ...the indoor climbing wall as compared to the mountain experience or viewing the CD-ROM nature series as compared to the misty morning 'nature' walk. The former, in all cases, might even provide more concrete 'skill' development, but the latter, the experience of self within the more-than-human realm, involves potential for a deep emotive relationship, an extending of the cognitive/physical process (p. 1).

Unless contrived adventure experiences can inspire us to begin thinking in terms of connectedness, context, and relationships, they are cutting short the depth of transformation possible.

A strong sense of individualism is another dominant myth sustained by contrived adventure experiences. Outdoor pursuits have been traditionally contextualized around strengthening one's sense of self, conquering internal fears, or creating better intra and interpersonal relations. The focus is overwhelmingly upon oneself, making the context within which the experience is taking place nearly irrelevant. Yet, how can healthy inter and intrapersonal relations exist independent of a relationship to place? As portrayed by Henderson (1998), "...our psychic relationship to the earth is innate, part of essential humanness, a yearning....Without this connection we are sensory undernourished. We become alienated from a part of our being" (p. 4). This ideological commitment to individualism and development of self is at the expense of discovering a broader sense of interdependence with the larger social and biotic communities (Bowers, 1993).

Adventure education's emphasis on self-actualization also exacerbates the erroneous notion of an autonomous and separate self. In contrast to this traditional Western outlook, there exists the potential to actualize more of a relational perspective and expanded sense of Self; one which extends beyond a mere bag of skin and bones. The ecological self, as described by Naess (1989), encourages us to experience ourselves as one part of a much larger whole; one link in a web of interconnected relationships. Realizing this would require moving beyond simply acknowledging the presence of the natural world, and toward fuller engagement with non-human beings. The depth of experience to be sought is one in which humankind are able to acquire a relational perspective, thereby transforming us into participants of the natural world's existence. As Kaza (1993) advises, "...in the course of studying mountains and rivers in depth, one sees them explode into all the phenomena that support their existence—clouds, stones, people walking, animals crawling, the earth shaking" (p. 129). And so, I ask adventure educators: How often does a river bagger, so intently focused upon the self and the eddy line; come away from an experience knowing anything at all about the texture of the river's rock or the creatures living below the surface of the water?

Following from this focus on the autonomous individual, emerges yet another cultural pillar strengthened by contrived adventure experiences: anthropocentrism. Contrived adventure experiences unarguably bolster an anthropocentric worldview by supporting the notion that humankind is believed to be the epitome of creation, around whom the rest of the world revolves. The natural world, viewed from a wholly instrumental standpoint, is perceived as being separate from ourselves; its very existence determined and controlled by our use of it as a 'resource'. *We* are in control. More often than not, contrived adventure experiences are framed around our need to overcome and conquer the water, the mountain, or the rock wall; thereby reinforcing a sense of separation and need for control and domination over the rest of the world. Indoor climbing walls and wave pools not only afford humans control over variables such as weather and level of risk, they also falsely lead us to assume that we even have the know-how and ability to re-create natural world systems, in all of their complexity. The truth of the matter is, however, that one's level of success in these types of scenarios stems, in fact, from the differences inherent within the simplicity of the contrived environments. Ultimately, fortification of this control paradigm is antithetical to opening up to the more-than-human world.

Anthropocentric assumptions also surface innocently within the language used in contextualizing adventure experiences. 'Success' more often than not implies 'to overcome'. Parks and wilderness areas are referred to as 'ours' and are often described in terms of how they can serve humans. Indeed, their very existence reinforces the belief that we *can* control and corral the natural world. The weather is said to be "good" or "bad" dependent solely upon whether or not it is conducive to our chosen activities. We speak of the natural world as the environment, as a resource that is "out there" separate from ourselves. At the same time "progress" suggests that new and improved equipment and techniques be continually generated by the outdoor industry so as to further enable us to *overcome* the natural world with new and better ideas and/or tools.

The following passage, excerpted from a World Wide Web description of an adventure education course, clearly conveys how a pre-developed way of thinking, one geared towards anthropocentrism, is deeply imbedded within the field of adventure education's chosen language: "...a challenging exhilarating journey that takes place against the backdrop of some of Canada's most beautiful wilderness, from the snowy peaks of British Columbia's Coast Mountains to the shores of a northern Ontario lake". A backdrop?! How engaged can we become with a place that is relegated to merely serving as a backdrop, a stage for our human adventures? As Bowers and Flinders (1990) contend, language not only conveys our thoughts but also shapes our thinking. Unless we are able to modify our language to create symmetry with our intentions; we risk funneling both our thoughts and actions back toward a different reality. A reality in which neurosis abounds and we remain alienated from a part of our true being: the more than human world.

Furthermore, the above excerpt intensifies our media-generated perceptions of what is beautiful: mountain top panoramic views, pristine and remote locations, and mega-fauna (ie. bigger is better). This stereotypical view is supported through the natural areas most frequented by adventure educators along with the artificial environments we create for ourselves. Would we even consider simulating a prairie or swamp environment? Likely not. There is a deep need, I feel, to redefine *beauty* in the context of the natural world. And it is only in spending time immersed within the less glamorized natural areas that the subtleties and intricacies of the various landscapes can begin to pull deeply at our psyches and our souls.

In a nutshell, how often do we come away from adventure experiences asking ourselves how we are dwelling on the earth? Or how we can create more time and space to interact with other living beings? Do we consider how to simplify our lifestyles in order to minimize our negative impacts on these beings? Do we think of trying to live more mindfully—to even begin to question the actual manufacturing and energy extraction costs of all this 'essential' new gear? (let alone disposing of the old). Rarely. Likewise, as we find ourselves perched upon a twelve inch platform, thirty feet or so above the ground, struggling with our lack of self-confidence and a whole host of internal fears, we neglect to direct attention toward finding out where the struggles came from in the first place— an unhealthy society in which we are no longer conscious of our organic natural world reality. Healthy people cannot co-exist with a sick planet. We manage our experiences so as to turn our attention away from these necessary criticisms. And yet, critical and meaningful questions, about the human condition in relationship to the more-than-human world, are urging to be asked.

THE NOW WHAT: ENGAGING IN THE REAL ADVENTURE

It appears to be quite clear at this point that contrived adventure experiences have the potential to hinder, or thwart, our ability to create a space in which to remember our organic relationship to the earth. I find myself somewhat skeptical, however, in fully attributing this impediment to the contrivance itself. By that, I mean to question whether it is actually the fact that adventure experiences are contrived which is limiting our ability to regain our intuitive call to being in deep relationship with the earth or rather, is it the *way* in which we consciously or unconsciously *choose* to contrive these experiences? Is it not accurate to imply that we

could purposely and intentionally choose to create programs that would enhance and magnify our sense of relational identity with the more-than-human world?

Risk (perceived and real, physical, emotional, social, mental, and spiritual) is at the core of the adventure paradigm. And so, once again, I ask adventure educators everywhere: how deeply are you truly willing to risk? How profound is the adventure toward change to be? What if we were to redirect contrived experiences in the direction of challenging the Western worldview, rather than driving debilitating assumptions deeper into our culture and into our beings? We *could* choose to rework our cultural templates.

Imagine the adventure of spirit and soul that could dwell in experiences contrived toward dispelling the myth of dualism and separation while encouraging the feeling that humans are a part of, rather than apart from, the natural world. Experiences which would aim toward developing a sense of humility and grasping our insignificance in the greater scheme of things. Could we use the adventure education paradigm to challenge ourselves towards developing an awareness of, and redefining, the underpinnings of our language and how we use it? As formidable a task as it would be to awaken the perception of how our everyday constructed realities have distanced us from both the inner and outer realms of "nature" surely reconnecting with our innate relational sensibilities would be worth the effort.

While I do not claim to have all of the answers, I do know from the depth of my being that we are orienting ourselves towards escapism by engaging in the mimicry, rather than the reality, of the natural world. Contrived experiences are at best a poor imitation. Where is the wildness in a contrived experience? Is it in the storm clouds, rain, hail; the solidity and groundedness of the rocks and trees? There is no artificial substitute for the natural world. As we verge upon an age in which the reality of cyberspace environments could facilitate the use of high technologies to directly interface between mind and machine, it behooves us to not lose touch with the power of direct and authentic experiences with the natural world. With those experiences that elicit a sense of awe: the mixed emotion of reverence, respect, and wonder resulting in revelatory experiences that penetrate to the core of our beings. For as Abram (1996) suggests, we are only fully human in contact and celebration with what is not human. In all honesty, I believe that there is a need, and perhaps even an obligation, to re-contextualize contrived adventure education experiences in order to, as the Latin world "context" would suggest, learn to "weave together" with the rest of the natural world. Therein lies the *real* adventure.

REFERENCES

Abram, D. (1996). *The spell of the sensuous.* New York: Vintage Books.

Bowers, C.A. (1993). *Education, cultural myths, and the ecological crisis: Toward deep change.* Albany: State University of New York Press.

Bowers, C.A. & Flinders, D. J. (1990). *Responsive teaching: An ecological approach to understanding classroom patterns of language, culture, and thought.* New York: Teachers College Press.

Guralnik, D. B. (Ed.). (1980). *Webster's new world dictionary of the American language.* Second College Edition. William Collins Publishers, Inc.

Henderson, B. (1998). The place of deep ecology and ecopsychology in adventure education. In Miles, John C. and Priest, Simon (Eds.), *Adventure Education.* 2nd ed.

Kaza, S. (1993). Conversations with trees: Toward an ecologically engaged spirituality. *ReVision, 15,*(3), 128–136.

Naess, A. (1989). *Ecology, community and lifestyle.* Translated by David Rothenberg. rev. ed. New York: Cambridge University Press.

Senge, P. (1990). *The fifth discipline.* New York: Doubleday.

World Wide Web. (1998). http://www.outwardbound.ca.

Do Contrived Adventure Experiences, Such as Ropes Courses, Hinder Participants from Developing a Connection to the Natural World?

Stephen Streufert

One of my favorite stories about a person developing an amazing relationship with the natural world is the story of John Muir and his infamous tree ride. In *The Mountains of California* (1921), Muir recalls leaving the house of a friend as a "storm began to sound" (p. 249) and then spending half a day gaining "the summit of the highest ridge in the neighborhood" (p. 251) in search of a tree to climb. The December storm was intense, and Muir noted trees falling at a "rate of one every two or three minutes" (p. 249); with care, Muir selected a group of trees on the ridge top, as "under the circumstances the choice of a tree was a serious matter" (p. 249).

Muir (1921) continues:

After cautiously casting about, I made a choice of the tallest of a group of Douglas Spruce [Fir] that were growing together like a tuft of grass, no one of which seemed likely to fall unless all the rest fell with it. Though comparatively young, they were about 100 feet high, and their lithe, brushy tops were rocking and swirling in wild ecstasy. Being accustomed to climb [*sic*] trees in making botanical studies, I experienced no difficulty in reaching the top of this one, and never be-

fore did I enjoy so noble an exhilaration of motion. The slender tops fairly flapped and swished in the passionate torrent, bending and swirling backward and forward, round and round, tracing indescribable combinations of vertical and horizontal curves, while I clung with muscles firm braced, like a bobolink on a reed. (p. 250)

Muir (1921), while in this fury of storm and motion, clinging to branches making "arcs of twenty to thirty degrees" (p. 251), describes his connections to his surroundings with amazing detail. The fluid prose of his decriptions includes the smell of the wind, "...from the chafing of resiny branches...the gale was spiced to a very tonic degree" (p. 254), the sound of the storm,"...the quick, tense vibrations of the pine-needles, now rising to a shrill, whistling hiss, now falling to a silky murmur" (p.253); and the effect of light, "...reflected from the bent needles was so great as to make whole groves appear as if covered with snow" (p. 252). Clearly in this tree-top afternoon, Muir's adventure was filled with a deep awareness of his environment, contributing to his relationship with the natural world.

In reflecting upon the posed question, *do contrived adventure experiences, such as ropes courses, hinder participants from developing a relationship with the natural world*, I wondered what constitutes a contrived adventure experience, as well as the possible inclusion of "tree riding" as a component for an adventure based course. Would tree riding be considered a contrived adventure experience? Muir's experience of leaving a friend's home to spend an afternoon in a tree certainly seems in many ways contrived. Perhaps tree riding is more contrived than rock climbing, yet not as contrived as a ropes course? Or what about "raft riding" down a river, or "ski riding" down a mountain?

For purposes of this argument, I propose that an adventure experience can be defined as contrived if one or both of the following conditions are met. One, the experience must ultimately be unnecessary, that is not needed nor critical to survival; and two, that the experience is engaged upon for a specific purpose or range of purposes. With this as a definition, a comparison of the following three adventure activities will illuminate my belief that most, if not all, adventure based courses are initially comprised of well-designed, contrived adventure activities: (a) Muir's tree riding adventure in the Sierras, (b) a ropes course experience, (c) a river rafting expedition.

An examination of the first condition as set in the proposed definition suggests that none of the three events are critical for survival and are ultimately unnecessary. Muir chose to leave a friend's house to climb the tree, and similarly, participants in either a rafting expedition or a ropes course adventure also make a conscious choice to enter into the experience. No elements forced participation; all these adventure choices can be viewed as unnecessary acts to the state of survival.

After this initial choice is made, however, circumstances can arise that do challenge survival. At times, Muir's death-grip 100 feet up on the Douglas Fir may have indeed been a genuine act of survival. Similarly, the white-out and storm conditions that blow in suddenly during a peak ascent, or the quick-rising flood waters on an extended paddling expedition force genuine experience. Examples of the Oregon Episcopal School students on Mt. Hood and the mis-adventures of the rafting parties on the Illinois River in Oregon in the Spring of 1998 come to mind as very real and consequential outcomes of initial choices. Similarly, survival experiences can occur on a ropes course during rushed lowerings in the event of a sudden lightning storm. Yet, the initial choice to be exposed to the circumstances, in all examples, is indeed a contrived choice. And, I maintain, almost all adventure courses offer participants the initial choice to enter into similar contrived experiences.

The second condition necessary for an adventure experience to be contrived is that the experience is engaged upon for a specific purpose or range of purposes. Contrived implies some plot or scheme that is set forth in order for certain outcomes or set of outcomes to be achieved. A ropes course could be considered contrived because the experience is designed to create a circumstance where the challenges of gravity, foresight, balance and strength invoke a sense of dissonance followed by resolution and reflection. Could it not be said that rafting down a river creates a comparable circumstance as the challenge of current, foresight, strength and skill invoke a similar dissonance, resolution and reflection? In the probable words of the internal questions of participants: Can I do it? What if I screw up? How high am I? How long would I circulate in that nasty hole? What will it feel like when I finish? I wonder what it will look like from way up on the balance beam? I wonder what the canyon is like? Will I be supported by those around me? Will I freak out? If I can do this, in what else can I demonstrate mastery?

Perhaps Muir faced some of these same questions. He clearly had an expressed purpose as he left his friend's house to make his stormy tree ascent. Muir (1921) believed that the experience "had something rare to show," noting that the "danger to life and limb is hardly greater than one would experience crouching deprecatingly beneath a roof" (p. 249).

The purpose of the ropes course and rafting experiences then seem quite similar; a purpose at all implies a contrived experience. Not all adventure experiences are for the purpose of dissonance, resolution and reflection, as purposes and desired outcomes vary significantly between programs and components within programs. Yet, it is almost certain that almost all programs are designed with some purpose in mind.

And finally, as it is likely an argument that will be made, perhaps the definition of contrived is insufficient without inclusion of the concept of the influence of people and their creations. With the assumption that a rafting expedition initially represented a likely choice for a non-contrived adventure experience, a comparison of the similarities between rafting and ropes course adventures sheds some interesting light. Both adventures require human-created materials, one constructed to rest in water, the other to rest in trees; both have the potential to be located in "natural environments" as well as along roadsides and so forth; both experiences provide opportunities for travel in a medium that would otherwise be significantly less safe without the use of the necessary human

created tools. Both provide levels of perceived and actual risk. In 1997, the *National Safety Report* of Outward Bound USA suggests that in terms of accidents and incidents, the two events did not differ significantly. And finally, with regards to aesthetics, significant advantage either way would be tough to claim, pitting hypalon tubes, fiberglass oars, aluminum frames, coolers, and personal flotation devices versus harnesses, "lobster claws," cargo nets, "biners" and helmets. It seems to me that it would be difficult to develop standards of "contrived or not" based on the influence of human-created factors.

Thus, in using the proposed definition of a contrived adventure experience, I believe that most adventure based courses may initially be a series of well designed contrived adventure experiences. Though there may be arguments that would attempt to categorize and classify degrees to which one experience is more contrived than another, the outcomes of this would likely be unclear, inconclusive and controversial.

Therefore, given that contrived activities are a part of most adventure based courses, and that the degree to which an experience is contrived is difficult to assess, it would be imprudent to suggest that a participant's capacity to develop a relationship with the natural world would be dictated by the contrived or not contrived label. Muir's experience of the tree ride was contrived, yet his environmental awareness and relationship to the natural surrounding, as demonstrated by his writings, was significant. Research of adventure based courses that include contrived activities supports that gains are made in participant's environmental awareness (Gillett, Thomas, Skok & McLaughlin, 1991; Hanna, 1995; Purdue & Warder, 1981); though Shepard & Speelman (1986) suggest the need for further research.

If a contrived or not contrived label does not serve as a guideline in explaining the likelihood of developing a relationship with the natural world, what can guide practitioners in the design of adventure based courses?

IN WILDNESS IS THE PRESERVATION OF THE WORLD

I believe that environmental awareness and connections to the earth are not guided by what degree an activity is contrived, but rather by another, perhaps deeper concept. Henry David Thoreau gives a term to this connection, to this spirit; he calls it wildness. In his essay *Walking* (1862), Thoreau suggests that it is this spirit that preserves the world,"...that in Wildness is the preservation of the World" (p. 672). It is interesting to note the high frequency of a slight but significant misquotation of this phrase, replacing "wildness" with "wilderness." The spirit of wildness is significant in making connections to oneself, to others, and to communities, either social or environmental. It is in these connections that a participant's relationship to the natural world is strengthened.

In looking at a ropes course experience, away from the contrived or not contrived labels, can aspects of wildness be observed, awakening connections with oneself? I can imagine the faces of former students with wild looks in their eyes as they clutch with a Muir-like tenacity to the huge branches, 65 feet up in the giant Red Oak anchoring the ropes course at the Outward Bound School in North Carolina. Whether this is perceived risk or actual, contrived or not, these students are coming into contact with the wild, tasting the metallic flavor in their mouth and smelling the odors of real emotion of their bodies, perhaps for the first time in their lives. One contrived purpose of a ropes course experience is to awaken the wild feelings within oneself, creating connections to fear, relief/joy, balance, and belief.

Willi Unsoeld, philosopher, theologian, teacher and mountaineer, lectured extensively about the concept of "alienation" and the spirit of wildness prior to his death in 1979. In an audio taped lecture to a group of National Park Service employees, Unsoeld conducted an informal experiment of participants, asking audience members to raise their hands if they did not put on underarm deodorant that morning. By the show of hands he would presumptively conclude that we are indeed, alienated from ourselves. "How can I take pride in me if I got to head me off at the armpit?" he says (Unsoeld, 1974). Alienation from true self is promoted extensively in our media and perpetuated in society blocking our connections to the wild. Experiences in adventure based courses can promote the connections to ourselves through experiences like ropes courses or rafting.

Similarly, adventure-based programming has the ability to promote connections to others. Unsoeld continued in his discussion with an example of alienation from others, citing his horrible favorite, the story of Kitty Genovese who was murdered "very inefficiently" (1974) in New York City over a period extending up to nearly an hour. Some 38 people witnessed the murder, including one individual who opened up a window, scared off the attacker, only to have him come back and finish off the job while Kitty was scratching on the door and pounding on it for help. As Unsoeld said, we are "alienated from each other to a degree far beyond that which we think we're capable of" (1974). In the years since the Genovese murder, I'm sure we are all painfully aware of an increasing number of similar stories. The connections to others that adventure based programming can unleash through shared adventure are significant.

And finally, Unsoeld (1974) goes on, we are alienated from nature, unconnected to the wildness. It is in this absence of connection and awareness, absence in the understanding that all is truly of one fabric that our alienation allows us to treat the earth in exploitive ways. The manner in which we are able to treat things effects how we treat people, a concept echoed by many in the ecofeminist movements. The connections formed during an adventure based course between nature and a participant can be so sufficient as to cause a disappearance of the perceived separation, and create a knowledge that is "like the knowledge of a mate: carnal and intimate yet, in love, immune to exploitation" (Turner, 1992, p. 21). In the words of Stephen J. Gould (1991), "we cannot win this battle to save species and environments without forging an emotional bond between ourselves and nature as well, for we will not fight to save what we do not love" (p. 14).

Adventure based courses have the ability to help facilitate experiences that allow wildness to battle alienation from self, others and communities, both social and environmental. A basic model of some adventure based programs, including Outward Bound, suggests that if participants can understand and respect self, then respect and compassion can flow to others in their group. In process of this flow, participants have the opportunity to see the connections between their group, and the greater social and environmental communities. I believe that the direction of the flow in this learning model can be both ways: nature-others-self or self-others-nature. The critical factor is that the ele-

ments of the adventure based course provide opportunities for participants to touch the wild in their connections to self, others and community.

The creation of a tradition of "Deep Wild" was introduced by Jack Turner, writer and chief guide at the Exum School of Mountaineering, at the National Outdoor Leadership School Wilderness Education Conference in 1992. Turner (1992) argues our industry has sold adventure, but has not passed on the spirit "of independence and passion for experiencing the wild and the free" (p. 21); as such, "we have a clientele too often characterized by dependence (p. 21)," thereby creating repeat customers who lack "the spirit of our wilderness heroes and do little to further the cause of wilderness preservation" (p. 21). Turner (1992) challenges us as educators to develop a tradition of Deep Wild within our students, helping to break the belief that something special is required to experience the wild besides spirit—"special equipment, special knowledge, special abilities—a belief favored by our culture because it reinforces patterns of consumption" (p. 21). What is the dollar value of the media's image of the backpacker, fully outfitted with all the required bells and whistles? Perhaps the fully equipped backpacker is less in touch with the wild, alienated and insulated from the feeling of rain, the cut of wind, or the bite of a mosquito. The number of individuals experiencing wilderness travel has increased dramatically in the last years; how many of these wilderness travelers are exploring wildness?

Finally, David Orr in *Ecological Literacy* (1992) writes persuasively about our continuing and growing ecological illiteracy. He points out that environmental issues are complex and cannot be understood through a single discipline or department, and urges the study and appreciation to look at interactions across the boundaries of conventional knowledge and experience. Orr (1992) argues, perhaps most importantly, that "all education is environmental education" and that "by what is included or excluded, emphasized or ignored, students learn that they are *a part of or apart from* [italics added] the natural world" (p. 90). I have little doubt that adventure based course leaders could teach almost any portion of their courses in a manner that does not strengthen a participant's relationship with the natural world, nor forge connections. The challenge, however, is to allow participants to make connections through the wild to self, others and nature through careful framing, role-modeling, debriefing and sharing in the experience.

Though I've done no exhaustive study to find the average length of adventure based courses, I feel confident that the length is likely less than 10 days. Similarly, I've done no research on the percentage of youth, who in their 12–16 years of education, if that, have the good fortune of taking part in one of these adventure based courses; again, I'd guess the number is relatively small. I'd hope, though, that with these few individuals who are exposed to our industry, we as educators would ensure that their courses, whether contrived or not, are filled with experiences that cause them to feel the connections; to feel the wildness. As our industry continues to serve a clientele of increasingly differing abilities and backgrounds, the diversity of approaches to accessing the wild should not be discounted.

It is my belief that an experience that gives a connection to wildness in any area, whether with self, in union with others, or in awareness of communities; those experiences have the potential to influence other areas. Conventional wisdom suggests that the learning of a third language is more easily accomplished than the learning of the second. Similarly, if participants feel the connections, the wildness in one area, whether it be self, others, or community, the probability to feel comparable connections with and in other areas is increased. With relatively few individuals taking relatively short adventure based courses, we need to make the most effective use of our time, planting wild seeds that can take root on a variety of levels. We must provide these experiences with the belief that it is these connections to the wild that a lasting relationship to the natural world can be demonstrated by activism and lifestyle choices of participants long after their adventure based course experience is over.

REFERENCES

Gillette, D., Thomas, G., Skok, R., & McLaughlin, T. (1991). The effects of wilderness camping and hiking on the self-concept and environmental attitudes of twelfth graders. *The Journal of Environmental Education, 22*(3), 33–44.

Gould, S. J. (1991, September). Enchanted Evening. *Natural History*, p. 14.

Hanna, G. (1995). Wilderness-related environmental outcomes of Adventure and ecology education programming. *The Journal of Environmental Education, 27*(1), 21–32.

Muir, J. (1921). *The mountains of California.* New York: Century.

Orr, D. W. (1992). *Ecological literacy: Education and the transition to a postmodern world.* Albany, NY: SUNY Press.

Outward Bound USA. (1997). *Annual safety report.* Garrison, NY: Author.

Purdue, R., & Warder, D. (1981). Environmental education and attitude change. *The Journal of Environmental Education, 12*(4), 27–28.

Shepard, C., & Speelman, L. (1986). Affecting environmental attitudes through outdoor education. *The Journal of Environmental Education, 17,* 20–23.

Thoreau, H. D. (1862). Walking. In H. S. Canby (Ed.), *The works of Thoreau* (pp. 648–689). Boston, MA: Houghton Mifflin.

Turner, J. (1992). Creating a tradition of "the deep wild". *Proceedings of the National Outdoor Leadership School's 4th Annual Wilderness Education Conference, 4,* 21–23.

Unsoeld, W. (Speaker). (1974). *Nature of Wilderness Values* (Cassette Recording, 11.28.74). Albright Training Center.

CHAPTER 13

Should Wildlands Be Made Available to More People, as Opposed to More Restrictions and Limitations?

YES PERSPECTIVE: Alan Ewert, Ph.D. and Erin K. Smith, M.A.

NO PERSPECTIVE: Pam Foti, Ph.D.

Alan Ewert, Ph.D. is currently a Professor and the Patricia and Joel Meier Endowed Chair in Outdoor Leadership in the Department of Recreation and Park Administration at Indiana University. Prior to this he was a Professor in Natural Resources and Environmental Studies and Program Chair for the Resource Recreation and Tourism Program at the University of Northern British Columbia in Prince George, British Columbia and Branch Chief of Recreation, Wilderness and Urban Forestry Research with the USDA Forest Service. His books include *Outdoor Adventure Pursuits: Foundations, Models and Theories; Culture, Conflict and Communication in the Wildland-Urban Interface and Natural Resource Management: The Human Dimension.* He is currently an Executive Editor for the *International Journal of Wilderness* and is the 1998–99 President of the Academy of Leisure Sciences.

Erin Smith, M.A. is currently a doctoral student in Recreation and Park Administration at Indiana University. She received her M.A. from The University of Georgia in recreation resource management and has worked as a practitioner in recreation leadership, environmental education, and recreation administration. Her present research areas of interest are the sociological and social psychological aspects of the outdoor recreation and wilderness experience.

**Pam Foti, Ph.D.**, is an Associate Professor in the Parks and Recreation Management Program, School of Forestry, at Northern Arizona University. She has a Bachelor of Science in Park and Recreation Administration from The Ohio State University, Master's in Wildland Recreation from the University of Nevada-Reno, and a Ph.D. in Land Resources from the University of Wisconsin-Madison. She has been at NAU for over 10 years, maintains research projects in Human Impact Monitoring in several southwest canyon areas, and is a frequent Grand Canyon hiker.

Should Wildlands Be Made Available to More People, as Opposed to More Restrictions and Limitations?

Alan Ewert, Ph.D. and Erin K. Smith, M.A.

Imagine the following scenario:

A young man decides that he wants to leave the city and explore the wildcountry. He longs to see nature at its finest; to experience danger and test his mettle against the challenges that come directly from the natural environment. He wants to see what nature has to offer and sets off exploring the canyons, mountains, rivers and forests. He feels strength from the wilderness and is energized from his rambles over hill and valley. Because of this experience and the bond that is formed between this man and the wilderness, he decides to dedicate his life to protecting these and other wildlands so that others may experience the richness and vitality that he has experienced. John Muir starts the Sierra Club.

Now imagine a more contemporary scenario:

A young man decides that he wants to leave the city and explore the wilderness. He longs for the freedom of hiking over mountains, through forests, and into canyons of the backcountry. He looks forward to all the challenges and opportunities that the wilderness can offer him. He thinks these experiences may afford him a new course of action for his life; something more fulfilling than his current occupation. With the eagerness of youth he approaches the ranger station only to be told that

all the permits have been given out and he could possibly get to hike into the backcountry some time next week. John Muir goes back to his home and his job, never to fulfill his dream of adventuring in the wilderness, never to fight for the protection of these lands. He goes on to other things in his life but never again to wilderness.

While the above scenarios utilize a great deal of poetic license, they represent one of three treatises we make in this chapter. In essence we believe that wildlands* should be made more available to more people, as opposed to the implementation of more restrictions and limitations. We take this position for the following reasons: First, we are not convinced that wilderness areas are overused and moreover we believe that limiting use is a misleading and inappropriate management option.

Secondly, we believe that our interpretation of wilderness as a place where people are

---

*Note: In this chapter we will use the terms wilderness and wildlands interchangeably. In cases where we are referring to officially-designated areas as are usually contained in the National Wilderness Preservation System (NWPS) we will use the term Wilderness with a capital "W."

visitors but not inhabitants is essentially a North American concept that is not widely ascribed to elsewhere. If we look across other cultures, it is clear that there exists a wide range of human interaction with and use of wilderness. Even within North American culture, individual feelings and attitudes regarding wilderness and wildlands are subject to differing interpretations as to how the land should be used, what are acceptable impacts and what value they provide to society. Thus, we would suggest that an approach that automatically considers higher visitation levels as opposed to the concept of wilderness is only one way to manage these types of landscapes.

Finally, we believe that actions and behaviors that foster wildland protection depend largely on the relationship people have with the landscape. The stronger that relationship, the more likely that individuals will be willing to protect and safeguard those wildlands. Thus, actual use of wilderness is the prerequisite to wilderness protection. This does not say that we believe in a philosophy of "anything goes as long as someone wants it" or "wildlands should be allowed to be severely degraded." Rather, we are implying that there is a cost that managers and wilderness advocates face when individuals are overly restricted in their visitation to wildlands and wilderness areas. This cost comes primarily in lost opportunities and a consequent reduction in the individual's willingness to "protect" these areas.

This chapter seeks to address the issue of making wildlands more available to people, and uses the following sequence. We will first examine the present use of wilderness and discuss whether or not we believe it is really being overused. We will discuss the problems we see with limiting visitation in the context of the protection of the resource. This will be followed with a discussion of the

social-psychological construct of wilderness in North America and a comparison with the concept of wilderness in other cultures and countries. That is, what constitutes a wilderness or wildland and how much are these lands actually used? Finally, we introduce the idea that directly experiencing the wilderness is a precursor to protecting that wilderness. We will examine three rationales or frameworks in which we believe that the relationship between wilderness use and wilderness protection is evident: conservation leadership; attitude and behavior theories; and the concept of place attachment.

PRESENT WILDERNESS USE

The argument of limiting visitor use is essentially making the assumption that the present use levels of wilderness are too high and that the wilderness or the wilderness experience is being compromised. While the oft-used phrase "loving it to death" has been linked to the use of wildlands, a recent report on wilderness visitation states that less than one percent of all nature-based outdoor recreation on government managed lands actually takes place in wilderness (Cordell & Teasley, 1998). Cordell and Teasley (1998) report that in 1994–5, while an estimated 49.5 million Americans visited local or state parks and resorts and 8.8 million Americans visited national parks, the total estimate of visitors to wilderness was less than 1.5 million. Remembering that officially-designated Wilderness lands now total over 104 million acres (Loomis, Bonetti, & Echohawk, 1999), the use of wilderness totaled just over one person per acre per year. Does this relatively low density of wilderness visitation represent a situation of overuse? Moreover, when acreage is held constant, wilderness recreation use is forecast to increase from 0.5 percent to slightly less than 1 percent per year for the next 50 years (Loomis, Bonetti, & Echohawk, 1999), further suggesting that it is unlikely that there will be a huge spike in visitation rates in the foreseeable future.

Obviously, the use of wilderness is not distributed evenly and there are locations that clearly have a much higher yearly density of users; particularly those wilderness areas that are closer to large urban environments (Ewert, 1998). However, crowding perceptions and wilderness expectations are dynamic phenomena that can change in a variety of ways. As suggested by Ewert (1998), perceptions of crowding differ as a function of the wildland area visited and that visitors to wildlands near large urban environments are not as expectant of high levels of solitude or pristine environments as are their counterparts in more remote locations.

In addition to concerns over the actual overuse of wilderness, we also question the management strategy of limiting visitor use as an appropriate one for maintaining ecological quality. Hammitt and Cole (1987) note that it is not just the *amount* of use but also the *type* of use that impacts wildlands. In addition, ecological impacts caused by visitor use generally follow an asymmetric pattern (i.e., the rate of change is significant in the initial stages of use but then tends to flatten out as visitor numbers increase). We believe that the most significant reductions in impact to wildland areas would occur if managers restricted horses and campfires, not just numbers of users.

WILDERNESS AS A SOCIAL CONSTRUCT

Our concept of wilderness has been shaped by our legal definition of wilderness as a set-

ting that provides 'solitude and primitive recreation' in an area that is 'untrammelled' where a person is 'a visitor and does not remain.' These terms have defined wilderness as we know it in North America. However, has our codification of wildlands tended to influence how we define wilderness? In other words, is an area automatically precluded from being wilderness if it has human inhabitation or is relatively small in area? A comparison of the wilderness concept in North America with that of other cultures gives us a greater insight for reflection on the role wilderness plays in our society.

Western and Non-Western Concepts of Wilderness

As previously mentioned, wilderness as we know it is a Western concept. Most societies in the world do not set aside land where natural processes dominate but people are not permitted to live. An examination of other cultures, both Western and non-Western, challenge some of the basic assumptions we hold about wilderness. Two of these assumptions are: (a) wilderness experiences are inherently beneficial and contribute to the survival and well-being of an individual or a society, and (b) wilderness and civilization are incompatible and must be experienced separately.

Some cultures do in fact see wilderness as inherently hostile, and experiences in wilderness are believed to be detrimental to an individual and to the culture. An example of a culture with radically different views of wilderness is the Bantu culture in Kenya. Bantus do not parcel off land and preserve it in its natural state; in fact, there is no word in Bantu language that can be equated with the term wilderness. The closest term is *eli-gyinga* which roughly translates into "wild bush beyond any foreseeable human use" (Burnett & Kang'ethe, 1994). Travel into the wilderness is resisted; entering the wilderness provides an opportunity for the wildness of the land to enter the human world and bring evil and disease into the Bantu communities.

At the other end of the spectrum is the relationship of Native American cultures and the land. Again, there is no concept in these cultures of wilderness as Westerners perceive it, because the process of excluding a space from being lived in and experienced is equivalent to keeping people from understanding themselves. Native American cultures experience a 'oneness' with the land that is difficult for Western cultures to comprehend. For Native Americans, it is unimaginable to live apart from the land; human and nature are extensions of each other and cannot be separated (Booth & Kessler, 1996). This relationship is illustrated by Paula Gunn Allen (1979):

> We are the land. To the best of my understanding, that is the fundamental idea embedded in Native American life and culture in the Southwest. More than remembered, the earth is the mind of the people as we are the mind of the earth. The land is not really the place (separate from ourselves) where we act out the drama of our isolated destinies. It is not a means of survival, a setting for our affairs, a resource on which we draw in order to keep our own art functioning. It is not the ever-present "Other" which supplies us with a sense of "I." It is rather a part of our being, dynamic, significant, real. It is ourself, in as real a sense as our notions of "ego," "libido" or social network, in a sense more real than any conceptualization or abstraction about the nature of the human being can ever be. (p.191)

The relationship of the indigenous cultures with the land as an extension of themselves is reflected in the view they hold toward wilderness. A quote by Chief Luther Standing Bear of the Ogalala Sioux in which he addresses the Western view of wilderness highlights the differences in perspectives between the two cultures:

> We did not think of the great and open plains, the beautiful rolling hills, and the winding streams with their tangled growth as "wild." Only to the white man was nature a "wilderness" and only to him was the land "infested" with "wild" animals and "savage" people. To us it was tame. (In Hendee, Stankey, & Lucas, 1990, p.48).

The idea of setting aside land from which people are kept out is incomprehensible to the Sioux. There is no overcrowding in wildlands according to the Sioux; wilderness is home, spirit, life.

Alternative Western Views of Wilderness

Even within Western cultures there are differences as to what is considered an acceptable level of use on wilderness lands. Among these cultures, the restrictions placed on wilderness use in the U.S. are the most extreme. For example, Finnish wilderness areas are also used as a place to raise reindeer and drive snowmobiles (Kajala & Watson, 1997). In Britain, the American view of wilderness doesn't exist and nor do the British want it to. Wilderness as in the U.S. is perceived as a "museum piece" that offers no more benefit to the visitor than a well-managed natural area (Henderson, 1992). Just as Nash (1982) suggests that one man's [sic] wilderness may be another's roadside picnic ground, we can also say that one culture's wilderness may be another culture's home, backyard, sustenance, or park. Even among other Western societies, our views toward wilderness remain quite extreme and esoteric.

How does this perception relate to placing more restrictions on visitations versus allowing more people in wilderness? It points to the importance of understanding that wilderness and wildlands can be perceived in numerous ways, and that an elitist North American viewpoint is only one of many perspectives. In a similar fashion, how individuals define the concepts of solitude and naturalness influences their evaluation of what is 'good' and 'bad' in a specific wilderness or wildland experience.

Solitude and naturalness aside, perhaps the real issue is not in numbers of people but in behaviors—i.e. we need stewardship not restrictions. Indeed, the most highly rated potential problem of wilderness as rated by managers is lack of wilderness stewardship skills and knowledge (42%), even higher than the 29% who feel that policies should be more restrictive; perhaps stewardship skills would further reduce this (Gager, Hendee, Kinziger, & Krumpe, 1998). Beyond the issue of the concepts of wilderness use and stewardship, we believe there is an even stronger reason for making the wildlands more available to people, namely what happens when people experience the wildlands?

THE RELATIONSHIP BETWEEN USE AND PROTECTION

John Isle, a noted writer on natural resource and conservation policy once noted the following:

> The history of the United States is fundamentally a history of rapid exploitation of immensely valuable natural resources. The possession and exploitation of these resources have given most of the distinctive traits to American character, economic development, and even political and social institu-

tions....Thus, the question of conservation is one of the most important questions before the American people. (In Clepper, 1966, p.3)

By the middle of the nineteenth century, the cities of America had developed into highly urbanized and often undesirable entities. From this period there arose two distinct streams of thought concerning how Americans felt about nature. One approach, epitomized by Henry David Thoreau's, "In wilderness is the preservation of the world," spoke to the cathartic and cleansing effect wilderness could have on the individual city dweller. The other stream characterized nature and wilderness as an atavistic foundation for building the national character (e.g., hardy, stern, resolute).

Whether you ascribe to wildlands as catharsis or building a national character, the underlying assumption in both cases is that the individual is actively participating in the experience. The beneficial effects of wilderness were not viewed from an "armchair" perspective but rather from the perspective of being out in the wildlands and directly experiencing it. Nor was preservation of wilderness viewed from a biological diversity perspective but rather from the perspective of what wilderness could do for people (Wirth, 1966).

How do we see active experience in wildlands associated with wildland preservation? We contend that knowing wilderness through direct experience is an important and often first step in developing a meaningful relationship with the natural environment. In turn, this 'knowing' will result in an increased level of willingness to protect and safeguard these landscapes. To support this argument, we can work from both ends of the use-protection relationship. We look at wilderness protection leaders and examine their past use of wilderness, and we look at theories and concepts that support the link between use and protection, including the theory of planned behavior and the concept of place attachment.

Conservation Leadership

With few exceptions, this active involvement in wilderness and wildlands is present in many of the past proponents of wilderness. Individual wilderness advocates who also had significant personal interaction with the wildlands included the following: George Catlin, George Perkins Marsh, Henry David Thoreau, Theodore Roosevelt, William Cullen Bryant, John Muir, Bob Marshall, Frederick Law Olmsted, Aldo Leopold, Stephen Mather, John J. Audubon, Grey Owl (Canada), Bill Mason (Canada), and Ian Player (South Africa). More recent leaders in wilderness and environmental conservation who also have had an extensive personal interaction with the wildlands include Wallace Stegner, Edward Abbey, Roderick Nash, Rachel Carson, and Stewart Udall.

We acknowledge that it could be mere coincidence that the individuals listed above had direct involvement with the natural environment and that this interaction played little or no role in the formation of their attitudes and values toward those environments. What, then, does research suggest about this relationship between personal involvement in wilderness-type settings and pro-environmental attitudes?

A number of authors have documented conservation and environmental leaders and their past involvement with wilderness and wildland settings (Ibrahim, 1989; Nash, 1968). From a research perspective Nord, Luloff, and Bridger (1998) found a moderately strong correlation between frequency of visits to forest areas and pro-environmental behavior.

More specifically, Tanner (1980) looked at significant life experiences among selected conservationists in the United States. Of the life experiences listed, outdoor activities were the most prominent factor for 35 of the 45 respondents. In a similar fashion, contact with the natural environment was the second most prominent factor for 26 of the 45 respondents. Tanner concluded that experiences in outdoor pristine environments were dominant influencing variables in the development of the attitudes and value systems of the conservationists studied.

Building on Tanner's work, Palmer (1993) looked at categories that influence the development of types and levels of knowledges held by selected environmental educators. Of the 13 categories examined, the outdoor environment was listed as the most important by 91 percent of the respondents. As suggested by Place (1998), the studies by Tanner and Palmer emphasize the power the outdoor environment can exert in developing images as well as subsequent attitudes and behaviors associated with conservation and environmentalism.

In developing our position we also consider the theory of planned behavior developed by Ajzen (1985, 1991) and others which suggests that behavior is often a result of past experience and subsequent attitude formation. Within this context, we believe that attitudes are strongly influenced by past experience and behaviors are strongly influenced by attitudes. Moreover, a significant amount of research suggests that direct experience is the most powerful and influential way to learn and effect attitudes (Bandura, 1977; Driver, Brown, & Peterson, 1991; Manfredo, 1992). Thus, our logic is as follows: direct experiences in natural wildland settings develop attitudes and values that result in behaviors that are pro-wilderness. Reduce or eliminate these direct experiences and subsequent pro-wilderness attitudes and resultant behaviors are not formed. In essence, reducing the opportunity to visit a wildland or wilderness setting can and will result in a reduction in the public's willingness to protect and safeguard these areas.

Place Attachment

The concept of *place attachment* purports that people can develop attachments to places in a similar way as they do to other people or objects. What results from a wilderness experience is a formation of emotional bonds and memories tied to the wilderness area. In essence, what was once an abstract symbol (i.e. 'wilderness') becomes a personally meaningful place after you experience it for yourself. Instead of wilderness being an image in the mind of a visitor, it becomes, a place where personal challenges are faced, where a person feels free to express him or herself, or where an individual can experience the natural environment with friends or family. Upon returning, wilderness is no longer a spot on the map; it has become an integral part of the memory and identity of the visitor, and to be without it would to also be without a part of oneself.

The place attachment concept has been applied to people's relationship with natural landscapes in the fields of environmental psychology and human geography. Within this context, Tuan (1977) defines place as space that has been given meaning, and what begins as undifferentiated space becomes place as we get to know it better and endow it with value and a sense of attachment. Attachment can be defined as an affective relationship between people and the landscape that goes beyond cognition, preference, or judgment (Riley, 1992). Inherent in the concept of place attachment are the elements of emotion, meaning, and identification; as people become attached to a place, the place becomes a significant part of their lives. Numerous authors report that people are invested and linked to places to which they are attached (Hummon, 1992; Hunter, 1978). Through interaction with places, people develop what Relph (1976) terms an "existential insideness" which is characterized by an unselfconscious identification and feeling of belongingness to a place. The place becomes perceived as a living, dynamic relationship full of meaning and significance that is known and valued.

Researchers have applied the place attachment concept to wilderness (Brandenburg & Carroll, 1995; Williams, Patterson, Roggenbuck & Watson, 1992). While Williams et al. (1992) only examined actual wilderness users, they noted that across all the wilderness settings examined, individuals with more previous visits and more years since their first visit to the wildland area were more attached to it, suggesting that personal interaction in wilderness has some influence to the level of attachment a person feels toward it.

Brandenburg and Carroll (1995) compared the attachment to a wildland river drainage between people who had personally interacted with it and people who had not. Their phenomenological study revealed that people who visited the wildland area perceived it as "unique" and "special" as suggested in the following quotation:

> The [river drainage] is a place of secrets. When I am there I feel like nature is whispering in my ear, telling me of the things that most people don't take time to hear. I know there are other places that are remote and natural and stuff, I've spent my life in the woods, but [this river drainage] is a special

place, there is something mystical about it. (Brandenburg & Carroll, 1995, p.387)

It can be argued that meaningful place attachments can be developed in settings other than wildlands. However, in our cities and communities, many of the opportunities for making connections between people and natural places have been removed. The homogenization of our environment via business franchises, strip malls, and planned developments has removed the uniqueness of our communities and, as Godbey (1997) argues, removed meaning and authenticity from our lives.

We argue that wildland settings have inherent qualities that make them particularly salient for attachment. In wildlands, every place is clearly unique as it is created and recreated by natural processes and not from the plans of an architect or designer. Moreover, the individual often must exert considerable energy and self-motivation to get to these sites. This increased cost often results in a perception of higher value. Opportunities to experience the unique environments of the wildlands increases the potential for people to develop meaningful and emotionally rewarding relationships with their surroundings. For example, the interaction with wildlands can serve as a catalyst for awakening people to the natural processes going on around them and their place in that system; suddenly their impact on the ecosystem is recognized. The following is a quote from an individual explaining his motivation for beginning to recycle:

> When you started getting more...step out of doors...fishing, stuff like that, where you, I don't know, get in touch with nature, whatever you want to call it. You started to get a little bit responsible feelings for it...I think getting out into nature has a big deal to it...I

think that's where I got it from...getting out into nature, you started to see the things that you could actually be harming...you started to see your victims, so to speak. (Hallin, 1995, p. 567)

People attached to wildlands also indicate a willingness to modify personal behaviors in order to protect the area. In fact, personal interaction with and attachment to wildlands developed pro-environmental views that can supersede broader views of resource management:

> Well, when you talk about the national forest as a whole it should be managed multiple use, we need to be logging this land. But the [river drainage] is a pretty special place, you just need to go up there to see that. (Brandenburg & Carroll, 1995, p. 387).

The willingness to alter personal behaviors and the process of reexamining social norms and standards that result from wildland visitation are the essential keys in wildland protection. If people return from the wilderness more willing to support as well as act to protect and preserve those landscapes, then would not the true value of wilderness be realized? That is, if we value these types of resources should we not also promote ways to strengthen their protection rather than simply "locking them up?"

The province of Alberta provides a case study of the effect of overly restrictive wilderness regulation. As Stankey, Martin, and Nash (1990) report, the Alberta Wilderness Areas Act is so restrictive of any type of wilderness recreation, preferring instead, to treat wilderness designated lands as ecological reserves; that there has been little pressure or interest on the part of wilderness advocacy groups or the general public to promote new areas for protection. Rather, the public has increasingly supported the idea of creating "Wildland Recreation Areas" that allow for various forms of traditional, dispersed recreational activities.

CONCLUSION

Many would suggest that wildlands should be protected for the sake of biological diversity rather than scenic beauty or recreational opportunities (Brandon, Redford, & Sanderson, 1998; Grumbine, 1994). Some would go so far as to suggest that emphasis on wilderness protection detracts from more immediate and important environmental concerns (Cronon, 1995; Gomez-Pompa & Kaus, 1992). We are not disputing the importance of biodiversity but would point out three items for consideration. First, many if not most wildland/wilderness areas are in locations not suitable for extensive biodiversity considerations (e.g., high mountains, glaciated peaks, desert areas, etc.). From a global perspective, if you are concerned with maximizing biodiversity, protecting wilderness areas would not be the most efficacious way to achieve it. Second, in its complexity, biodiversity is a difficult term for the public to understand, whereas remembering that wilderness trip to a beautiful backcountry lake is much more accessible to both their memory and comprehension. Third, some believe that in order to achieve sustainable development within park systems, the parks must be used. A view promoted as a win-win situation at the 1992 World Parks Congress in Caracas in which human use of wildlands and parks is considered the best long-term way to preserve them (Brandon, Redford, & Sanderson, 1998).

Thus, we conclude our argument that *more* rather than *fewer* people should be allowed in wildlands. This is not to discount the numerous concerns surrounding the management and allocation of wilderness and wildland areas such as biodiversity, specific impacts such as horse use; and non-point sources of pollution from locations outside of the wilderness (e.g., air pollution).

Moreover, we contend that wildlands and wilderness areas are essentially social constructs and as such, will only receive continued protection if society supports this protection. Given the fact that resource impacts generally occur as a function of type of use rather than simply the amount of use, restricting use may do little to elevate use impacts to specific areas but may very well serve to reduce long-term support for wildland protection in general. As a result, specific locations may be preserved at the expense of support for the continued existence of system-wide protection. In other words, individual parks may be preserved at the expense of saving park and wilderness systems. This loss will probably not occur in the near future, but who can say how our progeny will feel about "locking up" significant areas of landscapes which few would be able to visit? Will wildland and wilderness areas become only an abstract concept in their mind from which they are expected to continue with the same level and intensity of preservation and conservation that we currently possess? Will our generation be the last that has the wide-spread opportunity to actually visit these precious bits of landscape; visits from which we emerge determined not to let them disappear?

"Go forth, under the open sky, and list to Nature's teachings."

William Cullen Bryant, 1817

REFERENCES

Ajzen, I. (1985). From intentions to actions: A theory of planned behavior. In J. Kuhl and J. Beckmann (Eds.), *Action-control: From cognition to behavior* (pp. 11–39). Heidelberg, Germany: Springer-Verlag.

Ajzen, I. (1991). Benefits of leisure: A social psychological perspective. In B. Driver, P. Brown, & G. Peterson (Eds.), *Benefits of Leisure* (pp. 411–417). State College, PA: Venture Publishing.

Allen, P. G. (1979). The Sacred Hoop: A contemporary Indian perspective on American literature. In G. Hobson (Ed.), *The Remembered Earth* (pp. 222–239). Albuquerque, NM: Red Earth Press.

Bandura, A. (1977). Self-efficacy: Toward a unifying theory of behavioral change. *Psychological Review, 84*, 191–215.

Brandenburg, A. M. & Carroll, M. S. (1995). Your place or mine? The effect of place creation on environmental values and landscape meanings. *Society and Natural Resources, 8*, 381–398.

Brandon, K., Redford, K. & Sanderson, S. (Eds.). (1998). *Parks in peril: People, politics, and protected areas.* Washington, D.C.: The Nature Conservancy/ Island Press.

Booth, A. & Kessler, W. B. (1996). Understanding linkages of people, natural resources, and ecosystem health. In A.W. Ewert (Ed.), *Natural Resource Management: The Human Dimension* (pp. 231–248). Boulder, CO: Westview Press.

Burnett, G.W. & Kang'ethe, K. (1994). Wilderness and the Bantu Mind. *Environmental Ethics, 16(2)*, 145–160.

Clepper, H. (Ed.). (1966). The conservation movement: Birth and infancy. *Origins of American Conservation* (pp. 3–15). New York: The Ronald Press Company.

Cordell, H. K. & Teasley, J. (1998). Recreational Trips to Wilderness. *International Journal of Wilderness, 4(1)*, 23–27.

Cronon, W. (1995, August 13). The trouble with wilderness. *The New York Times Magazine, 144(50152)*, 42.

Driver, B., Brown, P., & Peterson, G. (Eds.). (1991). *Benefits of leisure.* State College, PA: Venture Publishing, Inc.

Ewert, A. (1998). A comparison of urban-proximate and urban-distant wilderness users on selected variables. *Environmental Management, 22*, 927–936.

Gager, D., Hendee, J. C., Kinziger, M., & Krumpe, E. (1998). What managers are saying—and doing—about wilderness experience programs. *Journal of Forestry, 96(8)*, 33–37.

Godbey, G. (1997). *Leisure and leisure services in the 21st century.* State College, PA: Venture Publishing.

Gomez-Pompa, A. & A. Kaus. (1992). Taming the Wilderness myth. *BioScience, 42*, 271–279.

Grumbine, R. E. (1994). Wildness, wise use, and sustainable development. *Environmental Ethics, 16(3)*, 227–249.

Hallin, P. O. (1995). Environmental concern and environmental behavior in Foley, a small town in Minnesota. *Environment and Behavior, 27(4)*, 558–578.

Hammitt, W. & Cole, D. (1987). *Wildland recreation: Ecology and management.* New York: John Wiley & Sons.

Hendee, J. C., Stankey, G. H., & Lucas, R. C. (1990) *Wilderness Management.* Golden, CO: North American Press.

Henderson, N. (1992). Wilderness and the Nature Conservation Ideal: Britain, Canada, and the United States Contrasted. *Ambio, 21(6)*, 394–9.

Hummon, D. M. (1992). Community attachment: Local sentiment and sense of place. In I. Altman & S.M. Low (Eds.), *Place Attachment* (pp. 253–278). New York: Plenium Press.

Hunter, A. (1978). Persistence of local sentiments in mass society. In D. Street (Ed.), *Handbook of urban life* (pp. 133–162). San Francisco: Jossey-Bass.

Ibrahim, H. (1989). *Pioneers in leisure and recreation*. Reston, VA: AAHPERD Publishing.

Kajala, L & Watson, A. E. (1997). Wilderness—Different Cultures, Different Research Needs. *International Journal of Wilderness, 3(2)*, 33–36.

Loomis, J., Bonetti, & Echohawk, C. (1999). Demand for and supply of wilderness. In H. K. Cordell (Principal Investigator), *Outdoor Recreation in American Life* (pp. 351–375). Champaign, IL: Sagamore Publishing.

Manfredo, M. (Ed.). (1992). *Influencing human behavior: Theory and applications in recreation, tourism, and natural resources management*. Champaign, IL: Sagamore Publishing Inc.

Nash, R. (Ed.). (1968). *The American environment: Readings in the history of conservation*. Redding, MS: Addison-Wesley Publishing Company.

Nash, R. (1982). *Wilderness and the American Mind (3rd ed.)*. New Haven, CT: Yale University Press.

Nord, M., Luloff, A., & Bridger, J. (1998). The association of forest recreation with environmentalism. *Environment and Behavior, 30(2)*, 235–246.

Palmer, J. (1993). Development of concern for the environment and formative experiences for educators. *Journal of Environmental Education. 24(3)*, 26–30.

Place, G. (1998). Conservationist and environmentalist: The outdoor influence. Unpublished paper.

Relph, E. (1976). *Place and Placelessness*. London: Pion.

Riley, R.B. (1992). Attachment to the Ordinary Landscape. In I. Altman & S.M. Low (Eds.), *Place Attachment* (pp. 13–35). New York: Plenium Press.

Stankey, G., Martin, V., & Nash, R. (1990). International concepts of wilderness preservation and management. In J. Hendee, G. Stankey, & R. Lucas, *Wilderness Management* (pp. 45–96). Golden, CO: North American Press.

Tanner, T. (1980). Significant life experiences: A new research area in environmental education. *Journal of Environmental Education, 11(4)*, 20–24.

Tuan, Y. (1977). *Space and place: The perspective of experience*. Minneapolis, MN: University of Minnesota Press.

Williams, D. R., Patterson, M. E., Roggenbuck, J. W. & Watson, A. E. (1992). Beyond the commodity metaphor: Examining emotional and symbolic attachment to place. *Leisure Sciences, 14*, 29–46.

Wirth, C.L. (1966). Parks and wilderness. In H. Clepper (Ed.), *Origins of American conservation*. New York: The Ronald Press Company.

Should Wildlands Be Made Available to More People, As Opposed to More Restrictions And Limitations?

Pam Foti, Ph.D.

The Paria River flows intermittently from its headwaters in Bryce Canyon National Park, through Utah and Arizona to deposit silt and sediment in the Colorado River. The spectacular beauty of Paria Canyon, especially the 40 miles from Whitehouse Trailhead to Lee's Ferry, is known internationally. Hikers and backpackers are drawn to the colorful, winding corridors of stone, the narrow passages, and the constricted gorges. In addition, a trip through Paria Canyon becomes a fascinating geological adventure as visitors are treated to a stunning display of seven major geologic formations, including the 1200 foot Navajo Sandstone formation.

In 1986, 2400 people hiked through Paria Canyon, this number swelled to 5060 people in 1992 and then jumped to 6925 in 1994. In 1996, 10,200 people hiked either all or a portion of Paria Canyon—a 375% increase in use over 10 years. The tremendous increase in visitors left its toll.

Intensive wilderness monitoring began in Paria Canyon in 1995. A 1997 report indicated that out of 23 monitoring sites, two were extremely impacted, nine were heavily impacted, seven were moderately impacted, and five were slightly impacted and none were unimpacted. The major problems noted in Paria Canyon included human waste disposal, fire impacts, vegetative damage, litter, and general "pioneering behavior" of visitors as they continued to carve out new camp/use sites. By 1997, the extent of impact had reached a level where managerial action was necessary in order to protect the environmental parameters of the resource base and the wilderness values of the visitor's experience. Finally, in January of 1998, overnight use was restricted to 20 entries per day for all trailheads.

Coyote Buttes is a Special Management Area within the Paria Canyon-Vermilion Cliffs Wilderness Area. The thoroughly wild, swirling ridges of rock within Coyote Buttes contain small and fragile formations which create a feeling of wonder and amazement. Not long ago, the colorful sandstone swirls and cone-like "hoodoos" of Coyote Buttes existed in relative obscurity—in fact, virtually unknown. National recognition came slowly at first through national publications, magazines, landscape photography, and word-of-mouth. International recognition came through similar modes, but at an almost exponential rate, especially with the addition of Coyote Buttes' photos and information on the Internet. Today, Coyote Buttes is a much sought after "trophy" hike with almost all hikers focused on viewing a frequently photographed formation called "the wave".

Like Paria Canyon, the significant increases in visitor use between 1990 to 1996 resulted in human and environmental impacts. Unlike Paria Canyon, Coyote Buttes had neither the size nor the resource tolerance for significant increases in visitor use. The area is small and the rocks are extremely fragile. In fact, the values so highly treasured in Coyote Buttes can only be maintained by limiting treasure hunters. While the area is currently assessed in monitoring reports as being "unimpacted to slightly impacted", the potential for impacts is so great that managerial decisions related to visitor use were highly recommended. In 1996 visitor limits were initially established to protect the site and the visitor experience, these limits were increased in 1998 to allow additional access within the tolerance levels of the site.

The two examples above are representative of canyons and sandstone areas throughout the Southwest. A 1990's hobby is to "bag" slot canyons; a new passion is to photograph colorful sandstone swirls. As the masses of visitors seek to satisfy their drives, the resource base suffers the impacts, and the blows to wilderness values are further undermined. Do resource and human values inherent in wildland areas need to be protected from the numerous visitors who seek to enjoy the area through the imposition of limits and permits? I would argue a resounding "yes".

A question which has plagued resource managers for decades has been "how many" in an area; what is the carrying capacity of a wildland area? Many answers have been proposed, but few have been completely successful. Whether or not there is a "magical" number which represents the true carrying capacity of a site remains to be seen; beyond the "true number" though, the fact remains that recreational impacts do exist and do decrease the quality of the resource base and the social system of wildland areas.

One way to consider recreational impacts to wildlands is through the PBS system: physical, biological, and social. In considering this system, the ultimate question is "given the recreational impacts, is the level of use 'worth' the impact to the site or the user?" The answer to this question is only apparent within managerial philosophies and environmental ethics of both visitors and managers.

Physical impacts to wildland recreation sites are well known. Recreationists impact soils through compaction and erosion and they impact fragile rock formations through breakage and vandalism. Wildland sites' water impacts from recreationists include eutrophication, contamination, and suspended matter/turbidity. There is no doubt that at some level of use, which can be assessed through site monitoring, the physical impacts of visitors exceed the ability of the site to sustain a healthy, balanced system.

Biological impacts are also frequently the result of visitors to a wildland area. Site flora may be trampled, broken, or bruised. Tree roots become exposed as a result of excess site use and sometimes result in the death of the tree. One of the largest impacts, especially in southwestern canyon areas, is the damage to trees as a result of campfire woodgathering. In popular wildland areas, managers grapple with questions such as, "how many new campsites should be allowed in an area?" or "how much vegetative loss of a site is appropriate before the integrity of the site is compromised?"

Biological impacts related to recreation also include things such as wildlife habitat destruction, harassment of wildlife species, and interference with breeding cycles and habits of animal populations. Should areas be closed off to recreationist to allow breeding? Again, it is a question of managerial priorities and user ethics. Is the action worth the impact?

Of course, wildland site visitors have impacts on the site's social system. Relationships to consider in the social system include individual to individual, group to group, groups to multiple users, and groups to administrative agencies. The dynamics of each of these relationships are complex and varied, but critical to the successful experience of each visitor. Is there a point where there are too many people in the same area to provide a wild experience? Are wildland areas simply amusement parks filled with natural features instead of human-made features? The social values of a wildland site are as important as the physical and biological components. These values may become degraded and, once lost, can result in the deterioration of a site and of an experience.

The existence of human recreational impacts is obvious and can be documented in every canyon in the Southwest; in many cases the same impacts occur in canyon after canyon. And, managers can be persuaded to implement limitations, restrictions, and permits in canyon after canyon. But the real focus of limits and restrictions should be on user ethics.

Permits are annoying to deal with and difficult to obtain, sometimes taking up to three months for an educational group permit. Restrictions are frustrating and may result in being denied access to an area on the

"best" weekend; or users might have to plan ahead to ensure entry into a site or schedule their visit during the off-season.

Is it all right for enthusiastic users to "love an area to death"? Rather than reacting negatively to limits and restrictions, don't conscientious users have an ethical responsibility to embrace the role of limits and restrictions for the good of the site? The final question in considering site impacts really draws upon the environmental ethics of the user: Is recreational use above and beyond the physical, biological, and social limits "worth" the impact I might cause? Realistically, only the user can address this question based on his/her ethical principles. But regardless of an individual's ethical approach, the conscientious user must be able to accept and respect site limits and restrictions.

Ethics may be defined as the voluntary restriction of behavior based on the understanding of the need for restriction. An individual may not "like" restrictions, limits, and permits; but ultimately they may understand the "need" for them to protect wildland values. Wildland users may approach the ethical questions by concentrating on the consequences to the site of their actions (End-Result Ethics). Or, they may choose behavior based on a set of moral principles, like scientific principles which relate to a site (Rule Ethics). Some users may elect to value limits and restrictions by understanding that these are merely part of the social contract which protects the good of a site for all users, present and future (Social Contract Ethics). Finally, a user may understand the need for permits, limits, and restrictions through personal convictions which guide his/her behavior (Personalistic Ethics). Whatever ethical approach an individual might take; in all cases, the person has the option of ultimately making an individual choice related to site use and overuse. Is the action worth the impact?

I frequently teach outdoor leadership using scenarios for the students to work through; perhaps a short permits/limits/ restrictions example is appropriate.

"You and your three hiking partners have been planning a hike in the Great Canyon for the last eight months. You know that you can apply for a hiking permit at least four months in advance of the hike. It was your responsibility to obtain the permit. Your work schedule has been hectic and the permit slipped your mind until last week, three weeks before the trip. You call the back-country office and inquire about the availability of a permit in the hiking area of your choice. You discover that there are no permits available in that area for your hiking time. With a silent curse, you hang up the phone and consider your options. First, you know that the area you have chosen is large in size and receives little use. The area is unimpacted and the resource base is in very good condition. Second, you know that the probability of seeing a backcountry ranger is slim to none during the time of year that you will be hiking. Third, you know that you probably won't even see the other permitted hikers in the area. And, fourth, you know that your hiking partners have depended on you to get the permit. What do you do? What are the impacts? Are the impacts worth the action?"

Permits, limits, and restrictions are part of our world in the 21st century; and they are part of the formula to protect our wildland areas into the future. Managers need to use the tools available to protect all of the environmental components of a site and to re-spect all of the social components of an experience. It is incumbent upon wildland users to find, within their ethical systems, the ability to understand and accept the tools of protection.

REFERENCES:

Bureau of Land Management. (1997). User Statistics (unpublished). Kanab Field office, Kanab Utah.

Cole, D. N. (1982). Wilderness campsite impacts: effect of amount of use. USDA Forest Service Intermountain Research Station. Research Report INT-284.

The Wilderness Threats Matrix: a framework for assessing impacts. (1994). USDA Forest Service Intermountain Research Station. Research Report INT-475.

Cordell, K. H., Bergstrom, J. C., Hartman, L. A., and English, D. B. K. (1990). An analysis of the outdoor recreation and wilderness situation in the United States: 1989–2040. Washington, DC: USDA, Forest Service.

Hendee, J. C., Stankey, G. H., and Lucas, R. C. (1990). Wilderness management (2nd edition). Golden: Fulcrum Publishing.

Marion, J. L. (1991). Developing a natural resource inventory and monitoring program for visitor impacts on recreation site: a procedure manual. Denver: National Park Service, Natural Resources Publication Office. National Resources Report NPS/NVRT/NRR-91/06.

CHAPTER 14

Is It Possible to Justify a "Value-Laden" Position for Ecologically-Based Adventure Education?

YES PERSPECTIVE: Holly Bickerton, M.S. and Bob Henderson, Ph.D.
NO PERSPECTIVE: Daniel Vokey, Ph.D.

Holly Bickerton is a recent graduate of the Faculty of Environmental Studies, York University, Toronto, Ontario. She has worked in a number of OEE settings, including the Boyne River Science School and Charleston Lake Provincial Park. She is also a graduate of the Queen's University Co-op Program in Outdoor and Experiential Education.

Bob Henderson, Ph.D. teaches Outdoor Education and Environmental Inquiry with the Departments of Kinesiology and the Arts and Science Programme at McMaster University, respectively. He is currently the chair of the editorial board of *PATHWAYS: The Ontario Journal of Outdoor Education.*

Daniel Vokey, Ed.D., has taught outdoor adventure education at Strathcona Park Lodge on Vancouver Island, B.C.; W3 Adventure in Montreal, Quebec; Queen's University in Kingston, Ontario; and The Canadian Outward Bound Wilderness School, Northern Ontario. Daniel served on the Advisory Board of the Journal of Experiential Education and as Guest Editor of the Journal of COBWS Education. He currently facilitates activity-based team-building workshops on a contract basis and teaches in the Faculty of Education of the University of Prince Edward Island.

Is It Possible to Justify a "Value-Laden" Position for Ecologically-Based Adventure Education?

Holly Bickerton, M.S. and Bob Henderson, Ph.D.

Moments of profound clarity are rare in life. When they occur, we should hold onto them and refer to them often for ourselves and others. The story below offers one of those moments, and we share it in the spirit of understanding the many links between adventure education, and educating for wider social and ecological change.

Recently, one of us was riding down a hill into an apple orchard, the tractor bouncing along with outdoor educator Pete Herlihy behind the wheel. It was the last day of a week-long residential stay at the Boyne River Natural Science School in southern Ontario. Keen grade six students were bounding through the spring blossoms. Pete's task was to debrief the week stay at Boyne River, where frequently, the program offers a balance of adventure and environmental education. This particular week, the students had taken part in some seemingly disparate programs. On one hand, they had all participated in both group initiatives, and in the individual challenge of an aerial course. On the other hand, their program had a strong environmental focus, with elements of the Institute for Earth Education's Earthkeepers

programme scattered throughout the week. Smoothly, Pete rallied the group and began to review their week together. At the end of the session, Pete provided the following summary for the students. This is where the clarity of expression struck deeply, for Pete seamlessly combined the goals of adventure, outdoor, and environmental educators into four main objectives.

Pete began by stressing the kinds of individual challenges the students had undertaken: some low-ropes initiatives over the river, the aerial course. He explained how important our *self* is; how we need character skills such as confidence and self-esteem. All our actions come from a sure understanding of ourselves; without this, we can't begin to sort out social and environmental challenges. Second, Pete reviewed the activities that required co-operation: the group initiatives, the challenges. The group discussed how we need to work together and co-operate as a *community* because we can't solve the big problems on our own. Third, we reviewed some of the concepts we'd learned about nature: cycles and interdependence, and natural change over time. We needed *knowledge* to understand our place on the earth; for without knowledge and a respect for the mystery of nature, we would have no understanding of the challenges we face in learning how to act wisely, for our local homes, and the earth as home. And, finally, we remembered the exciting, magical and fun-filled activities we'd done: a drink from a clear, cold spring, discovering, a muddy hike, a campfire. Above all, our time in nature should be fun and should feed the *spirit*. It is only through deep appreciation and enjoyment, even love, that we will find the motivation and foster the values that we need for responsible action towards ourselves, our communities, and the earth.

So succinct, so true, so rich in meaning, such a clear linking of adventure and environmental-based teaching! In four straightforward points, Pete had brought these sentiments together into clarity. When asked where the clarity came from, Pete humbly commented that he'd "had some time to think about it" while driving the tractor through the sunshine. Not bad for a morning's work!

These four statements capture a clarity of expression for those outdoor educators who consciously and intentionally combine adventure and environmental education objectives and practices; with an aim toward cultivating ecological consciousness. Many of us go about these same four objectives in our practice intuitively, or we may tend to express our practice in more complex language and meaning. Whatever the case, we were then, and remain, struck by Pete's seamless review of the aspirations for an outdoor education programme.[1] But this is not an end to our story; it serves rather as a beginning.

Certainly adventure education and environmental education are compatible; as Pete suggested, we need to change ourselves and our interactions with others, as well as learning about the environmental and social challenges we face. But as adventure educators, we feel that we can't just leave our work after Pete's second objective; that is, focusing on self and community. In this paper we hope to suggest that as educators, we have an ethical duty to work toward meaningful social and environmental change. To do this, we need to teach students the knowledge they require in order to contribute to lasting social and environmental change, and to foster and encourage a spirited commitment and an ethic of care toward the natural world.

The educator could stop us anytime now with a resounding, "But wait! Certainly you are aware that this assumes the need to *change* how we live. The implicit message is that we dwell wrongly, and that there is a socio-cultural environmental crisis to which we must ethically respond. It represents a value-laden stance by the educator assuming problems and challenges we must respond to." To all these connected statements, we would answer: yes. We are aware of these grounding assumptions to our practice. As educators who actively encourage students to re-vision the place of human kind in nature, we are aware of our difficult ethical position. Indeed, we regularly find ourselves asking the questions: am I advocating or educating? This constitutes the main discussion of this paper: is it ethical to suggest that students change their values? (Of course, it is the student who elects to change by learning, but we provide the important context in which this occurs.) How is it possible to explain, and even to justify, our ethical position as adventure and environmental educators?

In this paper we will explore these questions. First, why is it important that we, as adventure educators, maintain an educational goal of socio-environmental change?

And second, if we do, how do we respond to charges of being "biased", single-sided, and propagandist? To these questions, we offer three main points, upon which we elaborate below. First, let us emphasize that we really do believe that we are facing a social-cultural ecological crisis that implores our responsible action as educators. Second, we will discuss the point that the environmental crisis is essentially one of values and morals, and suggest reasons why discussions concerning fundamental moral issues leave us grasping for words in our own defense. Finally, we hope to discuss teaching values as adventure educators, and to make the point clear that in education, there is no neutral position: we are all advocating something.

This is equally true in adventure education, and we raise these issues because we believe that, by avoiding this controversial issue in our practice, we exist in a grey area, a sort of black hole, that confounds and confuses intentions. And therefore, we need to make some confirmed stance for our professional practice. The silence on this issue of our environmental-based ethical agency in education may also serve to silence deeply relevant discussion on difficult, but important student issues of lifestyle and worldview pertaining to self, community, knowledge, and spirit. It seems a shame, even an injustice, to shirk this place of relevance.

THE ROOTS OF OUR SOCIO-ECOLOGICAL CRISIS

The prediction of eco-catastrophe is now so commonplace that it has begun to lose its power to shock (Cayley, 1991, p. viii).

To begin with, we'd like to make a simple point: that we believe there really is ur-

gency to the socio-environmental situation in which we find ourselves, and that it demands our attention as educators. Certainly education serves two main functions: first, it helps to establish and maintain the socio-ecological order, and second, it helps to challenge the culture into new and needed directions when the socio-ecological order proves to be out of step with emerging larger realities. As educators, we often tend to perform the function of the former, not the latter. In adventure education, we may be more inclined to serve the latter, but less inclined to address it directly. Our purpose here is to note that social-ecological change needs to be as much a part of our goal as the intra- and inter-personal change which adventure education tends to highlight.

The evidence of environmental crisis is mounting from all angles. A "Scientists Warning to Humanity" states:

> We, the undersigned, senior members of the world's scientific community, hereby warn all humanity of what lies ahead. A great change in our stewardship of the earth and the life on it is required, if vast human misery is to be avoided and our global home on the planet is not to be irretrievably mutilated.[2]

As environmental educator David Orr (1991, p.99) eloquently laments, "the fabric of life is becoming more threadbare." Even our consciousness, perhaps especially our collective consciousness, shows signs of ecological crisis. Well-known author and park warden Edward Abbey (1989, p.100) once said, "Among politicians and businessmen, Pragmatism is the current term for 'to hell with our children.'" Naturalist John Livingston (1994, p.177) asserts that, as ecological misfits, our ideology creates

> ...a theatre of the grotesque, a pageant of the deviant...a being estranged from [our] roots

and [our] natural context committing the most improbably and aberrant acts under the self-justification provided by [our] obsessive narcissism.

If there is truth in such claims (and it is important to note that we could continue to cite both evidence and opinion along these lines from a wider variety of disciplines for several pages) then we have an *ethical responsibility* to aspire and work toward a society that is a function of a socio-ecological education. As adventure educators, to be part of such an education is indeed our greatest adventure, and the one to which all other adventures aspire.

But somehow, despite our best efforts, our concerted destructive activities continue, unabated. Educator Bert Horwood (1989) notes that, in the nearly three decades since the landmark Earth Day 1970 celebrations, we have become "smarter polluters, not non-polluters." Despite mountains of data that support claims of environmental degradation, we appear to possess a collective "conceptual integument" that prevents the acceptance of this crisis in to our everyday consciousness (Evernden, 1993). This implies that, while facts and figures seem important, the debate is not only an empirical one.

Other authors, particularly those within the deep and social ecology movements,[3] have suggested that the so-called "environmental crisis" is a manifestation of a larger, societal crisis with deep roots in our concept of nature and our relationship to it. While our public debate centres on potential instrumental[4] solutions to the physical predicament; a decade of writing in social theory and environmental thought has suggested the "crisis" to be one that is inherent not in "nature," but in the social organization of human society:

The environment is not something that has a reality totally outside or separate from ourselves and our social milieux. Rather, it should be understood as the conceptual interactions between our physical surroundings and the social, political and economic forces that organize us in the context of these surroundings (DiChiro, 1987, p.23).

Naming the environmental crisis as a social, political and economic one is arguably more common than placing its roots in morality. Our emphasis in expressing this as a moral crisis is to pinpoint the importance of questioning the *mores* that reveal the conceptual core of North American society. Naming the environmental crisis as a moral crisis is to pinpoint the human value system which underlies the same political and economic decisions that were to perpetuate large scale environmental degradation.

Unfortunately, changing the focus to discuss the environmental crisis as amoral, one does not simplify our dialogue at all: in fact, it complicates matters. Contemporary North America resists discussion of *morality* and *values* even more strenuously than it resists political, economic, or scientific arguments. The ensuing public debate surrounding "the good life" for humans and all other beings inevitably becomes clouded with instrumental arguments, that is to say, arguments which define nature as a means to an end:

To the environmentalists, what is at risk is the very possibility of leading a good life. To the industrialist, what is at risk is the very possibility of leading a good life. The debate, it appears, is actually about what constitutes a good life. The instance of physical pollution serves only as the means of persuasion, a staging ground for the underlying debate. (Evernden, 1994, p.5)

INARTICULATE MORALITY

If the environmental crisis is a moral crisis, then what can we say about values, and about right and wrong? If we, as educators, plan to cultivate a different set of values (i.e., environmental values), on what ground do we stand to express them? Perhaps the best-known expression of an environmental ethic is Aldo Leopold's now-famous dictum: "A thing is right when it tends to preserve the integrity, stability, and beauty of the biotic community. It is wrong when it tends otherwise" (Leopold, 1966). But already with talk of "right" and "wrong", many of us shudder these days, and already we are grasping for words. This underscores the difficulty of raising adventure-based environmental education as a question of values; it is very difficult to speak in moral terms.

The loss of the discourse of morality can perhaps be seen as the result of a profound misunderstanding of liberal individualism. In an individualist society, when it is claimed to be permissible for each of us to have our "own" value system; how do we justify educating for a societal change in values? If all values are equal, then discussion about good ways to act in relation to the natural world becomes either "preachy" or futile. This situation is problematic to the adventure/environmental educator; who does not believe that "value systems" of corporate gain and consumptive practice are as valid, or may be as equally held as those which suggest elements of ecological sustainability.

Philosopher Charles Taylor (1991) argues that this misunderstanding results in our society, where it has become a moral imperative to valorize individualism; that is, it becomes an imperative to "be true to oneself." To challenge any value position is to challenge a fundamental moral position. The result is a type of ethical relativism in which no one opinion can be any more or less valid than any other. In Taylor's words, "the vigorous defense of any moral ideal is somehow off limits," and critics are forced, if not into an involuntary silence, at least into profound "inarticulacy". The only argument left is an instrumental one, stripped of moral implication, and necessarily barren in ethical possibility.

To restate the dilemma we face as environmentalists and educators, we begin to see the scope of our work as it relates to morality. While we face environmental degradation of an unprecedented scale, we must acknowledge that it is a question not only of our damaging actions, but of the *mores* that guide them. Embedded in the languages of instrumentalism and individualism, we are prevented from conceiving of (let alone speaking of) "morality" in any meaningful way that will guide us out of our dilemma. With the stakes high, this seems to be a checkmate of near-unimaginable dimensions. And yet, with all of this in front of us, some of us maintain hope and assert our overtly or covertly "value-laden" position as adventure educators. Why we do this, and how we can begin to justify the teaching of values, is the subject we turn to next.

EDUCATION AND VALUES

It would be the height of pessimism to believe that our society could go on in its present direction without bringing down upon itself catastrophes. To believe the foregoing would be pessimism, for it would imply that the nature of things does not bring forth human excellence (George Grant, 1970).

As we've noted, to speak in terms of "values" and especially "morals" is very challenging. Archaic to the modern ear, the words conjure up images of stifling repression, and even oppression. At its most fundamental, educating students with a moral goal seems to be like *telling them how to live*. In referring to morality, we are broadly questioning what constitutes a good way to live, particularly for adventure educators, in relationship to each other and in relationship to the natural world. It is important to emphasize that this concept need not be narrow and rule-bound; its focus is on *morality* rather than on *moralizing*. By this we mean that it is too easy, even an abdication of responsible inquiry, to set too narrow a focus on morality as "what it is right to do" rather than "what it is good to be" (Taylor, 1989, p.5). We hope to express morality as a questioning approach that pervades our practice. On what "morality" then, do we rely as adventure educators with a goal of social change?

Educationally, the well-intentioned "Values Clarification" movement of the 1960s and 1970s allowed students to articulate their values (i.e., their moral position) in the absence of judgement on them (Raths, Merrill and Harmin, 1978). Teachers were to share all possible views, the many sides of each issue, garnering around them the recognition found in an "objective" stance. The fear of losing this objectivity of an opinion, or worse, a proclaimed personal stance on the subject (say, the state of our environment and our relation to it) was to be labelled with moral imposition and manipulation. At the very least, the educator was giving an imbalanced view in exposing bias; at worst, such views were labelled as indoctrination.

What was less addressed was the relativistic, abstracted and dispassionate nature of such inquiry. Also poorly articulated was that this "neutral" stance did not readily lend one to action of any kind other than knowledge gathering for knowledge's sake. In it was an inherent failure to address intentional change for other visions of society. In this position of morality avoidance, we lose the ability to question "what it is good to be." We lose our personal responsibility to act for something (i.e., for the earth or for a better way of dwelling with the earth). It follows that education becomes a function of society, and accordingly, serves society without challenging the ethical status quo. Acknowledging the inherent environmental values we teach can ensure that society becomes a function of education, which is to say, education becomes able to challenge social and ethical norms through a focus on service, individual accountability, and agency (Tappan and Brown, 1989).

And what about the fact that educating for social change in adventure education implies a non-neutral, value-laden position? As environmental educator David Orr (1994, p.12) succinctly notes, "all education is environmental education". In other words, in what we include or exclude in each of our educational activities, we are somehow teaching about the environment and our place in it. As an example, Orr (1991) offers:

> To teach economics, for example, without reference to the laws of thermodynamics or those of ecology is to teach a lesson that is fundamentally wrong: that physics and ecology have nothing to do with the economy.

This is no less true of adventure education. When we fail to acknowledge our value-oriented goals as adventure educators, we risk assuming that our work is neutral. In losing our openly, inherently moral goals as educators, we may also become champions of the status quo, whether inadvertently or not. When we avoid issues of humans and environment, we risk teaching (by implication) that the value of a rock face is only in its climbing, or that the value of a canoe expedition is merely its potential for self-growth. But these are not neutral positions either: they imply an instrumentality to nature, and encourage a view of nature as a backdrop, rather than as a sustaining place to which we are bound in responsibility, action, and celebration.

This is why we cannot end our educational goals with a focus only on self and community: as necessary as these are, our situation demands the attention of concerned citizens committed to viable-socio-cultural change. Adventure education is ideally positioned to provide knowledge about our place in the natural world, and to contribute to fostering an ethic of commitment and care. As educators, we need the hope and faith that spins forth from envisioning a viable consciousness, with roots in a clearly articulated ethical position, and wings in positive action.

CONCLUSION

For the adventure educator, we recall Pete's summary: we need individual character skills and we need to learn how to work collectively. However, our situation requires that we encourage further goals in adventure education. One of these implies that, within the context of adventure education, we actively teach a knowledge of the earth and our place within the fabric of life. But perhaps most importantly, through enriching experiences in nature, we also need to encourage a spirited ethic of caring. We need these because we cannot solve the problems of social disparities and environmental degradation without such an education. At the same time, we are bound by responsibility to begin to teach such values.

To concerns that this implies teaching from a value-laden position, we agree, but note that all positions are value-laden. With no position

neutral, it becomes even more imperative to identify and make open our ethical stance, to raise clear issues for dialogue with others. If, as Orr (1991) suggests, "all education is environmental education," then it seems to be our responsibility to situate our own value position, and to work at sustaining open and accountable dialogue on the issues which underlie our current socio-environmental crisis.

We maintain hope, because as adventure educators, we can see the fruits of our labours. Some of our students do gain empowering self character skills that foster personal agency; that is, they become self-determined rather than determined. Some of our students do learn through our teaching to work together in problem-solving settings for a social agency. Some gain knowledge and understanding of how the earth functions and how we function on it from within. And most importantly, some of our students find enjoyment and the energy of a caring spirit; a participatory consciousness with the earth that inspires the challenge of accountability and responsibility. As adventure educators, we are ideally poised to contribute to this change; as citizens of the earth, we are ethically bound to it.

REFERENCES

Abbey, Edward (1989). Cited in *A voice crying in the wilderness: Box clamantis in Deserto*, New York: St. Martin's Press.

Cayley, David (1991). *The age of ecology.* Toronto: James Lorimer & Company.

DiChiro, Giovanna (1987). "Environmental Education and the Question of Gender: A Feminist Critique." In *Environmental education: Practice and possibility*, ed. Ian Robottom. Geelong, Australia: Deakin University Press.

Drengson, Alan (1994). *An ecophilosopher's dictionary: Basic concepts for ecocentric exploration*. Victoria: Lightstar Press.

Evernden, Neil (1992). *The social creation of nature*. Baltimore: John Hopkins.

Grant, George (1970). *Lament for a nation*. Toronto: House of Anansi.

Horwood, Bert (1989). "Introducing Spiritual Dimensions in Outdoor Education." *Pathways: The Ontario Journal of Outdoor Education, 1*, 2 (April).

Leopold, Aldo 1966 (1949). *A sand county almanac*. New York: Ballantine Books.

Livingston, John (1994). *Rogue primate*. Toronto: Key Porter.

Orr, David (1991). *Earth in mind: On education, environment and the human prospect*. Washington, D.C.: Island Press.

Raths, Louis, Merrill and Harmin (1978). *Values and teaching*, 2nd ed. Columbus, Ohio: Charles E. Merrill.

Tappan and Brown (1989). "Stories Told and Lessons Learned: Towards a Narrative Approach to Moral Development and Moral Education." *Harvard Educational Review, 59*(2):182–205.

Taylor, Charles (1991). *The malaise of modernity*. Toronto: House of Anansi.

Taylor, Charles (1989). *Sources of the self: The making of the modern identify*. Cambridge, Mass: Harvard University Press.

"World Scientists' Warning to Humanity" (1993/1994). *Green Teacher, 36*, (Dec/Jan), pp.34–37.

ENDNOTES

1.   A later conversation with Pete revealed that this week had been particularly rewarding, because the week's curriculum had allowed him to bring together the goals of adventure education and environmental education, in a way that unfortunately doesn't always occur. Such a week, he pointed out, "is what you always aim for" as an outdoor educator at a residential centre.

2.   See *Green Teacher*, no. 36, Dec/Jan 1993/94. This warning was signed on 18 November 1992 by 1575 scientists from 69 countries, including 99 out of the 196 living Nobel Laureates in science.

3.   See in particular: Alan Drengson and Yuichi Inone (eds.), *The Deep Ecology Movement: An Introductory Anthology*. Berkeley, CA: North Atlantic Books, 1995; Carolyn Merchant, *Radical Ecology: The Search for a Livable World*. New York: Routledge, 1992; David Rothenberg with Arne Naess, *Ecology, Community and Lifestyle*. New York: Cambridge University Press, 1989.

4.   As opposed to intrinsic arguments, instrumental arguments are a means to an end; actions, materials, or beings are valued for their functional use in attaining other valued items or states. Intrinsic arguments are those actions, states, beings or relationships which are valued for their own sake, not for what they lead to, or produce (Drengson, 1994).

Is It Possible to Justify a "Value-Laden" Position for Ecologically-Based Adventure Education?

Daniel Vokey, Ph.D.

What does it mean to adopt a "value-laden" position advocating ecologically-based adventure education? In my interpretation, it means commitment to at least three beliefs. The first belief is that adventure educators have an ethical duty to promote social and environmental change. The second belief (a belief that illustrates how advocating ecologically-based education is a "value-laden" position) is that the deterioration of our social and natural environments is at root a *moral* crisis. The third belief is that adventure educators are well-positioned to promote more socially-just and ecologically-sound ways of life through their programs. In what follows, I will critically examine each of these three beliefs. My goal is to argue that more work needs to be done before adventure education can effectively challenge the socio-ecological status quo.

THE ETHICAL DUTY OF ADVENTURE EDUCATORS

To begin with, let us consider the belief that adventure educators have an ethical duty to promote social and environmental change through their programs. At first glance, this appears to be a reasonable view. The deterioration of our social and natural environments is serious enough to be considered a real crisis. Furthermore, because all education is value-laden, adventure educators could embrace social-ecological change as a goal without necessarily slipping from education into indoctrination. Indeed, because all educational interventions are designed from one or another value-laden perspective, we misrepresent our programs if we naively present them as "value-neutral". In contrast, being explicit about our moral commitments will actually help us avoid imposing our views upon those participating in adventure education programs. Do we then, not have a duty to take up the cause of social and environmental change?

The answer is: not necessarily. We can accept both that the deterioration of our social and ecological environments is serious and that value-neutral education is impossible, and still not accept that we have an ethical duty to challenge the socio-ecological status quo. To arrive at this latter conclusion, we would have to provide additional arguments or reasons demonstrating that *socio-ecological change should be given priority over all other worthy educational objectives*. These additional arguments or reasons are required before we can say that either we must explicitly challenge the socio-ecological status quo in our programs or we have necessarily failed in our responsibilities as adventure educators. Such additional arguments or reasons are required because, without them, it remains an open question whether or not we have other responsibilities as adventure educators that should take priority over promoting social and environmental change.

In questioning the view that we have a duty as adventure educators to promote more just and environmentally sound ways of life, I do not wish to suggest that challenging the socio-ecological status quo is necessarily indefensible. It is one thing to propose that we are *ethically justified* if and when we add social and environmental change to our adventure education program goals. It is quite another thing to believe that we are *ethically required* to adopt such objectives. We have yet to see if the reasons cited to this point are sufficient to justify the first belief. They certainly are insufficient to justify the second.

What kinds of reasons do we need to justify beliefs about our responsibilities as educators? In other words, what kinds of reasons should serve to persuade people to accept statements about their educational duties? Thomas Kuhn (1962) shows how productive scientific enquiry presupposes a community of investigators who share a common paradigm of scientific enquiry, where *paradigm* refers to an interrelated set of beliefs, attitudes, interests, norms, priorities, and practices. MacIntyre (1988) extends Kuhn's account to show how *all* forms of productive inquiry and de-

bate, whether scientific, historical, literary, religious, moral, or otherwise, presuppose a community whose members share at least some basic agreements. One consequence of this is that *in order to be persuasive in a rational way, moral arguments must take place within a community defined by certain basic shared agreements*. Basic shared agreements are necessary because they represent the "common ground" to which we appeal in our arguments. Here, then, is the problem. Both Kuhn and MacIntyre have observed that, because members of competing communities of inquiry operate within competing paradigms, they speak different "languages". For example, those working within competing scientific paradigms typically have very different views of the world, and so formulate their theories in terms that do not have equivalents in the conceptual frameworks of their rivals. Moral discourse is no different: moral beliefs and arguments are necessarily framed in one or another moral "language" that corresponds to the point of view of a particular social and historical tradition. Christians speak of grace and sin, Buddhists of *karma* and *samsara*, Kantians of duties and obligations, modern liberals of rights and freedoms. Consequently, if you and I do not share the same tradition and corresponding moral point of view; then there is a good chance that we will find each other's moral arguments unintelligible and unpersuasive.[1]

In MacIntyre's (1984, 1988) narrative of its history, liberalism as a moral and political tradition has become susceptible to ethical relativism in part because it has lost sight of the proper role of community in moral discourse. Liberalism incorrectly imagines that moral arguments should and could be persuasive to "all rational persons", forgetting that even whom is considered a "rational person" varies from community to community, culture to culture, tradition to tradition.

Because it has thus been abstracted from specific social and historical contexts, public moral discourse has failed to resolve ethical questions in modern pluralistic democracies, creating fertile ground for ethical relativism on the one hand and moral/religious fundamentalism on the other (MacIntyre, 1984, pp. 6–8; 1988, pp. 5–6). To avoid these sterile alternatives, we need in moral discourse, as in other aspects of community life, to recapture a sense of "place". In other words, to construct persuasive moral arguments about ethical duties educational and otherwise, we need to locate ourselves in specific historical, social, and geographical contexts.

In light of these remarks, we can address the question raised above: What kinds of reasons do we need to justify our beliefs about our duties as educators? The answer is: it depends upon which particular moral community we inhabit, and which moral tradition we appeal to in justifying the aims and norms of our programs. Consequently, before we could conclude that we have an ethical duty as adventure educators to promote social and environmental change, we would need to say more about the set of background beliefs that the very idea of an "ethical duty" requires in order to be intelligible and persuasive.

THE ROOTS OF THE SOCIO-ECOLOGICAL CRISIS

What of adventure educators who are already committed to promoting social and environmental change? Are they not justified in taking up ecologically-based adventure education as a value-laden position? My reservations here have to do with the second belief listed in my introduction, that is, the belief that the deterioration of our social and natural environments is at root a *moral* crisis in the sense that it results from the *instrumental values* that are structured into our economic, political, and social orders. On this analysis, those adventure educators who wish to achieve significant social and environmental change must explicitly challenge instrumentalism, that is, the practice of treating people and natural resources as commodities to be exploited. To challenge instrumentalism effectively, adventure educators must design their programs to help people appreciate the *intrinsic value* of all life forms and the natural environment itself. That is to say, adventure educators must help people see how all strands in the web of life have value in and of themselves, quite independently of their use to humans. It is only by thus enhancing respect for others and for the environment, that adventure educators will be able to address at a deep enough level, the instrumentalist roots of the socio-ecological crisis.[2]

My reservations with this noble endeavor have to do with what makes education different from indoctrination and rational argument different from intimidation. The difference lies in the willingness to give good reasons why some beliefs or values are more correct than others. Another way of making this point is to observe that we cannot educate in a given area until we can explain how inquiry in that area is open to correction. For example, in order to teach mathematics, we need to know how to arrive at solutions to mathematical problems and how to identify errors in mathematical reasoning. To teach science, we need to know what should and should not count as valid ways of supporting scientific theories in different scientific disciplines. In the same way, if our task as adventure educators is to help people learn what is wrong with instrumentalism, then we need to know what should and should not count as good reasons for commitment to some moral values over others.

Herein lies the problem. In our modern, pluralistic democracies, we lack a widely-shared understanding of how conflict among competing sets of values should be rationally resolved. One symptom of this is what MacIntyre (1984, pp. 6–8) describes as the interminability of moral debate, the inability to bring rational resolution to disagreements among rival moral points of view. When MacIntyre argues that productive moral discourse occurs only within communities characterized by certain shared agreements, he does not mean to suggest that all members of modern societies are also members of one or another moral tradition. On the contrary, he attributes a large part of the inconclusive character of contemporary moral debates precisely to the fact that many people are not committed to any one tradition of moral inquiry and practice, and perhaps do not even appreciate that different traditions exist, with the consequence that their moral arguments juxtapose fragments from incompatible moral perspectives. In short, the inability to reach agreement in modern societies is a consequence of the *breakdown* as much as the *plurality* of moral communities and traditions. This is a problem for adventure education because, although we may have personal conviction in the rightness of our ecological and other values; we cannot educate for social and environmental change without being able to provide good *moral* reasons why relations of respect are better than purely instrumental ones. Otherwise, we are stuck in the awkward position of trying to use instrumental reasoning to argue against instrumental values. In the absence of shared agreement within our society on how to justify one set of moral values over another; it is

hard to see how adventure education could do more than preach to the converted.

ADVENTURE AND ENVIRONMENTAL EDUCATION

The third belief mentioned in my introduction is that adventure educators are well-positioned to promote more socially-just and ecologically-sound ways of life through their programs. Again, this might seem at first glance to be a reasonable view. After all, there is considerable common ground between adventure-based experiential education on the one hand and deep-ecology oriented environmental education on the other.

> Both are products of the late twentieth century. Both take the form of a modern rediscovery and recreation of ancient ideals gradually lost in the materialism and alienation of Western culture. The two movements have experienced an increasingly powerful impact from the work of women. Both have uncomfortable relations with their respective mainstreams; they are somewhat radical and touched with a distinctly disreputable air. (Horwood, 1991, p. 23)

Horwood attributes the commonalities among the two educational movements to their shift away from mainstream values: adventure educators typically want to shift from an over-emphasis upon cognitive content to a more holistic conception of teaching and learning, while deep ecologists typically advocate a shift from a human- to an ecologically-centered world view.

These commonalities notwithstanding, I question whether the confidence and self-esteem that adventure education programs can inspire is enough to effect the profound changes in lifestyle that deep ecologists desire. To my eyes at least, it would seem as if neither adventure nor environmental education have resulted in significantly less consumption and pollution since the inception of their programs. Generally speaking, we in North America continue to ignore and/or deny the ample evidence that we are destroying the very environment that we depend upon to live. We are like doctors who continue to smoke even though we appreciate intellectually that we are irreversibly damaging the lungs we need to breathe. Consequently, if adventure education is going to make a difference, then I believe that *we need to look more deeply into the dynamics of denial as a form of resistance to change.* What drives us, individually and collectively, to do what we know is against our long term interests: indeed, our very survival? What forms of education could undo our deeply ingrained habits of exploitation and self-destruction? Adventure education programs market themselves as catalysts of personal transformation, but even their instructors, myself not least, continue to consume more than our share of non-renewable resources. How can we help others unlearn their resistance to change when we have yet to deal effectively with our own?

A similar point could be made with respect to the social side of the socio-ecological crisis. The hard truth is that, inside and outside of North America, we live in a global context of oppression. Our human interactions are disfigured by unequal and unjust relations of political power, cultural privilege, and economic opportunity. In simplest terms: the rich continue to get richer, the poor poorer. This oppression is systemic: unequal relations are reinforced by social structures such as systems of public education, forms of mass media, economic relations, legal systems, and religious/political ideologies. Inequality is perpetuated by the efforts of those

in positions of privilege to maintain and enhance their advantages. Inequality is also perpetuated by the internalization, by both the privileged and the victimized, of oppressive attitudes, beliefs, and behaviors (Freire, 1970, 1985).

I refer to the global context of oppression because I believe that, if adventure education is to address world-wide injustice and environmental exploitation, then we will have to begin by locating ourselves, personally and institutionally, within existing hierarchies of power. In considering my roles and responsibilities to effect social change, I should not ignore the implications of my multiple positions of privilege as (for example) a white, male, university-educated, able-bodied heterosexual. I should not forget that I am a descendent of immigrants from the European nations that have taken possession of North America by conquest, and a member of the class that continues to use legal, economic, and military force to protect its "rights" to exploit the land and its resources. Similarly, I should not overlook how the educational institutions with which I am associated are deeply integrated within, dependent upon, and attached to the socio-ecological status quo. How many of us do not rely, directly or indirectly, on corporate profits?

I have had the good fortune to work with many adventure educators who, with great courage, have uncovered the subtle and not-so-subtle ways in which we reproduce hierarchies of race, class, gender, sexual orientation, and more in our programs. Even in the light of such work, however, adventure education institutions seem no less conservative than public schools when it comes to acknowledging the persistence of systemic oppression. I see little evidence that we have any special expertise or experience as a profession in giving up the social advantages we have inherited. The work of exceptional individuals notwithstanding, then, I believe that we need to know more about how "we" (the privileged) can dismantle the hierarchies of power from which we benefit before adventure education is ready to tackle the economical and political structures that perpetuate injustice and exploitation.[3] If past experience is any guide (Durning, 1997), raising prices on non-renewable resources would do more to promote conservation, in the short term at least, than participation in typical adventure education activities.

Our complicity with, and dependence upon the economic-political-socio-ecological status quo is not my only reason for doubting that adventure educators are well-positioned to promote more socially-just and ecologically-sound ways of life. I am here anticipating the point that, in order to promote change in larger social structures, we must start by changing ourselves. The belief that we need to heal our profound alienation from ourselves and our world in order to reverse our destructive habits is a recurring theme in ecological writing (e.g., Brown, 1997). I do believe that adventure education programs, particularly those that are wilderness based, can afford moments of genuine re-connection with the larger wholes in which we participate. However, there is a profound difference between such momentary experiences and the total transformation of perspective that deep ecologists prescribe (e.g., Chamberlin, 1997, p. 84). The nature of human alienation and the path to the recovery of wholeness is described in different ways in various religious and spiritual traditions. Their differences notwithstanding, virtually all such traditions speak of the path of self-transformation as fraught with peril. As adventure educators, we should be particularly sensitive to the risks involved in setting forth on a journey into unknown terri-

tory without the help of an experienced guide. I agree wholeheartedly that a solution to our socio-ecological crisis will necessarily involve a spiritual dimension. But, I wonder how many of us within adventure education have the experience and training required to serve as reliable guides to those entering the spiritual wilderness.

CONCLUSION

There are many different kinds of adventure education programs, run by a wide variety of individuals and organizations, so it is difficult to make generalizations that would apply to them all. The people responsible for designing and instructing particular programs are, I expect, better positioned than I to judge whether they are ready and able to educate for socio-ecological change. I have no wish to dampen any individual's or organization's enthusiasm for working toward more just and environmentally sound ways of life. Yet I can't help noticing that environmental and moral education programs are too often thought of as something that *other* people need. Without questioning the value of adventure education, I think it is perhaps overstating the case to say that we who offer such programs are ready to lead the way into a new ecological age. Let us show that we can change ourselves: that we can run programs that are more socially-just and ecologically-sound, before we try to change the world.

REFERENCES

Brown, Kirk. (1997). From the inside out: Building a sustainable environmental movement. *The Trumpeter Journal of Ecosophy, 14*(2), 57–60

Chamberlin, Chuck. (1997). The practice of citizenship as support for deep ecology. *The Trumpeter Journal of Ecosophy, 14*(2), 82–85.

Durning, Alan T. (1997). After the deluge: The changing worldview. *World Watch,* Jan–Feb, 25–31.

Freire, Paulo. (1970). *Pedagogy of the oppressed* (trans. M. B. Ramos). New York: Continuum.

Freire, Paulo. (1985). *The politics of education: Culture, power, and liberation* (trans. D. Macedo). South Hadley, MA: Bergin & Garvey.

Horwood, Bert. (1991). Tasting the berries: Deep ecology and experiential education. *The Journal of Experiential Education, 14*(3), 23–26).

Kuhn, Thomas. (1962). *The structure of scientific revolutions.* Chicago: University of Chicago Press.

MacIntyre, Alasdair. (1984). *After virtue.* Notre Dame: University of Notre Dame Press.

MacIntyre, Alasdair. (1988). *Whose justice? Which rationality?* Notre Dame: University of Notre Dame Press.

Pivnick, Janet. (1997). Speaking from the deep: The problem of language in deep ecology education. *The Trumpeter Journal of Ecosophy, 14*(2), 53–56.

ENDNOTES

1.   Deep ecologists have spoken of the difficulty of communicating across paradigms, e.g., "of finding the language to make sense of an 'ecological approach' within the confines of 'the dominant, modern worldview' held by the majority of students and educators" (Pivnick, 1997, p. 53).

2.   The first "basic platform principle" of the Deep Ecology Movement as listed by Chamberlin (1997, p. 82) is "The well-being and flourishing of human and nonhuman life on Earth have value in themselves (synonyms: intrinsic value, inherent value). These values are independent of the usefulness of the non-human world for human purposes."

3.   I do not, of course, assume that all adventure educators enjoy the same multiple positions of privilege as I do. At the same time, however, I do think that most adventure education programs rely directly or indirectly on the profits generated by the exploitation of people and the natural worlds within liberal capitalist democracies.

CHAPTER 15

Should Gender-Specific Programs, Such as All Women Courses, Be Offered in Adventure Education?

YES PERSPECTIVE: Karla Henderson, Ph.D.
NO PERSPECTIVE: Juli Lynch, M.S.

Karla A. Henderson is Professor and Chair in the Department of Recreation and Leisure Studies at the University of North Carolina at Chapel Hill. Her research and writing interests have focused on gender and leisure, women in the outdoors, and research/evaluation methods. She has written extensively on each of these topics. When not academically inclined, she enjoys the outdoors especially when she is running, canoeing, sea kayaking, or snowshoeing.

Juli has been facilitating national and international experience based learning programs since 1988. Her clients include a long list of organizations from Fortune 500 companies to small businesses. Her expertise is in the area of team development, specifically in the design and delivery of team development programs. She draws from her own experiences as an internationally recognized adventure racer, competing in multi sport, ultradistance races such as the Raid Gauloises, Eco-Challenge, and ESPN Extreme Games. She is also in the process of completing her Ph.D. in Organizational Development Psychology. Her research interests are human performance and human process in group and team settings.

Should Gender-Specific Programs, Such as All Women Courses, Be Offered in Adventure Education?

Karla A. Henderson, Ph.D.

In 1986, my colleague and I (Henderson & Bialeschki, 1986) proposed a session for the Association of Experiential Education (AEE) conference in Connecticut entitled "Outdoor Experiential Education (For Women-only)." We wanted to build upon the work being done by Miranda and Yerkes (1982) and Mitten (1985) to discuss the issues surrounding the little publicized women-only programming that had been growing. That presentation title in the program, unbeknownst to us at the time, created a stir among conference participants. A misunderstanding existed about who could come to the session. We had no intention of suggesting that men were not welcome but we wanted to also emphasize the importance of women. Therefore, the title was misleading. In retrospect, we realize we should have put a question mark after "only" because the title was meant to raise the query. Underlying the misunderstanding, however, was also the apparent "threat" that such a topic, especially if only women could discuss it, might present.

In that presentation and the paper published in the proceedings (Henderson & Bialeschki, 1986), we identified many of the points that are still salient today when we examine the value of gender targeted, specifically all women, groups. Now, many years later, gender-specific programming is still a controversial issue for some people. In this paper, I will briefly summarize what has or has not happened regarding new understandings of this topic in the past few years. I will also try to set a framework for a more in-depth analysis of the ongoing questions which any programming for a targeted group might engender.

As a point of information, I personally do not think adventure education should be either gender-specific or coeducational. I believe that all individuals should have choices about the types of experiences they would like to have. I do believe, however, that a place exists specifically for all-girls or all women programming as well as perhaps all-boys or all men programming. I am pleased that the authors of this text have stated the issue in the way they did because a broader question is raised about targeted programs of any kind. The debate may not be whether gender-specific programs ought to be offered, but how to provide a variety of experiences to enhance the growth and development of all individuals through adventure programming.

Some of the misunderstanding regarding the issue of gender-specific programming surrounds the terminology used. "Women-only" sounds more discriminatory than "all women" groups. This distinction is semantic, but when targeting particular groups; inclusion exemplifies the goals better than exclusion. Misunderstandings also exist surrounding the use of sex and gender and female versus girls and women. Sex usually refers to biological sex; when an individual is labeled as female, biological sex is connoted. Gender refers to the cultural construction that exists regarding sex. The concepts of gender, man, and woman are socially constructed. Just because one is born either male or female does not mean that all boys and all girls will be alike. Therefore, I prefer to use the terms female and male only as adjectives because they suggest a biological description and not a social construction. I also recognize that in the field of adventure education, we work with girls and boys as well as women and men. I will use the terms women and men to include boys and girls for simplicity of writing.

A final caveat to this paper relates to any definitive conclusions drawn from this discussion. Although some girls and women MAY have different needs and expectations in adventure programming, we must not be too essentialist about what women need. Great differences exist in gender-specific groups (Fischer, 1985). All men groups may tend to display competitive and aggressive behavior in interactions. All women groups may tend to spend considerable time expressing personal feelings. In mixed groups, men often share more while women sometimes fade into the background. With most male groups, leadership is stable and held by designated leaders. With women, the leadership often rotates. Although these characteristics may be tendencies because of the ways in which boys and girls are socialized at an early age, they do not always occur and they are not absolute conclusions. Competition and aggression can occur and may be problematic in all women groups.

The more we are learning about gender-specific programming, the more we are also learning that great variability exists among groups. Therefore, although girls and boys are socialized toward certain tendencies, many exceptions exist. The desirability of examining the uniqueness of every programming opportunity rather than focusing totally on the meanings of gender in a group may be worth considering.

Even with those cautions, the question of gender-specific programming merits further discussion. The question in adventure education, as well as in other educational institutions, relates to the consequences of gender-specific and coeducational programs. Riordan (1990) suggested that today in elementary and secondary schools we have largely ignored the topic because we think we know the answers. I applaud adventure educators for not making sweeping generalizations and setting the potential controversy to the side as most public educators have done. Continuing examination can reveal new insights as we note changes occurring in society and in the way that adventure programming is evolving.

When I agreed to write this chapter and began to work on it, I wondered what more could be written that had not already been said. From my perspective, it is hard to refute the value of all women groups. As I reread our 1986 paper and examined the plethora of recent work, I found many similarities. Yet, I believe adventure educators should be credited with continued examinations of how to provide the best possible programming. Quality inclusive programming as an issue is much bigger than whether gender-specific programming should be done. A tie exists, nevertheless, between both discussions. The best ways to achieve the outcomes of adventure programming, not disregarding structure, is the salient question. If gender-specific programming has the potential to reach desired objectives, then it ought to be examined critically.

WHY ALL WOMEN GROUPS?

The research and writing done about gender-specific groups has been predominantly about all women groups. This literature has come from other fields and from qualitative data collected from women, mostly in gender-specific outdoor groups. Most recently, Hattie, Marsh, Neill, and Richards (1997) conducted a meta-study of outcomes of Outward Bound programs. They concluded that few researchers have examined differences in outcomes between mixed and single-gender groups. In analyzing mixed groups, they concluded that little difference existed in the outcomes between male and female participants. Studies using experimental and control groups also do work to answer these questions. Further, many variables enter into what happens in an adventure education experience such as group composition, leadership effectiveness, resources available, talents and skills of the individuals, and philosophy of the program. To really understand the outcomes and consequences of adventure programming, gender may be just one of several variables to consider.

To examine the efficacy of gender-specific groups in adventure education programs, the literature from educational research offers some insights. Riordan (1990) provided an interesting background perspective on the evolution of single sex schooling. During the 19th century in the United States, school was single sex and only for boys. The inclusion of women was considered a progressive move. For girls to have educational experiences, single-sex was sometimes the only option. Separate, however, did not always mean equal in terms of resources available. Where resources were equal however, Riordan (1990) found that all girl schools have consistently provided a better educational environment. The educational literature regularly suggests that overall coeducational experiences are better for boys but gender-specific opportunities (given equal resources) generally are better for girls. Although the passage of Title IX in the US in 1972 assured that educational institutions should have equal resources for male and female students/participants, it also assured that all public programs that were previously separate must now be coeducational.

Educational researchers have uncovered results that have implications for adventure educators. Henderson & Bialeschki (1986) reviewed educational literature through the mid 1980s and found that in classrooms, boys usually receive more attention than girls (e.g., Sadker & Sadker, 1986). This finding carried on into higher education settings (Krupnick, 1985). Riordan's (1990) more recent review of the literature showed that males are more likely to assume leadership positions, be more orally active, and more influential than females in all types of groups and situations.

Riordan (1990) also found that in examining coed interactions, they were often sex segregated. Girls were more likely to talk to girls and boys are more likely to interact with boys. The challenge in mixed gender groups may be to increase cross sex interaction if that is an important goal of mixed gender groups. Mixed schools are essentially boys' schools because they are dominated by their interests in general.

hmmm

The explication about all women groups in outdoor settings has changed little in the writings of the past 15 years (cf. Fox, 1997; Henderson & Bialeschki, 1986, 1987; Hornibrook, Brinkert, Parry, Seimens, Mitten, & Priest, 1997; McClintock, 1996; Miranda & Yerkes, 1982; Mitten, 1992; Nanschild, 1996; Nolan & Priest, 1993; Warren, 1990). Although mutable, many girls and women do have fears about the outdoors as traditionally considered a male domain. The growing number of new opportunities for women in the outdoors has resulted in more women going outdoors and making choices about its value in their lives.

Girls and women continue to make similar statements about why these gender-specific groups are good for them. If not familiar with the positive values, I encourage you to pursue this literature cited below. In summary, McClintock (1996) described several themes that transcend the literature and are evident in research done in other fields:

1.   The emotional and physical safety (e.g., Mitten, 1992; Nanschild, 1996; Pottinger, 1994).

2.   The freedom to throw out gender role stereotypes (e.g., Henderson & Bialeschki, 1987; Miranda & Yerkes, 1982).

3.   The opportunity to develop close connections with other women (e.g., Hornbrook et al., 1997; Miranda & Yerkes, 1982; Mitten, 1992; Nanschild, 1996; Warren, 1990).

4.   A comfortable environment for either being a beginner (e.g., Lueck,

1995; Nolan & Priest, 1993) OR being highly skilled (Fox, 1997), and

5.   Opportunities to have or be a role model/leader (e.g., Fischer, 1985; Nanschild, 1996).

As we address contemporary controversial issues in adventure education, these conclusions are difficult to debate. They are important outcomes of adventure programming. Could they be accomplished in mixed gender groups? Maybe. The value of these outcomes may lie in how we broaden our thinking about what happens in adventure education groups to both female and male participants. The underlying issues that these findings evoke are what can help adventure educators move ahead in the future. These issues provide the foundation for examining the consequences of targeting any specific group

ISSUES THAT GENDER-SPECIFIC ADVENTURE EDUCATION RAISES

Questions regarding separate but equal have not been solved. In education, we have assumed that coeducation is equality while single sex is inherently unequal (Riordan, 1990). Does gender-specific programming give women the skills to reach equal opportunities in the outdoors or do all women groups undermine women's attempts to gain equality? The answer is clearly not always obvious. One interesting new program developing across the United States is the "Becoming an Outdoor Woman (BOW)" (Lueck, 1995). This "remedial" program, aimed to get women outdoors hunting and fishing, may not be equivalent to programs organized for boys or men, but the proposed outcome is to provide female participants

Is it about equality

with a more level playing field to access these opportunities.

A related question concerns whether mixed or gender-specific programs perpetuate stereotypes. For example, because all women groups tend to focus on interaction and sharing, does that mean that competition is further downplayed? Further, individuals have argued that if we want to change attitudes about differences, contact is necessary. Does the contact between male and female participants in adventure programming result in reducing prejudices or further promoting them?

Another issue that is seldom discussed regarding gender-specific programming or education is the underlying homophobia inherent in the arguments. Many years ago the fear was that separating the sexes for a long period of time might cause homosexuality. Although that concern is seldom voiced, other issues of choosing with whom one is most comfortable enter into the picture. With a growing acceptance of gays and lesbians in society, opportunities to be with individuals with the same lifestyle might be valuable in some adventure programming situations. Lesbians or gay men may not necessarily be drawn to gender-specific groups but if they are; the environment must be perceived as safe for them.

Another topic raised concerns what gender-specific programming should model. Should all women groups be modeled from traditional male leadership styles (Jordan, 1992; Henderson, 1996)? What might mixed group leaders learn from gender-specific leaders? The structure of a group does not necessarily dictate how the group will function, and yet, questions underlie the value of using traditional models for targeted groups. Perhaps the reason why some coed groups have not attracted girls and women is be-

cause of the male models that have been used. To be of the most value, leaders must reexamine what leadership styles might be best for any given group.

The biggest implication of gender-specific programming is how it parallels other broad questions about diversity and social justice. Some individuals would argue that all women programming is a regressive step. Through civil rights legislation in the United States, we have pushed for ending segregation of any type. Unfortunately, research is not conclusive enough to suggest that ending any type of segregation necessarily results in better educational or social outcomes; given that resources are equal (Riordan, 1990). Others would argue that gender and race are not good comparisons. Gender is something that most people cannot escape. Our families usually are mixed gender and almost all public spaces, except perhaps rest rooms, are mixed. On the other hand, most of our families are not mixed races and many white people for example, in the United States, can avoid situations of dealing with someone who does not share the same skin color, if desired. Therefore, race and gender may not be comparable. Yet despite much or no contact, gender stereotypes continue to be slow to modify (Riordan, 1990). We can learn more about inclusion by examining how all aspects of diversity intersect.

CONCLUSIONS IN PROGRESS

The questions that continue to need answering relate to how we can be most successful in reaching the goals of adventure education, and how our work results in inclusive quality programs. Are gender-specific groups necessary in adventure education? I definitely believe a place exists for gender-specific programming, but not to the exclusion of mixed groups. Most people agree today that the answer to that question is "it depends." To move this question further, we need to address two issues. How can adventure educators give people choices in what they want to do and how they want to learn? Second, once a choice is given, how can we ensure that the leadership is such that all individuals feel included and get an opportunity to gain the most from the experience? No one group structure is always going to be the best. Just because a group is all women, all men, or coed does not mean that specific outcomes will always occur. I believe we must accept the value of a variety of program offerings whether they are mixed, gender-specific, race-specific, or disability-specific; and determine the common denominators that make for effective leadership and desired outcomes, regardless of the group structure.

ARE THERE VARIABLE DENOMINATORS?

REFERENCES

Fischer, M.L. (1985). On social equality and difference, a view from the Netherlands. *Management Education and Development*, 16(2), 201–210.

Fox, R. J. (1997, July). *Women, nature, and spirituality: A qualitative study of exploring women's wilderness experience.* Paper presented at the 1997 Australia and New Zealand Association of Leisure Studies Conference in Newcastle, NSW, Australia.

Hattie, J., Marsh, H.W., Neill, J. T., & Richards, G. F. (1997). Adventure education and outward bound: Out-of-class experiences that make a lasting difference. *Review of Educational Research*, 67(1), 43–87.

Henderson, K. A. (1996). Feminist perspectives on outdoor leadership. In K. Warren (Ed.), *Women's voices in experiential education* (pp. 107–117). Dubuque, IA: Kendall/Hunt Publishing Company.

Henderson, K. A., & Bialeschki, M. D. (1986). Outdoor experiential education (for Women-only). In M. Gass & L. Buell (Eds.), *AEE 14th Annual Conference Proceedings Journal* (pp. 35–41). Boulder, CO: Association of Experiential Education.

Henderson, K. A., & Bialeschki, M. D. (1987). A qualitative evaluation of a women's week experience. *Journal of Experiential Education*, 10(6), 25–28.

Hornbrook, T., Brinkert, E., Parry, D., Seimens, R., Mitten, D., & Priest, S. (1997). The benefits and motivations of all women outdoor programs. *Journal of Experiential Education*, 20(3), 152–158.

Jordan, D. (1992). Effective leadership for girls and women in outdoor recreation. *Journal of Physical Education, Recreation, and Dance*, 63(2), 61–64.

Krupnick, C. G. (1985, May). Women and men in the classroom: Inequality and its remedies. *On Teaching and Learning* (pp. 18–25).

Lueck, D. H. (1995, Summer). Opening the great outdoors to women. *Outdoor America* pp. 16–19.

McClintock, M. (1996). Why women's outdoor trips. In K. Warren (Ed.), *Women's voices in experiential education* (pp. 18–23). Dubuque, IA: Kendall/Hunt Publishing Company.

Miranda, W., & Yerkes, R. (1982). The need for research in outdoor programs for women. *Journal of Physical Education, Recreation, and Dance, 53*(4), 82–85.

Mitten, D. (1985). A philosophical basis for women's outdoor adventure programs. *Journal of Experiential Education, 8*(2), 20–24.

Mitten, D. (1992). Empowering girls and women in the outdoors. *Journal of Physical Education, Recreation, and Dance, 63*(2), 56–60.

Nanschild, D. L. (1996). *Women's perceptions of a wilderness experience in a women-only setting.* Unpublished thesis, University of Adelaide.

Nolan, T. L., & Priest, S. (1993). Outdoor programmes for women-only? *The Journal of Adventure Education and Outdoor Leadership, 10*(1), 14–17.

Pottinger, R. R. (1994). Mountain leader training Why women-only courses? *The journal of Adventure Education and Outdoor Leadership 11*(1), 15–16.

Riordan, C. (1990). *Girls and boys in school: Together or separate?* New York: Teachers College Press.

Sadker, M., & Sadker, D. (1986, March). Sexism in the classroom: From grade school to graduate school. *Phi Delta Kappa.*

Warren, K. (1990). Women's outdoor programs. In J.C. Miles & S. Priest (Eds.), *Adventure Education* (pp. 410–417). State College, PA: Venture.

Should Gender-Specific Programs, Such as All-Women Courses, Be Offered in Adventure Education?

Juli Lynch, M.S.

In the 1990 publication of *Adventure Education* (Miles & Priest, 1990), Warren's article *Women's Outdoor Adventures*, advocates for women-only outdoor adventure programs. Warren labels women as a special population with special needs in regards to experiences in the wilderness. Arguing from a feminist perspective, she claims that women need to learn by doing, need to develop self-confidence, need to bond with the natural world, and need shared leadership and consensus decision-making. Warren goes on to argue that the feminist model for adventure education is distinct from a traditionally white male-dominated adventure education philosophy because it embraces diversity; where the differences and needs of each group member are heard and considered in the cooperative development of the experience (Warren, 1990).

Is this true? According to Wurdinger (1997), the philosophy of adventure education includes three primary components: experiential learning, risk taking, and the aim of moral development. He also suggests that the process of experiential learning in adventure education allows groups of individuals to work together toward common goals. This process promotes a diversity of ideas which encourages individuals to learn more about themselves and how they interact with other participants. The tenets contained in this philosophy do not appear to be dominated by white males, but rather, are inclusive of the feminist perspective.

If the philosophy of adventure education is truly inclusive; then should the field be promoting gender-specific programming? This paper will argue that the philosophy of adventure education already meets the "needs" that gender-specific and women-only programs lay claim to. And that adventure education, by definition, accomplishes this while embracing a philosophy of inclusivity.

There are a number of arguments that can be found, especially in feminist literature, that defend all-woman adventure programming. One of the aims of this paper is to present these arguments and to discuss how, in many respects, these arguments have perpetuated myths that move the collective community of adventure educators, facilitators and participants away from the intended or "true" definition of adventure education.

254

One of the struggles with debate in this area is the lack of empirical evidence related to gender-specific adventure education programming. Most of the articles on the subject are anecdotal discussions about the benefits of gender-specific programming (Henderson, 1991; Lichtenstein, 1985; Mitten, 1992 ; Yerkes & Miranda, 1982), with little to no empirical evidence about whether or not these outcomes actually occur in gender-specific adventure education programming.

DIFFERENT NEEDS OR NEED TO BE DIFFERENT

"There are many objects of great value to people which cannot be attained by unconnected individuals, but must be attained if at all, by association."

—Daniel Webster

One of the arguments supporting gender-separate programming in education is based on the notion that women and men have different natures. Those who adopt this position argue that men and women are fundamentally different, that they have different interests, abilities, and aspirations and that these basic and different dispositions result in different ways of knowing and experiencing their world. (Gilligan, 1982).

Jordan (1992) discusses differences between women and men related to leadership in the outdoors. She suggests that men are more apt to initiate structure by taking control when given a task, whereas women are more adept with human relations functions such relationship building. In addition, Jordan argues that women have stronger process-oriented capabilities such as communication, trust building, group dynamics, and handling personality conflicts. Hender-

son (1991) argues that women, through years of exposure to particular social roles, have been ingrained with an "ethic of care." Mitten (1992) makes a number of statements that presume women have emotional needs in adventure education programs that are different than men's, including unconditional support, attention, acceptance for who they are, and personal time.

Such arguments about what is "natural" for males and females have been attacked on a number of grounds. First, these claims often ignore cross-cultural evidence (Bank, Biddle, & Good, 1980; Baker & Jones, 1992). Second, even within similar cultures, the "natural" differences between the sexes are based on relatively small differences in average performance (Bank & Hall, 1997). Third, the notion of "natural" differences ignores differences across situations and historical periods, both of which have been shown to have major effects on the definitions of what is "natural" behavior for males and females. Fourth, many of the "natural" differences between females and males are based on subjective opinions.

The assumption of "natural" gender differences as a reason to advocate gender-specific programming in adventure education could be considered to be a sexist argument designed to resist change, justify the oppression and separation of women, and preserve male power and privilege. A more plausible discussion would revolve around asking what myths are perpetuated about adventure education's views of gender differences when we rationalize gender-separate programming due to these differences? Does the definition and underlying philosophy of adventure education offer a pedagogy that already accounts for these differences?

How can these "natural" differences, if they exist, be made into a meaningful part of the "relationship" aspect of adventure education? (Bartley & Williams, 1988). Can these differences exist and still allow for women and men to co-exist in structured learning environments, such as adventure education experiences?

[handwritten: Wrong question — of course!]

FEMINISM OR HUMANISM

Most of the arguments for woman-only programming embraces a feminist perspective (Henderson, 1992; Henderson & Bialeschki, 1990–91; Mitten, 1992; Warren, 1990; Yerkes & Miranda, 1982). These authors argue that the content and pedagogy of adventure education, although projecting the "illusion" that it speaks to everyone, ignores the needs, experiences, and perspectives of women. Henderson (1992), for example, argues that women choose outdoor activities because of the "journey" and empowerment, and that this differs from the "quest," traditionally associated with the male experience in the outdoors. "How many mountains are climbed or the difficulty rating on one's climb are irrelevant to how women generally experience the process of climbing" (Henderson, 1992).

[handwritten: Does it?]

[handwritten: Sexism?]

[handwritten: Why do we do AE?]

Feminist pedagogical approaches and dynamics in education evolved from the consciousness-raising practices derived from the women's movement of the 1960's and the progressive tradition in American education created by John Dewey (Maher & Terreault, 1994). Advocates argue that it is unique because of its attention to the particular needs of women students and its grounding in feminist theory which emphasizes relational rather than "separate" approaches to learning, democratic rather than authoritarian approaches to leadership, and cooperative rather than competitive group dynamics (Gilligan, 1982).

A number of questions arise when we question the value of creating all-women ad-

venture education programs because these programs tend to be grounded in feminist theory. First, what makes this or that teaching practice "feminist"? For example, Project Adventure's learning goals which include: increased sense of personal confidence, increased mutual support and decision-making within a group, and increased joy in one's physical self and in being with others appears to coincide with feminist theory (Rohnke, 1986). Second, are the tenets of feminist pedagogy a commitment to taking women students seriously, a consciousness of the extent to which gender is embedded in social structures, and an understanding of the differing needs of women participants only possible in women-specific adventure education programs?

[handwritten: no but also very present in...]

One of adventure education's missions is to perpetuate the values, ideas, and attitudes of its definition or philosophy. Since society itself does not completely live up to these ideals, what *should be* and *what* is may differ.

Are adventure education programs products of a white-male Western society in which achievement and objectivity are valued over cooperation and connectedness? Or, is this a myth perpetuated by a feminist perspective? Will separate programming continue to cultivate a myth? Are there ways in which adventure education can make commitments to break the myth of a white male-dominated model as the prevailing content and pedagogy? Is it possible to address this neglect by adopting a content and pedagogy of inclusivity? Can inclusive programming move theory into action?

[handwritten: no... in education though]

[handwritten: Isn't this happening already?]

REMEMBER? SEPARATE IS NOT EQUAL

Among the groups who adopted the 1960's civil rights slogan "separate is not equal" in the United States were those who constituted the women's movement of the 1960's. By using the "separate is not equal" slogan, feminists sought to undermine romantic notions of women existing in separate spheres from men in education, business and society (Bank & Hall, 1997).

With the passing of Title IX of the Educational Amendments of 1972 and the Women's Educational Equity Act (WEEA) of 1977 in the United States, legislation provided policy that prohibited sex discrimination and evaluated educational programs and activities that eliminated gender stereotyping and promoted gender equity.

Despite historical precedence for women fighting "against" exclusion from educational opportunities and activities that include men, one can notice a trend toward gender-specific programming in many "spheres" of adventure education (Mitten, 1992). Advocates of "single-sex" schooling in formal educational settings argue a number of reasons that may well parallel similar intentions in adventure education. First, advocates of same-sex schools point out that Title IX and WEEA were past over twenty years ago, and women and girls still face sexual discrimination in educational settings (Riordan, 1997). Second, advocates of single-sex education employ feminist and emancipatory arguments suggesting that women are an oppressed group with many strengths. The proper education for them is one that builds upon their strengths, recognizes their "different voice" (Gilligan, 1982), and incorporates "women's ways of knowing" (Belenky, Clinchy, Goldberger, and Tarule, 1986). A third argument favoring single-sex schooling stresses protection for girls and women (Tyack & Hansot, 1990).

Should we, if we believe in gender equity, accept these arguments for women-only adventure education programs? Do similar arguments arise for male-only adventure education programs, such as they have arisen in support of single-sex, single-race schooling for African American males? (Hudley, 1995).

Does gender-specific programming eliminate "sexism?" A study on single-sex schools and classrooms found a type of sexism called "gender reinforcement," where the gender of the single-sex group is reinforced as being superior to the other gender. It was prevalent in both boys' and girls' programs. Another type, "embedded discrimination," where opposite gender individuals were discriminated against in the single-sex setting was also observed in both boys' and girls' programs (Lee, 1997).

CONSCIOUS INCLUSION OR UNCONSCIOUS EXCLUSION?

A dramatic shift in thinking should be considered by practitioners in this field. This shift is toward an inclusive philosophy of adventure education. When examining a philosophy of inclusion, three major concepts emerge: dispelling the myths, creating partnerships and promoting community.

Dispelling myths as related to adventure education and gender-separate programs, advocates revisiting the definitions and philosophies that encompass the field. Recognition that adventure education roots are embedded in philosophies of human virtue challenges us to consider the structurally embedded assumption that adventure education is like historic or traditional social institutions.

Creating partnerships encourages us to address one another as "different, similar and equal." It emphasizes the importance of partnering to achieve richness of meaning and outcome. It challenges us to fully dimensionalize our perceptions of the larger society by gaining knowledge and understanding of others' experiences and hearing opposing viewpoints (Benton & Daniel, 1996). It demands that we explore ways to discuss all topics of diversity, including race, ethnicity, gender, socio-economic class, sexual orientation, religious affiliations, and physical abilities.

Finally, promoting community reminds us that pursing similar goals and embracing similar philosophical beliefs in isolation limits the breadth of our experiences. While this may achieve depth of purpose, such as promoting women's "ways," ultimately, such behavior stunts the larger community's ability to grow. It is important for leaders of adventure education programs to promote the building of relationships amongst participants in order to create a community. It can be as simple as investing time in learning each other's names and sharing individual interests (Benton & Daniel, 1996). We cannot talk for anyone else; we must encourage our participants to find their own voice and tell their own story. As leaders, we model and encourage the need to talk with each other. Although avoidance might reduce the chances for conflict; it also reduces the chances for understanding (Sleeter, 1992).

"E PLURIBUS UNU" (OUT OF MANY....ONE)

If the challenges of the 21st century are to be met successfully, adventure education must consider the liabilities of exclusion and the possibilities of inclusion. It is my belief that people are social creatures who desperately need each other, not only for company but for meaning in their lives. Adventure educators are in a unique position to foster inclusive communities by the contextual nature of their work.

Are there inherent inequities in adventure education? Does this warrant gender-separate or gender-specific programming? From a philosophical perspective the answer is no, for the inherent inequities, like the inherent risks of adventure education, become the vehicle for arriving at the interpersonal and intrapersonal growths that define adventure education. Does this require that a programs actions and behaviors match this philosophy? Of course. Does this mean that facilitators need to attend to and bring out into the open the issues of gender; recognizing that they do, in fact, affect the whole group process of adventure education? (Smith, Roland, Havens & Hoyt, 1992). Of course. Will this be a challenge that carries us into the 21st Century? As Knapp described in 1985, "this may be the ultimate challenge for experiential educators" (Knapp, 1985). According to Miles (1999), "Adventure education is people work. Love, will, dedication, compassion, and deep resources of energy are necessary to do this work." Is worth it? In my opinion, it may be more than worth it. Our survival may depend on it.

REFERENCES

Baker, D. P., & Perkins-Jones, D. (1992). Opportunity and performance: A sociological explanation for gender differences in academic mathematics in J. Wrigley (Ed.) *Education and Gender Equality*. London: The Falmer Press.

Band, B. J. & Hall, P. M. (1997). *Gender, Equity, and Schooling: Policy and Practice*. New York: Garland Publishing.

Bank, B. J., Biddle, B. J. & Good, T. L. (1980). Sex roles, classroom instruction, and reading achievement. *Journal of Educational Psychology*, 72: 119–132.

Bartley, N. L. & Williams, D. R. (1988). Gender issues in outdoor adventure programming. *The Bradford Papers Annual*, 3.

Belenky, Field, M., Clinchy, Goldberger, N. R., & Tarule, J. (1986). *Women's Ways of Knowing: the Development of Self, Voice, and Mind*. New York: Basic Books.

Benton, J. E. & Daniel, P. L. (1996). Learning to talk about taboo topics: A first step in examining cultural diversity with preservice teachers. *Equity and Excellence in Education* ((29)3, 8–17.

Gilligan, C. (1982). *In a Different Voice: Psychological Theory and Women's Development*. Cambridge, MA: Harvard University Press.

Henderson, K. (1991). The ethic of care: Leisure possibilities and constraints for women. Society and Leisure, 14(1)97–113.

Henderson, K. A. (1992). Breaking with tradition: Women and outdoor pursuits. Journal of Physical Education, Recreation and Dance. (1), 49–51.

Henderson, K. A., & Bialeschki, M. D. (1990–91). Ecofeminism: Recreation as if nature and woman mattered. Leisure Information Quarterly, 17(1), 1–5.

Hudley, C. (1995). Assessing the impact of separate schooling for African-American male adolescents. Journal of Early Adolescence (15), 38–57.

Jordan, D. (1992). Effective leadership for girls and women in outdoor recreation. Journal of Physical Education, Recreation, and Dance, 63(2), 61–64.

Knapp, C. (1985). Escaping the gender trap: The ultimate challenge for experiential educators. Journal of Experiential Education, 8 (2).

Lee, V. E. (1997). In B. J. Bank & P. M. Hall (Eds.) Gender Equity, and Schooling: Policy and Practice (pp. 135–158). New York: Garland Publishing.

Lichtenstein, G. (1985). Getting beyond machismo. Outward Bound, 1, 74–79.

Maher, F. A. & Thompson-Tetreault, M. K. (1994). The Feminist Classroom. New York: Basic Books.

Miles, J. C. (1990). In J. C. Miles and S. Priest (Eds.) Adventure Education (pp. 467–471). State College, PA: Venture.

Mitten, D. (1992). Empowering girls and women in the outdoors. Journal of Physical Education, Recreation, and Dance, 63(2), 56–60.

Priest, S. (1990). The semantics of adventure education. In J. C. Miles & S. Priest (Eds.) Adventure Education (pp. 119–128). State College, PA: Venture.

Riordan, C. (1997). Equality and Achievement: An Introduction to the Sociology of Education. New York: Longman.

Rohnke, K. (1986, May/June). Project adventure: A widely used generic product. Journal of Physical Education and Recreation.

Sleeter, C. E. (1992). Keepers of the American dream: A Study of Staff Development and Multicultural Education. London: Falmer Press.

Smith, T. E., Roland, C. C., Havens, M. D., & Hoyt, J. A. (1992). The Theory and Practice of Challenge Education. Dubuque, IA: Kendall/Hunt.

Tyack, D. & Hansot, E. (1990). Learning Together: A History of Coeducation in American Public Schools. New Haven CT: Yale University Press.

Warren, K. (1990). Women's outdoor programs. In J. C. Miles & S. Priest (Eds.), Adventure Education (pp. 410–417). State College, PA: Venture.

Wurdinger, S. (1997). Philosophical issues in adventure education. Dubuque, IA: Kendall/Hunt Publishers.

Yerkes, R., & Miranda, W. (1982). Outdoor adventure courses for women: Implications for new programming. Journal of Physical Education, Recreation and Dance, 53(4), 82–85.